THE SECRETS OF CEOs

In loving memory of Sylvia Tappin and Sir John Harvey-Jones

THE SECRETS OF CEOs

150 global chief executives
lift the lid on business,
life and leadership

Steve Tappin & Andrew Cave

NICHOLAS BREALEY
PUBLISHING

LONDON · BOSTON

First published by
Nicholas Brealey Publishing in 2008

3–5 Spafield Street
Clerkenwell, London
EC1R 4QB, UK
Tel: +44 (0)20 7239 0360
Fax: +44 (0)20 7239 0370

20 Park Plaza, Suite 1115A
Boston
MA 02116, USA
Tel: (888) BREALEY
Fax: (617) 523 3708

www.nicholasbrealey.com
www.theSecretsofCEOs.com

ISBN 978-1-85788-513-2

Library of Congress Cataloging-in-Publication Data

Tappin, Steve.
  The secrets of CEOs : 150 global chief executives lift the lid on business, life, and leadership
/ Steve Tappin & Andrew Cave.
    p. cm.
  Includes bibliographical references and index.
  1. Chief executive officers. 2. Executive ability. 3. Executives. I. Cave, Andrew. II. Title.

HD38.2.T37 2008
658.4'2--dc22

2008032051

British Library Cataloguing in Publication Data
A catalogue record for this book is available from the
British Library.

Printed in the UK by Clays Ltd
on Forest Stewardship Council certified paper.

FSC

CONTENTS

FOREWORD

by Sir Richard Branson

I must admit I'm not a great reader of business books. To be honest, when we started Virgin almost 40 years ago now we totally ignored the established business theories and strategies and struck out determined to do things differently. There weren't any business books where actual CEOs, from a range of different organizations, shared real experiences and lessons learnt with people just starting out. I wish there had been – perhaps I might have saved myself a few headaches along the way!

Let's face it, the world is constantly changing – no big surprise there – but the sheer pace of that change can be staggering, confusing and downright terrifying at times. Steve and Andy have identified the new facts of life that most businesses are hit by on a daily basis, especially hard globalization, sustainability and the war for talent. The developments on the internet, particularly when it comes to reaching out to your customers with new and interactive content, fascinate and totally baffle me. I hadn't gotten my head around Web 2.0 when someone in my team told me not to worry about it, that was yesterday and today we're looking at Web 3.0!

Hard globalization is a reality for Virgin. I have always had the dream that Virgin would one day become one of the world's most respected brands. As we expand outside of the UK across America, India, Australia, Asia, and the Middle East, I feel that dream is getting closer to becoming a reality. But hard globalization brings with it very specific challenges and *The Secrets of CEOs* highlights many of these. All businesses need to be aware of their global footprint.

One of the most impressive developments within businesses today is the belief that to truly become a successful, thriving company (whether that be a firm of 10 or a global organization employing

50,000 people) you have to place corporate responsibility and sustainability at the heart of your business. As recently as ten years ago this was unheard of. Every large business had a charitable foundation, but this was seen very much as a "nice to do" rather than a core strategy within your organization. Customers expect the companies they are purchasing from to act in an ethical, sustainable way. As business leaders it is crucial we repay that trust by going the extra mile to ensure best practice at all times. On a global level, the behavior of people, industries, and enterprises has immediate and often long-term effects on our world. If mankind makes a mistake, it can be catastrophic.

I believe that it is up to companies like Virgin to lead the way with a holistic approach to business. It was this belief that led me a few years ago to pledge Virgin Group's profits from our transportation businesses over the next ten years (approximately $3 billion) to clean energy initiatives. I hope that through the strides forward that our airline and transport companies across the world continue to initiate, trial, and invest in – successes such as our most recent biofuel trails on Virgin Atlantic and Virgin Trains – other airlines and transport businesses will also follow suit. When all businesses put sustainability at the heart of what they do, we will see a radically positive change in the impact we have on our planet. I believe that day is not too far away.

I was heartened to read Part III of this book. For a long time I have been drawn to the Gaia theory, a hypothesis formulated by James Lovelock almost 40 years ago, which states that the Earth is a living entity, like a single cell. This way of thinking can apply to business too. I have never been a fan of command and control and believe that the authors' model of a cell-like organization could be a really powerful way of running a business in the future. I have always believed that one of my strengths has been my ability to trust the people around me 100 percent and to be able to truly delegate responsibilty to the managers of our businesses. You cannot expect those who you rely on to run your companies every day to really put their neck out and go that extra mile if you do not give them a sense of ownership. Let them make mistakes, support them through the bad and the good

times, and instill in them a sense that your business is *their* business
– and most importantly, mean it.

Your people are everything – without them you don't have a business! This book touches on this very point throughout, whether it is
delegation, ensuring you encourage creativity and innovation, or simply letting your hair down with your staff and having some fun. I can
hand on heart say I am only one of many entrepreneurs at Virgin. We
employ like-minded people who love to innovate and challenge the
norm. To quote my good friend Stephen Murphy, who you'll hear a lot
more from in this book, "We employ rock climbers, not people who
need ladders." At Virgin it is this creativity and the ability to challenge
the norm that mark us out from the rest and ensure we continue to
grow. Employing the best people who will not only be loyal to your
company but are also not afraid to challenge it when things become a
bit staid is the best way to ensure you stay ahead of the curve.

At Virgin we not only know how to work hard, we know how to
party hard! It was great to see that many of the other CEOs interviewed for this book remind us that working is meant to be fun. We
spend most of our lives working: what a shame it would be if you're
spending that time doing something you hate. Even when things get
a bit rocky you can still learn from it. Had a bad day or week? Take the
team out and have some fun. It's amazing how a little downtime gives
you a new perpective on what you thought was an insurmountable
problem.

Naturally, and more's the pity, it can't all be party, party, party – so
check out Chapter 13 on building a career. I agree in the future the
best thing is not to be limited by traditional corporate careers but to
be clear on what you want from life and get as much varied experience as you can pack in. I still get some of my best and most memo-
rable experiences from setting up and launching new businesses
around the world – that's probably why I can't stop doing it! I was
glad to see that the authors recommend this as a great way to learn.
Read and enjoy...

I'll end as Steve and Andy do, by asking: Why not you?

THANK YOU

To Hugh Lloyd-Jukes, the third member of our fellowship, for his clarity of thought, relentless intellectual challenge, and driving execution without which this wouldn't be the book it is.

To Thea Dettmann for setting up over 150 meetings, patiently rescheduling most of them, and at the same time developing the book's graphics.

To Michelle Marin-Dogan, Nele Van Ginneken, and Gaston Dolle for the steely focus that allowed us smoothly to double the revenues of the practice while we focused on the book.

Thank you also to our colleagues at Heidrick & Struggles for their support and contribution to making this project happen. In particular, to Kevin Kelly, Steve Langton, David Peters and Bernard Zen-Ruffinen. Also to Alice Au, Aysegul Aydin, Patsy Buchanan, Derek Boshard, Claire Davies, Richard Emerton, Scott Eversman, Pascal Gibert, Tashi Lassalle, Sheng Lu, Arun Das Mahapatra, Keith Meyer, Charles Moore, Steve Mullinjer, Christine Stimpel, and Alicia Yi. In addition, to Rajiv Inamdar and the rigorously analytical teams at the Knowledge Management Centre, to Ankush Marwah and to Amy Qian. Finally to Narda Shirley, MD of Gong Communications, for invaluable support.

Andrew would also like to thank Damian Reece, Head of Business, The Daily Telegraph, for his role in setting up the partnership that led to this book. Thanks to Ra Tickel and Martin Strydom for their encouragement and enthusiasm for the project, and to Matthew Bishop, Helen Dunne, and Claire Anderson for their support in the tricky moments.

We would both like to thank Nick Brealey for his challenge to make the book truly global and his diplomatic guidance. Thank you also to Sally Lansdell for helping us to find "one voice" and for developing and stucturing the content without losing the essence of the book.

Thank you to our reviewers for giving so generously of their time to provide such detailed and thought-provoking feedback: Mark Armitage, Richard Baker, James Bilefield, Andrew Kakabadse, Kathleen Klasnic, Tony Manwaring, John Neill, Dwight Poler, Emma Reynolds, Tom Standage, and Frank Tang, and in particular Alan Watkins. Also the hundreds of people we've informally bounced ideas off over the last year or so.

Most of all, thank-you to our families – Jo, Lauren, Hannah and Jessie, and Paula, Roy, Margaret, Wendy, David and Lisa – for their love and understanding.

Steve Tappin & Andrew Cave
London, June 2008

THE CEOs

Thank you to all the CEOs who gave up so many hours of their precious time to this project – and to their miracle-working assistants who managed to match our diaries.

Adams, Paul, CEO, British American Tobacco
Amelio, Bill, president & CEO, Lenovo
Armitage, Mark, president US, The CarbonNeutral Company
Arora, Nikesh, president, EMEA operations, Google
Bailey, Sly, CEO, Trinity Mirror
Bajaj, Rahul, chairman, Bajaj Auto
Baker, Richard, former CEO, Alliance Boots
Banga, Vindi, president, foods, home and personal care, Unilever
Barry, Mike, head of corporate social responsibility, Marks & Spencer
Basing, Nick, former CEO, Paramount Restaurants
Beeston, Kevin, executive chairman, Serco
Bell, Chris, CEO, Ladbrokes
Bell, Sir David, chairman, Financial Times
Berrien, James, president and publisher, Forbes Magazine Group
Bilefield, James, former CEO, OpenX
Bolland, Marc, CEO, Morrisons
Bond, Sir John, chairman, Vodafone
Breedon, Tim, CEO, Legal & General
Brikho, Samir, CEO, AMEC
Broughton, Martin, chairman, British Airways
Brown, Frank, dean, INSEAD
Browne, John, Baron Browne of Madingley, former CEO, BP
Butler-Wheelhouse, Keith, former CEO, Smiths Group
Carayol, René, leadership expert
Carr, Neil, vice-president, Rohm & Haas
Carson, Neil, CEO, Johnson Matthey
Castell, Sir Bill, former CEO, GE Healthcare; chairman, The Wellcome Trust
Cheung, Stanley, managing director, Walt Disney China
Clare, Mark, CEO, Barratt Developments
Clarke, Tim, CEO, Mitchells & Butler
Clifford, Leigh, former CEO, Rio Tinto
Conde, Cris, CEO, Sungard
Coull, Ian, CEO, Segro
Cox, Phil, CEO, International Power
Crawshaw, Steven, former CEO, Bradford & Bingley
Crombie, Sandy, CEO, Standard Life
Daniels, Eric, CEO, Lloyds TSB

Johnson, Peter, former chairman and CEO, Inchcape
Judge, Barbara, chairman, UK Atomic Energy Authority
Kakabadse, Andrew, professor of international management development,
    Cranfield University, School of Management
Kelly, Kevin, CEO, Heidrick & Struggles
Kemp, Harriet, former vice-president human resources excellence, ICI
Kent, Muhtar, president and CEO, The Coca-Cola Company
King, Martina, former managing director of country operations for Europe, Yahoo!
Laidlaw, Sam, CEO, Centrica
Larcombe, Brian, former CEO, 3i
Leahy, Sir Terry, CEO, Tesco
Leighton, Allan, chairman, Royal Mail
Levy, Gigi, CEO, 888 Holdings
Makin, Louise, CEO, BTG
Mallya, Vijay, chairman, Kingfisher Airlines and United Breweries
Manduca, Paul, senior independent director, Morrisons
Manwaring, Tony, CEO, Tomorrow's Company
Mayfield, Charlie, chairman, John Lewis Partnership
McCaig, Ian, CEO, Lastminute.com
McCall, Carolyn, CEO, Guardian Media Group
McGregor-Smith, Ruby, CEO, MITIE
Middleton, Julia, CEO, Common Purpose
Mills, Brad, CEO, Lonmin
Moore, Philip, former CEO, Friends Provident
Moraitis, Thras, head of group strategy and corporate affairs, Xstrata
Mordashov, Alexey, CEO, Severstal
Morton, Bruce, co-founder, Ask Gen Y and e3 unlimited
Moulton, Jon, founder and managing partner, Alchemy Partners
Murdoch, James, chairman and CEO, Europe and Asia, News Corporation
Murphy, Gerry, former CEO, Kingfisher
Murphy, Stephen, CEO, Virgin Group
Murray, Alan, former CEO, Hanson
Murthy, Narayana, chairman and chief mentor, Infosys
Nadar, Shiv, founder, HCL; chairman and chief strategy officer, HCL Technologies
Neill, John, CEO, Unipart
Norman, Archie, former CEO, Asda; founder, Aurigo Management
O'Donnell, Sir Christopher, former CEO, Smith & Nephew
Parker, Alan, CEO, Whitbread
Parker, Sir John, chairman, National Grid
Patel, Ketan, founder partner, Greater Pacific Capital
Philipps, Charles, CEO, Amlin
Pindar, Paul, CEO, Capita
Pluthero, John, executive chairman of Europe, Asia and US and international, Cable
    & Wireless
Poler, Dwight, managing director, Bain Capital Europe
Premji, Azim, chairman and CEO, Wipro
Pym, Richard, former CEO, Alliance & Leicester
Quintana, Bob, president and founder, RLQ Consulting Group
Rake, Sir Michael, chairman, BT
Reece, Damian, head of business, Daily Telegraph

INTRODUCTION

This is the first book in which more than 150 top chief executives from across the Western and developing worlds, with more than 1,000 years of CEO experience between them, explain in their own words:

- ❑ What it's really like to be a CEO – and the health warning that should come with the job.
- ❑ The secret to dealing successfully with the five hard facts of life that will be critical to business success in the coming decade.
- ❑ What motivates and drives some of the world's top CEOs and how they really lead their businesses in practice.
- ❑ How businesses and leaders need to evolve to win in the coming years.
- ❑ The leadership experiences required to succeed in the new world of work.

We provide advice to chief executives on how to be better business leaders, as well as practical guidance for today's young and aspiring managers.

OUR RESEARCH

As well as 15 months of research, this book builds on more than 30 years of working with CEOs as an adviser on strategy, personal leadership, and talent in Steve's case, and as a financial journalist in Andrew's.

We have interviewed CEOs who lead more than 150 companies with total revenues of $1.8 trillion – about the same as the economy of Italy. Their businesses range across the globe. In Europe they incorporate two-thirds of the FTSE100 index, including leading businesses such as Tesco, BT Group, and WPP Group. They include new corporate champions of India such as Tata, Wipro, and Infosys, leading Chinese and Russian companies like Lenovo and Severstal, and US corporate giants such as Google, Dell, and News Corporation. Altogether they span a broad cross-section of corporate life, from industrial groups like BP, Xstrata, and BAE Systems to virtual worlds like Second Life.

Overview of research methodology

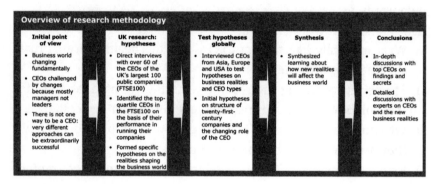

WHAT DID WE FIND?

First, we need to issue a warning.

Being a CEO should be one of the best jobs in the world. It offers the chance to make a real difference. However, real life for most CEOs is tough and many are not enjoying it. Rather like Frodo Baggins in *The Lord of the Rings*, while they are heavily burdened by the responsibility and ultimate accountability of their role, they cling to their position and can't bring themselves to stop. We uncover the real lives of CEOs in Chapter 1.

The rest of the book is in three parts.

CEO HEALTH WARNING
Even if you succeed in this role, you may ultimately be forced to leave it prematurely. There is a high risk that while in the role you will have a limited life outside work and that the job will put tremendous strain on your health, happiness, and close family relationships and friendships.

PART I: FACING UP TO THE FACTS OF LIFE

Leaders from Western companies as well as the new champions from Asia and Eastern Europe describe the secrets of winning in the face of five important business realities that companies will encounter in the coming years.

Profiting from "hard globalization"

Almost without exception, top CEOs believe that we are entering a period of fundamental change on a scale not seen for several hundred years. The world has moved beyond the two-way flow of Western organizations heading East en masse and top Eastern companies entering Western home markets. These opposing competitive flows are merging into a turbulent storm of full global competition for the first time: the start of what we call hard globalization.

Most Western leaders believe that they understand this new competitive environment, but their approaches are often parochial and incremental. Eastern CEOs are more open to learning the new rules. Chapter 2 shares top leaders' views on the mindset, strategy, and tactics required to make the shift from a domestically focused international business to an integrated global company.

Decoding sustainability

Five years ago nobody talked about sustainability. The mindset was still that business and society could continue operating in the ways they have done for the last couple of hundred years. Now, along with globalization, sustainability is a corporate buzzword. But what does it really mean?

Our interviews found that most business leaders remain confused, largely because the definition of sustainability continues to change. For more than a decade there has been increasing pressure on CEOs to take responsibility for their companies' carbon footprints and to address environmental concerns. A tipping point has been passed and corporations have largely woken up to the need to operate in an environmentally sustainable fashion. Those who haven't face a decade of growing regulatory pressure, particularly in Europe.

However, there is more to sustainability than going green. Ethical and social considerations are being taken much more seriously by an increasing number of leaders who believe that doing the "right thing" is also great business in the long term. They foresee that stakeholders will push businesses to embrace a role in society that goes beyond the environment. These CEOs are engaged in various activist social forums and signpost the corporate social responsibility agenda for the next ten years. We'll take you through what they are doing and how to strike a balance between running a successful business and saving the planet, both environmentally and socially.

Surfing the third wave of the web

With the exception of bosses of technology companies, a majority of CEOs confess to not having a strong handle on the latest developments in technology. This is a major concern, given that the web and related technologies will be the pre-eminent platform for connecting the world in the next decade.

Chief executives will have to ensure that their organization can properly exist in and navigate between real and virtual worlds. Most companies are not moving fast enough to profit from the social networking revolution of Web 2.0 and have not adopted an interactive way of doing business. They will be fundamentally challenged by what is to come. We uncover the secrets of leading web CEOs and experts in related fields.

Dealing with alternative capital

In mid-2008, most CEOs' agendas were dominated by the "credit crunch". Western capital markets were effectively closed to many companies and the financial crisis was spreading out to pose the risk of a wider recession across the West and of depressing emerging markets. However, even before this situation developed, the "capital" in capitalism was becoming much more sophisticated, complex, and globally diverse. Institutional investors are being supplemented as sources of capital by the modern-day conglomerates of increasingly global private equity firms, sovereign wealth funds from Asia and the Middle East, and opportunist hedge funds.

This chapter examines both these trends and explains how one could help provide solutions for the other. CEOs share strategies for ensuring your business survives and being ready to capture opportunities when the economy improves. They advise on how to deal with the intense personal pressure of being where the buck stops when the market's in freefall. And they explain how to navigate the developing maze of capital and that some of its newer forms may be key to your business's survival, by suggesting ways in which public company CEOs can apply some private equity techniques to survive and thrive during the credit crunch.

Waging the first world war for talent

CEOs reveal that, alongside the battle for the customer, the most important battleground for competing global companies is now for talent. This decade will see the first world war for the globe's top 1 percent of talent. The key drivers are poor demographics in the West, shortages of skilled workers in the East, and the lack of global leaders.

Chief executives do understand the importance of recruiting and promoting exceptional talent and claim to make it a top priority, but we found that many give it insufficient focus or time. In fact, many CEOs believe that their firm's current talent development activities are ineffective.

Top CEOs reveal that the first world war for talent will require a fundamental rethink of ways of attracting and developing talent. Chief executives will have to be much more heavily involved in development and new breeds of human resources professionals and external search partners will need to step up to the task. CEOs explain how they are responding to the big challenges posed by a new world of work, which increasingly involves directing a diverse and remotely located talent base, and dealing with the inevitable tensions generated by a global workforce containing a new mix of babyboomers, Generation X, and Generation Y.

The collective and related impact of the new global business realities will be fundamental and on a scale not previously experienced in our lifetimes. These new facts of life will mean that the majority of international companies operating traditional Western management techniques, even those run by highly capable professional CEOs, will not be able to cope without changing the way they operate. Most of the new champion companies from Asia and Eastern Europe will also be severely tested.

Part II: Leading at the top today

Part I gives you the latest insights from CEOs into the critical trends shaping the world. In Part II it's time to understand the common secrets for success: What have the best CEOs learnt about how to lead?

During our research we identified the most highly regarded CEOs by talking to their peers and observers of their businesses and by conducting our own research into their performance. We thus identified the top quartile of UK CEOs running international businesses. When we studied this group, we found that there were five main leadership approaches that remained consistent among top CEOs in Europe, America, and Asia alike:

❑ **Commercial executors** have a driving focus on achieving the best results in their industry, combined with a relentless attention to detail in order to ensure that operational and strategic ambitions become a reality. Sir Terry Leahy is a prime example as a leading international retailer and chief executive of Tesco. We hear his philosophy at first hand in Chapter 7.

❑ **Financial value drivers** aggressively pursue shareholder value. They understand the metrics of their industry and are often highly skilled at identifying value-enhancing corporate transactions or realizing value from portfolio disposals. Mick Davis has led the creation and rapid growth of miner Xstrata, masterminding a set of acquisitions that have transformed it from a small collection of coal and mineral assets into one of the top ten UK companies by stock market capitalization. He is profiled and interviewed in Chapter 8.

❑ **Corporate entrepreneurs** have something to prove. They disrupt industries because they believe in a better way of doing things. They excel in spotting breakthrough opportunities and making them reality; their vision for their companies is their life vision. In Chapter 9 Sir Martin Sorrell tells how he founded WPP, now one of the world's largest advertising and marketing businesses, and describes the experience as "the closest that a man can get to giving birth".

❑ **Corporate ambassadors** have a worldwide vision that has a broader societal impact. This involves operating at a geopolitical level and delivering transactions that transform industries. Lord Browne, the former CEO of BP who is now forging a new career in private equity, propelled BP from a mid-ranking European company into the third largest oil company in the Western world. Our interview with him in Chapter 10 illustrates the work of an exceptional corporate ambassador.

❑ Finally, **global missionaries** are on a personal mission to make a significant difference and a corporate mission to make their companies great. They are typically customer champions and they lead by inspiring people and energizing them to tap into their potential. Ben Verwaayen, the former chief executive of BT, is a good example and tells how his mission became increasingly clear from the outset of his career.

Part II examines these approaches. Each chapter starts with a detailed profile, based on extensive interviews, of a CEO who clearly illustrates one of the five types. We take you through their upbringing, what motivates them, and how they really lead their business. We then set the profiled leader in context with comments from other CEOs of their type and show how they typically measure success, the situations and industries in which they generally perform best, and their relative strengths and weaknesses.

This part of the book should help you understand how you lead and where the gaps and shortfalls may be in your own leadership approach, as well as which industries and situation are most appropriate for your skill set.

PART III: LEADING INTO THE FUTURE

Part III sets out how CEOs will lead in the future, taking account of the new facts of life from Part I and drawing on the experience and insight of the chief executives profiled in Part II.

Top CEOs believe that the current leadership model of many traditional Western "command-and-control" businesses is destined to fail because the challenges we describe in Part I will be too overwhelming for the structure to survive. Our research found that top chief executives believe that they must organize their businesses more organically. In the next decade many successful companies will replace command and control with more fluid and fast-moving cell-like organizations.

We describe how a chief executive provides business leadership at the nucleus of the cell by giving greater freedom to act to much more decentralized operations, while still policing performance. Our interviews found that most CEOs are better business leaders than personal leaders – they are generally comfortable with strategy and formulating operational plans, but are rarely good at lifting an organization, injecting pace or fresh energy. So in Chapter 12 we give examples of the new leadership qualities required to maintain the faster-moving, more entrepreneurial and energetic businesses of the future.

Individual CEOs will not have all the answers and skills; even if they did, they would not have the personal bandwidth to follow up on every action required. Top chief executives will require a small team of confidants (between three to five people) at the center of the business. These extremely talented global players will have the skills required and the appetite and values to sustain a world-class company. We give some guidance on how to pull together this new fellowship of the CEO and how to get it to work in practice.

What if you're not yet a leader but are determined to be one? In Chapter 13 today's rising stars advise you on the apprenticeship you'll need to follow to become a leader for tomorrow.

Finally, the last chapter revisits our CEO health warning. Chief executives offer specific advice on how to have a winning career and a successful life. We show how developments in the fields of elite sports, personal performance, and neuroscience can be applied to help leaders be and remain at their best.

THESECRETSOFCEOS.COM

We have set up www.theSecretsofCEOs.com, a website that reveals further secrets via CEO video interviews, webcasts, blogs, and community forums to help you continue your development as a leader. You'll also have an opportunity to register and join our community of tomorrow's leaders.

But first let's find out what it's really like to be a CEO.

1

THE REAL LIVES OF CEOs

L ife at the top isn't all it's made out to be. That's one of the main findings from our interviews with the leaders of top global companies. So what are their lives really like?

The chief executives leading our biggest companies are still largely twentieth-century leaders. About 60 percent of them can be more accurately classed as professional managers than leaders. They're running organizations with tens or hundreds of thousands of employees all over the world, but have become overburdened with processes, red tape, and day-to-day minutiae.

Today's chief executives are wrestling with their professional lives. They don't have long to prove themselves to impatient stakeholders and this task is made all the harder by huge confusion about who they are actually running their companies for and what to focus on most.

Our chief executives are grappling with leadership. About 50 percent admit that they find the job intensely lonely and don't know who to turn to for advice. A common response was: "I can't talk to the chairman because in the end he's the one who is going to fire me. I can't talk to my finance director because ultimately I'm going to fire him, and I can't tell my wife because I never see her and when I do, that's the last thing she'll want to talk about."

Many top chief executives also find it difficult to have time for a fulfilling personal life. They spend years getting to the top and then give up virtually all their personal time to doing the job before they're either ousted with a payoff or, with luck, retire on a generous pension.

WHO ARE WE DOING THIS FOR?

One might think that it's clear enough who chief executives run their organizations for. After all, companies are owned by shareholders, who put up the capital for them to grow, whether organically or by acquisition. It is shareholders who can vote down a CEO's remuneration, as happened with Glaxo SmithKline chief executive Jean-Pierre Garnier. They can also, of course, liaise with the chairman and the senior independent director to force the CEO out.

However, our research found a surprising division of opinion on the issue of who the most important stakeholders of a public company really are. Some 38 percent of the CEOs we interviewed say that shareholders are their most important stakeholders, but 24 percent say that customers are more important and 13 percent value their staff above all others. The remaining 25 percent see all stakeholders as ranked equally.

Gareth Davis, chief executive of Imperial Tobacco, is typical of the shareholder lobby. "Everything revolves around the shareholder," he says. "We live for the shareholder." Another chief executive is even more voluble: "The most important stakeholder has to be the shareholder, Everyone says businesses have to do something in philanthropy to solve the world's problems, but it is not our money. It belongs to the shareholders."

Mike Roney, chief executive of plastics group Bunzl, shares this view: "Certainly in the UK and the US, you have to say that the shareholder is the leading stakeholder. Without that, you are not in business." Clearly, chief executives need to take account of their shareholders. After all, not many survive for long if they ignore them.

However, some chief executives believe with equal conviction that other stakeholders are more important. In part this reflects the management style of particular CEOs, but it also depends on the industry in which they operate. Retail and banking chief executives, for example, are almost unanimous in saying that they put customers above even shareholders. Mervyn Davies, chairman and former chief executive of international banking group Standard Chartered, explains: "You have got to keep your customers, You have got to think about them and be very customer-centric. The reason why chief executives become chairman at so many banks is because of the importance of continuity in the relationships with customers. A non-executive cannot provide those sorts of important relationships with customers, governments, and regulators."

Peter Johnson, former chairman of international motor distribution group Inchcape, adds: "Ultimately the most important people are customers because if they don't like what you're doing, you have nothing." James Bilefield, former CEO of internet advertising technology group OpenX and director at Skype, is another chief executive who is clear that customers have to come first. As he says, "It starts and ends with the customer, it has to be the customer. It's the customer, stupid. Technically and legally, you have to put the shareholders first, but to deliver for them you have to put delighting customers at the core of all that you do."

It starts and ends with the customer.
It's the customer, stupid

Then there are chief executives who say that they run their companies for their staff, before shareholders and customers. Such CEOs tend to be in multinational industrial or commodity-based businesses. For example Alan Murray, former chief executive of building materials group Hanson, says, "Employees are very important. We have 1,800 sites worldwide. We cannot supervise all the people all the time, so we need people to understand the culture and what they can do and cannot do. We have to make sure that everyone understands the message and that everyone understands the message in the same way." Brad Mills, chief executive of mining group Lonmin, also selects employees as his most important stakeholder, as does Chip Hornsby, chief executive of international plumbers' merchants Wolseley.

The most sensible approach for an aspiring chief executive, however, is probably to try to embrace all three major stakeholder groups. Sandy Crombie, chief executive of life insurance group Standard Life, believes that looking after the needs of shareholders, customers, and staff should be an "unbreakable circle" that helps each reinforce the other. Eric Daniels, chief executive of banking group Lloyds TSB, agrees: "Ultimately if you neglect any of your stakeholders you will have a problem. If you are about building a long-term customer franchise, you cannot do it without your employees, your regulator, and your shareholders giving you the luxury of the time to do it in."

Andy Harrison, chief executive of budget airline easyJet, is perhaps the most succinct at summing this up. "If you're not focused on your customers, nothing works," he says. "If you're not focused on your people it becomes very tough, and if you don't look after your shareholders that's very tough as well. You have to strike a balance. Choosing one is unsustainable."

BEING THE BOSS IS TOUGH

To be the final decision maker in a multibillion-dollar business with hundreds of thousands of employees and pensioners relying on you is an awesome responsibility. The stresses placed on CEOs almost require them to be superhuman and they are not always that well prepared for the role. As Graham Wallace, the former Cable & Wireless chief executive, says, "Often CEOs have excelled in a very different job and the skills that have made them successful are not necessarily the ones that will make them successful as a major company chief executive."

Many CEOs have particular weaknesses that they need help to address. Some find it difficult suddenly to be in charge of people who were previously their peers. Others consider that their position prevents them from forming close relationships with their teams and some feel forced to resort to rather unlikely sources of support.

One FTSE100 financial services boss brings an actress into head office every month to train him how to act out the CEO role. He justifies this by explaining that he is an introvert and has to learn to perform for staff, the media, shareholders, and analysts. "I am a very shy individual," he reveals. "I would not naturally engage with people. It's just a management style I have developed over the years. We all put on a show. We are all actors and I have learnt to act. The actress comes in and coaches me in body language, presentation style, and public speaking. I am an introvert and introverts get drawn in. I don't need to have a high regard for friendships or closeness. I can retain my intellectual distance with people who work for me."

Similarly, the boss of a FTSE100 services company chooses to bring a singer into group headquarters for much the same reason. "It's very difficult for someone like me who's quite reserved because I have to talk to a lot of people outside the business and to stakeholders so it is very challenging," he says. "I work with a voice coach who is an actress. She says, for example, 'What emotion do you want to convey?' and I say that maybe I want to convey more emotion in a presentation. She teaches me to do it."

A very widespread problem for CEOs is a difficulty in engaging with their emotions. Leaders are meant to be dispassionate about difficult decisions, but Alan Watkins, who runs executive coaching consultancy Cardiac Coherence, believes that some take this to extremes. "Their tendency not to be attached to the emotional side of things gets to be exaggerated," he says, "and this blindness to human needs really reduces their leadership effectiveness. Unfortunately, many chief executives are managing rather than leading." Watkins considers that chief executives are overworked and focused on driving out results while struggling with processes, so that they often achieve by perspiration, sheer willpower, and by shutting down their emotions. "Chief executives need to be motivated and more passionate," he says. "And to do that, they need to understand themselves better."

Unfortunately many chief executives are managing rather than leading

Another business coach recalls the case of a chief executive client who was particularly devoid of emotion. He recalls: "I asked him to think of a time in his life when he had felt really passionate about something and he sat in silence before eventually saying: 'No, I have never felt that.'" The coach asked him whether he had felt emotional when he scored a goal as a 9-year-old and again an unflinching "No" was the response. Then the coach asked the CEO to decide the emotion that would most describe him. "All he could think of was being even-tempered," says the coach. "He worked so hard to keep his emotions in check that the strongest one he felt was being controlled."

While these examples are extreme, many CEOs do find they need support to cope with the huge pressures of the role. They get this support from a range of sources. Tony Froggatt, the former chief executive of brewer Scottish & Newcastle, leans heavily on his wife, who is a former human resources director at Whitbread and Australian services group Brambles. "I'm fortunate she is so understanding of the pressures," he says.

Other CEOs draw strength from the advice of their chairmen, and many turn to professional coaches: 39 percent of the FTSE100 chief executives we interviewed said they have used one. Andy Harrison articulates the reason: "It's very hard if your team become friends because you may have to fire them," he says. "You should get close enough to your team to talk about business issues but not get too close to them and risk losing a degree of objectivity." However, coaches are not universally praised. "If you look at coaches and mentors, they are generally people who have not actually run big businesses themselves so how can they tell you how to do it?" asks Sir Martin Sorrell, chief executive of advertising giant WPP Group. "They're shrinks." Richard Pym, former chief executive of banking group Alliance & Leicester, agrees. "Some of these coach people are just weird," he adds.

We'll unpack the different sources of support top CEOs draw on and what they're best used for in Chapter 14. It's clear that, whatever support network they build, loneliness is part of the role. "If you are lonely, get a dog," says Mike Roney somewhat unsympathetically. "But the chief executive's job *is* solitary. You really don't have a peer group in the same way that you have when you're one of a number of executives working at a larger company. It's not like the times when you could meet up with your peer group and listen to someone say that your boss is an idiot." Ultimately, CEOs have to learn to be tough, resilient, and self-sufficient. For some this comes naturally; for others it needs to be learnt.

Despite support networks, the pressure does sometimes get too great and a few chief executives adopt some approaches we'd not like to see repeated. One is revealed by Shelley von Strunckel, the Californian who created the first astrological column in a UK broadsheet newspaper at the *Sunday Times* and has a sideline reading the fortunes of well-known executives from the worlds of business and entertainment. She uses an astrological chart of the heavens, sun, moon, and planets, based on an individual's place and date and time of birth, to examine a person's strengths and blind spots, and then looks at astrological trends to forecast what's going on around them. "Often chief executives are very focused on their strengths and are ignoring their weaknesses," she says. "I help them understand their weaknesses, based on their horoscope, so that instead of sidelining their weaknesses, they learn how to use them. Usually they come to see me because they are in crisis. People don't tend to seek support when everything is rolling along." Von Strunckel claims to have predicted takeovers and stock market crashes. She even says that she forecast the credit crunch that began in 2007. And she recalls once working out from the stars that the head of a major Hollywood studio was going to be on television explaining a major fraud in the company. "Not only could I see a fraud going on, I saw how the fraud would appear," she claims. "I clearly saw him being interviewed on television. He kind of went pale when I said that. There had been a huge scandal and it had showed up in his chart. And he was, indeed, later on television. It turned out later that he knew about it, although he did not acknowledge that to me at the time."

Although it's not in the least comforting to think that some CEOs may be relying on astrologers to guide their business decisions, it shows the possible effects of the tremendous stress associated with the role.

Don't get personal

It's all very well to be driving for top performance and getting the support you need to achieve it, but work isn't everything. Is it possible to have a healthy personal life as the chief executive of a major public company?

Most CEOs find it extremely difficult. More than half of those we interviewed said that they have little time for family or personal interests and passions, such are the demands of being the boss. Others accept that getting anywhere near a balance requires compromise. Inevitably, this involves CEOs' spouses and families and it sometimes begins from the moment of appointment.

"My wife knew what she was letting herself in for," admits Charles Philipps, chief executive of Lloyd's of London insurer Amlin. "Before we were married I had to go to some printers to sign off a document for a client. I was not expecting it to take long and thought that we could go out that evening afterwards, so she came to the printers with me. She was still there at 5 a.m. the next morning and she still married me."

Another boss, the chief executive of a power company, took the post despite protestations from his spouse. "Did I have a deal with my wife?" he asks. "Well, she said she did not want me to do this job and I kind of ignored it. She said, 'You've gone ahead' and I said, 'I didn't think you were serious, darling.' But she was half serious. She was asking if I had thought through all the consequences. Was I going to make sure I keep my family promises? How could I fulfill the promises I had made to my shareholders and not fulfill those I had made to her? It's a good question and I can't answer it. It's very difficult. Try going on holiday without your mobile phone. My wife says 'Your Blackberry is not coming', but there's no way I'm leaving it behind."

How could I fulfill the promises I had made to shareholders and not fulfill those I had made to my wife?

Both Johnson at Inchcape and Ed Story, chief executive of oil exploration group SOCO International, made formal arrangements with their spouses. "My wife has put up with God knows what," admits Johnson. "I was on a plane all the time, I was just never there. I once went to Australia twice in a week. I was on a plane to Japan three times in one month. Every Sunday night I was heading to airports and every Saturday morning I was arriving back at 5 a.m. I made a deal with her and said I am going to stop when I am 60."

"Ours is an evolving deal," adds Ed Story. "She says, 'When are you going to sell this? You always sell. What are you going to do when you sell? Are you going to stay here?' I say not very much. We're still negotiating it."

Maintaining a healthy work–life balance is much harder for chief executives of multinational companies who need to be constantly on the move. "My wife and I have lived in 19 houses since we married," says Leigh Clifford, the former chief executive of mining giant Rio Tinto. "I think chief executives try to kid themselves about how much time they have to spend on peripheral stuff. You have to be discerning with your time. You only get one dig at the crease. Your personal affairs can get into a bit of a mess. You don't tend to give them the time and attention they need."

Mervyn Davies believes that one of the most important differentiators between good and bad international chief executives is their ability to sleep on a plane, which has a knock-on effect on their family life. "If you're a bad traveler and run an international business, it's a nightmare," he says. "You're not sleeping and you're coming home wrecked. It's a job, for Christ's sake. When they put you in the box and it is over, you're not going to be judged on how much profit you made."

When they put you in the box and it is over, you're not going to be judged on how much profit you made

For Richard Baker, the former chief executive of pharmacy chain Alliance Boots, it's all about personal discipline. "You have to be quite disciplined and focused at a personal level with your family life," he says, "because if you're not careful, you'll arrive at a time where you're working non-stop. My wife says I'm terrible at dinner parties because I just recede. I spend my life talking and I like going to dinner where I can just sit and listen to someone else's conversation. One of the biggest issues is having time on your own."

Some CEOs manage to rationalize this lack of time for themselves and their families. "You have to have a life. My kids advise me: 'Dad, get a life,'" reveals Sandy Crombie. "I have a life. It is not the same life as everyone else's but it is my life. There are only 24 hours in a day and I sleep 7 of them. I have been married for 36 years. I don't tell myself to get a life because I have got one. It comes with the job."

Perhaps surprisingly, Crombie's lengthy marriage is not unusual. Only a handful of the CEOs we interviewed have been divorced, with the overwhelming majority of the rest married for more than 20 years. However, the job can bite deep into those marriages. Many CEOs end up compartmentalizing their work and home lives, living in company flats or traveling during the week and going home at weekends. "My family are used to not seeing me during the week," says Paul Adams, chief executive of British American Tobacco. "They see me at weekends but not all the time or every weekend. It's the life they've grown up with."

"I can't remember my boys growing up," states one CEO who has been married twice. "I can't remember them when they were young. People ask whether you make a choice between your family and your career. You definitely do. I don't think you can have both. You need to choose." And in fact Jon Moulton, managing partner of private equity group Alchemy Partners, actually prefers investing in companies where the chief executive has been divorced once, arguing that they are better motivated to succeed. "I take a lot of interest in the chief executive's marital status," he confides. "One divorce is slightly better than none, because managers are motivated and challenged and sometimes they need to rebuild their wealth. Two is more worrying and three is a catastrophe. I don't generally make private investments when I see three divorces."

People ask whether you make a choice between your family and your career. You definitely do

Sir Martin Sorrell, who went through a highly publicized divorce, believes that everyone is defined by the meeting in their lives of work, family, and society. "There are very few people who can get the intersection of those three circles perfectly balanced and I have not managed to do it," he admits. "Getting the balance right is very, very difficult. All the stuff I do outside the business is related to business."

It is therefore clear that a healthy work–life balance can be very difficult to achieve if you are running a major public company. Some of the most effective CEOs say that they only manage it by relying on their secretaries to send them home on time or by learning to be extremely disciplined. We'll come back to some of the disciplines used to achieve a fulfilling personal life in Part III.

THE GOOD NEWS

So you can see why we think being a CEO should come with a strong health warning: it's a grueling job and most chief executives don't have much of a personal life. However, there is good news: some CEOs do manage to juggle home life and business and really enjoy the job. We'll take you through how they do that in Chapter 14. This is heartening because the realities of doing business in the coming decade, such as companies increasingly becoming globally dispersed and the internet enabling faster information flows and swifter decision making, will make it even harder to be a chief executive.

If you do want to be a CEO or learn more about doing the job, the rest of this book will take you through the detail of the emerging global realities and how top CEOs cope with them. It will show you how some of the best of the current crop of CEOs got to where they are today and how they actually do their job, as well as offering suggestions on how best to lead in the coming decade.

PART I

FACING UP TO THE FACTS OF LIFE

Chief executives agree that in the next decade the global economy and business world will change on a scale not seen in 200 years. And most CEOs think that the secret to success in the next decade will be understanding how to:

- ❏ Compete globally in the first decade of hard globalization.
- ❏ Position your company to deal with the environmental challenge and play a wider role in society as a sustainable business.
- ❏ Exploit the promise of Web 3.0 and the increasing importance of virtual worlds.
- ❏ Lead your businesses through the capital crunch.
- ❏ Be a winner in the first world war for talent that will be waged in the new and very different world of work.

The following chapters set out how top chief executives and experts expect these trends to shape the world in the coming decade and lay out how CEOs who have to confront these emerging realities day in and day out expect to address them in the future.

2

PROFITING FROM
HARD GLOBALIZATION

"To succeed in the global bazaar requires a global mindset."
Narayana Murthy, chairman and chief mentor, Infosys

"The force of globalization and international growth is both underrated and overrated. Underrated because the world is not yet as globalized as it can be, overrated because many of the effects of globalization are identical to that of increased competition... It's a part of the dynamics of markets, not some alien force."
Azim Premji, chairman and chief executive, Wipro

Chief executives of major companies see coping with globalization as the single most important reality for the next decade. This may seem surprising given that globalization has been talked about for years. However, the shift we are currently seeing is on a dramatic scale as India and China reintegrate into the world economy.

This chapter will examine the extent of this shift and the way it is ushering in the age of "hard globalization", where for the first time everyone is competing in a truly global fashion. We'll also explore how the best companies will approach global competition in the next decade.

The reality of globalization

Emerging markets will produce superior growth

Globalization is not a new phenomenon; a meaningful global trading bazaar can be traced back several hundreds of years. In its current incarnation, however, globalization denotes the development of an increasingly integrated global economy, a marked feature of which is the shift of power that is expected to see emerging markets, particularly those in Asia, surpass developed economies in size.

Philip Green, chief executive of United Utilities, believes that what's happening in China is "the second industrial revolution", while for Ed Zore, chief executive of Northwestern Mutual in the US, "globalization is a trend for the next 200 years". Sir Martin Sorrell says, "We've not witnessed growth on this scale for 200 years and not at this speed. I think China and India are going back to where they

THE RISE OF CHINA AND INDIA: FOUR QUICK REMINDERS	
Massive population	India + China = 40% of the world's population
Fast-rising education levels	China and India expected to graduate 1.5m technical students in 2010[1]
Rise of consumer class	1.2bn (20 times UK population) middle class across the two markets by 2025 McKinsey expects the Chinese consumer market to be bigger than the German market by 2015 and the Indian consumer market to outstrip Italy[2]
Thirst for technology	40% of Chinese population already have a cellphone[3]

were in 1819." At that time China and India generated about 49 percent of worldwide gross domestic product (GDP) due to silk, spice,
and porcelain trading. By 1973 their share had shrunk to 8 percent,
but China and India are growing so rapidly that

1819: 49%   they are forecast to hit 49 percent again by 2025.[4]

1973: 8%   Sir Martin adds, "Asia-Pacific will dominate again.

2025: 49%   This really is back to the future." Given that China

China and India's % of world GDP   and India's real GDP growth in recent years has

been three to five times higher than that of the US,
he does not seem to be overstating matters by saying, "Anyone running a business is pushing an open door going into India and China."
Indeed, momentum is gathering: for example, China accounted for
the biggest portion of overall growth in advertising services in 2007.
"We are watching something unstoppable and it will cause a painful
transition. We in the West were on the right side for 200 years and
will be on the wrong side for 200 years," Sir Martin attests.

Share price growth depends on increasing profits year on year and
it's difficult to see better opportunities for sustained growth than in
Asia, where huge numbers of people are set to be lifted out of poverty
and into consumerism and the size of the educated labor force is mul-
tiplying. Because of their huge and young populations China and
India are leading the way, so any truly global business has to be there
in scale if it wants to deliver growth to its shareholders over the long
term.

It's important to keep a sense of perspective, however. There are
substantial risks to operating in emerging markets, not least the danger
of forgetting the strengths of the West. Furthermore, in the medium
term at least, the preponderance of economic power will remain in the
West in real terms: the US and the EU are each expected to have real
GDPs bigger than either China or India in 2025. Given their huge populations, this means that Chinese and Indian consumers will still be
much poorer individually than their Western counterparts.[5]

In addition, different industries are growing at different rates in
emerging markets and the West and there is plenty of growth left to
target in the US in particular. At Diageo, the world's largest spirits

group, chief executive Paul Walsh is in no doubt over his company's most exciting emerging market: "The most important developing market for us is the US. Spirits are increasingly being consumed instead of other forms of alcohol and there is a growing market in America, with 1m new consumers coming of drinking age every year for the next decade. It's heavily driven by growth in the populations of Asian-Americans, Hispanics, and African-Americans. These consumers are very brand conscious. They're seeking something different. Spirits are seen as being much more aspirational than beer. While everybody gets compelled with the growth story in China, for us the message is 'Don't forget the US'. It's a market that already has a wealthy infrastructure and our brands have consumer appeal. That market is going to be extremely attractive."

China and India mean volatility and risks

As international investors will testify, while the best returns usually come from the riskiest markets, these can also produce extremely heavy losses. Growth at the rates being achieved in China and India is unstable, unpredictable, and prone to sudden crises. China and India are also both facing structural issues. They're seeing wage inflation and a war for talent for the top skills in areas of high demand, such as Bombay for information technology staff and Bangalore for call center employees. They may be hostages to soaring commodity prices and heavily dependent on oil and coal. They've sacrificed large swathes of land and taken a huge toll on the environment in the quest for economic growth, especially in China.

There are massive infrastructure problems, with transport grinding to a halt in many major Chinese and Indian cities, and barriers to entry exist for Western companies in certain sectors. Both markets are also in the relatively early stages of liberalizing their economies and introducing full market forces.

"The problem is that, as Gandhi said, only 20 percent of what gets sent out by Parliament is spent at its destination," says Vijay Mallya, chairman of Kingfisher beer combine United Breweries, founder and chairman of Kingfisher Airlines, and one of India's wealthiest and most successful businessmen. "What's missing is not resources – India's a wealthy country – but accountability."

A cardinal error is treating the two countries similarly. For example, Narayana Murthy, chairman of Indian information technology group Infosys, says, "What's happening in China is well demonstrated. We do not need more data to applaud China on increasing its growth rate, increasing its per-capita growth rate and urbanizing. But China has a system of governance whereby leaders in Beijing can wave a magic wand and get action. In India the electoral strength is in the rural communities, where there are 650m people. Most economic progress has taken place in urban India, where the infrastructure is weak but better than the rural areas. If politicians seek to accelerate infrastructure development, they look pro-urban and lose elections. If they don't, they lose economic growth: it's a 'Catch 22' situation and we are muddling through."

Murthy is also quick to point out the tremendous progress made since economic liberalization in India in 1991, when he says it took two to three years to get a license to import a computer, ten to twelve days to get foreign exchange for an overseas trip, and three years to get a telephone line installed. "Now, we do multimillion-dollar acquisitions overseas and we install 100m telephone lines in India a year," he says. "Today, entrepreneurship is encouraged in India. We will, as we move forward, find a solution."

Looking beyond China and India, Eric Daniels offers a cautious perspective. "Traders thought they could make money with impunity in emerging markets," he says. "The problem is that the massive flows into these markets have not gone into plant and equipment or structural areas like fertilizer plants and bridges; they've gone in some part into an equity boom that could disappear overnight."

When planning a market entry in emerging markets, double the projected time and halve the projected profits

Daniels says that the danger of emerging markets overheating reminds him of the time he spent running businesses in Argentina in the 1980s, while Chris Bell, chief executive of betting group Ladbrokes, has a rule of thumb for working in developing markets. "When planning a market entry in emerging markets, double the projected time and halve the projected profits," he says.

Whether your business grew up in the East or West, a balanced portfolio of Eastern and Western market positions will serve to smooth earnings volatility and reduce the risk of calamity.

A BRIEF HISTORY OF CORPORATE GLOBALIZATION

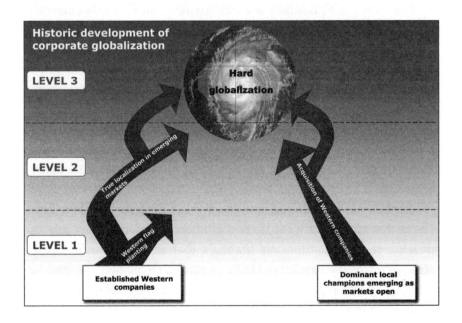

A review of the pattern of globalization by large corporations in the mid to late twentieth century shows two clear historical trends and an emerging pattern that will form the basis of developments in the coming decade.

Level 1: Flag planting doesn't work

Many Western companies have headed into emerging markets intent on achieving what Lord Browne, former chief executive of oil group BP, calls "easy globalization". They have tried to replicate their domestic models in emerging markets and failed because they did not understand local customs and practice.

"Those companies that have tried to impose Western prices, products, business model have not been so successful," notes Narayana Murthy, while Vijay Mallya recalls advice from his father: "He told me: 'If you want to sell beer, talk to the students. There are so many young people that if you are talking to the existing purchasers, you are talking to the wrong market."

The "wave one" mindset is a strategy for failure. "CEOs currently think of a 'go out' strategy," says Browne. "American firms are used to being top dog and thinking in terms of domestic operations versus the rest of the world. That's not right."

Ben Verwaayen, former chief executive at telecommunications company BT, adds: "When people talk about globalization and emerging markets and doing a joint venture in China in a product-type environment, that's not globalization. I think it is export-orientated internationalization. I've got nothing against it. It's not bad. It's something else."

The best Western companies operating in emerging markets have learnt to understand what their customers want and know how to develop reliable distribution channels that respond to the unique structural and geographical challenges of each market, as well as building quality pipelines of local talent. Having figured out the way to finesse their business models, they've then taken a long-term view. As Alan Rosling, executive director at Tata Sons, premier promoter company of Indian conglomerate Tata, notes, "Some foreign businesses have been in India for ever and know the market and are localized: some aren't even seen as foreign brands now. However, many entrants post-1991 were too short term in their thinking and used a lot of expatriates. Their cost bases were therefore too high. Lots came and then left in the 1990s. But those who stayed are doing well and some of the firms who left are trying once again."

Founder and CEO of Wipro, Azim Premji, underlines the key point: "All those who have thrived have done many things right, but one common trend has been the ability and willingness to construct solutions for India... rather than trying to force-fit solutions developed for other countries and societies. You have to be able to develop products, services, and solutions for India."

However, the biggest lesson of all from "wave one" globalization was humility. Vodafone chief executive Arun Sarin expanded into India through the acquisition of a majority stake in mobile operator Hutchison Essar in 2006. "When we did the acquisition, we thought it was all about taking skills to India," he told the CBI India Debate in London. "But in fact we've taken away as much as we have brought."

Unfortunately, in reality a large number of Western companies are still stuck in a flag-planting mentality.

Level 2: True localization

Level two globalization sees enlightened companies localizing their models effectively. Some have been doing this for years. Unilever's development of a business model designed for the Indian market, for example, is a rural tale that demonstrates that to succeed in foreign markets companies need to understand local consumer needs and tailor their products to match them.

Half of Indian sales of soaps and detergents are generated in rural India, so Hindustan Unilever developed and launched products like Lifebuoy, a product stressing health and hygiene. This brand has been synonymous with soap in rural India for decades, but the company realized that its products needed to be more affordable so also developed the low-cost detergent Wheel to graduate people from using soaps to detergents.[6] Wheel is now the world's largest detergent brand by number of washes per year. It touches 600m Indians, sells about 5m packets a year, and controlled about 20 percent of the Indian low-cost detergent segment in 2007.[7]

Hindustan Unilever also realized that poor rural consumers who have access to mass media are just as keen to get consumer products as are their urban counterparts. It therefore changed its pack sizes to bring prices within the reach of rural consumers. Today, sachets constitute about 55 percent of Hindustan Unilever's shampoo sales.[8] The company has also used the same strategy to sell its Surf Excel washing powder in sachets.

As Vindi Banga, president foods, home, and personal care at Unilever plc and former chairman of Hindustran Unilever, told us, in launching Wheel the firm "moved away from a cost-plus pricing approach to a target cost set by deducting a desired margin from a consumer price that we could get in the market for Wheel. At first, the target cost looked impossible – but we got there in two years with a cross-functional team. In addition, selling billions of very small sachets requires a core competence in supply chain and distribution. It is not easy to price at 2 cents and earn a decent margin!"

Hindustan's customer focus is indeed supported by a strong and distinctive supply chain. On the supply side it has 150 outsourcing units and 2,000 suppliers.[9] On the distribution front, third-party agents run more than 20 distribution centers to transport and store Hindustan Unilever products, serving 7,000 distributors that then use salespeople trained by Unilever to work with more than 8m retailers.[10] In addition, Hindustan Unilever has adapted its distribution network to harness locally available talent and meet social responsibility goals. For example, Project Shakti offers self-help groups the option of distributing Unilever products in rural India, helping them generate income while providing Unilever with access to rural consumers. A typical Shakti entrepreneur earns a sustainable income that amounts to around double his or her previous household earnings. Hindustan Unilever now wants to expand the project across India and has already extended it to about 50,000 villages in 12 states.[11] Unilever group CEO Patrick Cescau is proud of the way in which "Project Shakti shows how a lack of retail infrastructure in rural India encouraged us to develop new ways of reaching consumers through direct selling". He adds: "This requires a deep understanding of what consumers really think and need. That is why nine of out ten Unilever employees in developing and emerging markets, including our managers, are local inhabitants. They are drawn from the same communities as our consumers. They spend time living with some of the poorest people,

TATA GROUP: A NEW CHAMPION

Jamsetji Tata founded the Tata Group in the late 1800s with a view to helping to restore India's wealth. As India's pre-eminent business throughout the twentieth century, Tata has a long roll call of early innovations, including introducing the eight-hour working day in 1912 and profit sharing for employees in 1934. Equally, it suffered more than most from India's sluggish planned economy. Uniquely, control of the group rests largely with two charitable trusts.

Tata spent the 1990s rationalizing and consolidating its domestic position, but in 2003 Ratan Tata decided that the group had to globalize. Rosling recalls: "Tata decided we had to look at internationalization as an issue and he gave the challenge to the group to get interconnected with the international world. Tata told the businesses to look at every part of their value chain and look at what they could do internationally. Even pure domestic businesses were to look, for example by sourcing a power plant from China, or Chinese routers and handsets for telecoms."

Since 2003 Tata has pursued a measured expansion prioritizing developed markets, neighboring countries that are close geographically and culturally, then the big emerging markets and, finally, high-growth emerging markets in which it has yet to take a presence. The group has mostly grown through acquisitions and these have been gathering momentum in recent years: its single $407m takeover in 2000 contrasts sharply with $12bn spent buying Anglo-Dutch steel maker Corus in 2007 and the $2bn cost of buying Jaguar Land Rover in 2008.

Today, 30 percent of group revenues come from outside India and the principles of expansion seem clear:

❏ It is aggressive ("We need to stop taking baby steps and start thinking globally," says Ratan Tata).

❏ The aim is truly global operations. As Tata told the *Financial Times* in 2008: "We expect management to integrate with ours... we expect the integration to be easy, and [we] would not get involved with Indianising the company."

As a true global champion, Tata's aspiration is to be a great global business, not an international Indian company. Ratan Tata notes, "It would be great were we considered abroad as a globally operating company with a local touch – that just happens to be owned by a group of Indians."[12]

seeing how they live, what's important to them and the choices they have to make."

This example teaches us several critical lessons on localization. First, Unilever committed to complete localization and a long-term investment for success. Second, the company did not think of India as a single country. Rather, it approached tier 1, 2, and 3 cities and rural communities in subtly different ways. Third, it embraced a local mindset, asking what people really wanted and could afford rather than the maximum they could pay for pre-existing international products. Next, Unilever recognized that radical new distribution systems drawing on the existing infrastructure would be vital to success, rather than merely implementing the techniques it was accustomed to deploying in Western markets. Finally, Unilever drew on the opportunity to make a real difference to local communities.

Level 2: The rise of the new champions

Emerging market titans have leapfrogged level one. Having in many cases spent recent years solidifying their domestic position (Tata and Bajaj Autos, two of India's largest conglomerates, are good examples), these companies are now moving quickly to acquire global market positions.

These emerging champions are hungry and high quality. "I've never seen people who work as hard, who are as ingenious, and who also want to make money so much," says David Walton, former chief executive of engineering company API Group. "When we tried to work with a Chinese company in a joint venture, we found their manufacturing processes were better than ours."

These companies are also getting huge. In 2007 PetroChina became the world's most valuable company in the world after its partial listing in Shanghai nominally valued its shares at $1 trillion – nearly twice as much as America's most valuable company, oil giant Exxon Mobil. Overblown though the Chinese stock market may have been at that time, the Chinese are very serious players in the real economy: three of their companies – Sinopec, China National Petroleum, and State Grid – now feature in the Fortune Global 30 index.

Hungry and huge, the largest emerging markets groups are shifting westwards to move up the value chain, benefit from Western expertise, and improve their research and development and innovation capabilities. They're also buying positions in high-value markets with high-value customers, simultaneously diversifying their business risks and attracting new talent into their businesses. Tata's purchases, Lenovo's acquisition of IBM's personal computer hardware division, and Mittal Steel buying pan-European steel company Arcelor are but three examples.

Level 3: The secret of hard globalization

The truth is that a conception of globalization as either a westward or an eastward flow is flawed. Take Wipro. Azim Premji says, "We are building significant customer relationships in Canada and the Middle East and tapping talent bases in Eastern Europe, Mexico, and US locations outside the large metropolitan areas. Globalization for Wipro is not just about getting customers in the US and Western Europe and talent in India... which in itself is very, very important... but in addition it's about many other things and places."

Bajaj Autos chairman Rahul Bajaj agrees: "We have no choice but to globalize. It may be not only in our interest now but it will also be a question of survival in the future. This year, 20 percent of Bajaj Autos' production will be exported. This has to be 40–50 percent in five to ten years."

The reality is that true global competition has started. In their book *Globality*, three partners at strategy consulting firm BCG identified the same phenomenon. In their definition globality – what we term hard globalization – is "competing with everyone from everywhere for everything". "And by everything," they continue, "we mean just that – all the world's resources. Everybody will be trying to grab the same things that everybody else wants, especially the most precious and limited ones: raw materials, capital, knowledge, capabilities, and, most important, people: leaders, managers, workers, partners, collaborators, suppliers. And, of course, customers."[13]

And as Tim Clarke, CEO of Mitchells & Butler, reminds us, "Globalization can impact any business, even if all your operations are in the UK."

Below we distill what we learnt from conversations with CEOs who understand how to compete in the world of hard globalization from both Eastern and Western starting points.

Adopt a global mindset

In the future, "go-out" globalization will be a strategy for failure. The best leaders will draw on the plethora of instructive lessons from many attempts over past years, but twenty-first-century globalization really starts in the mind.

The essential first step is for the CEO, and then the business, to suspend their domicile, to stop thinking of themselves as having a "home" base. A global mindset attacks every question from the perspective of a citizen of the globe, not that of a territorial national. Every problem is solved by reference to global best practice and through the application of globally sourced resources.

Narayana Murthy sums it up:"To succeed in the global bazaar requires a global mindset." He argues that companies need to adapt and improve best global practices, accept global-level competition, and produce products and services that compete with those from the best global companies. In addition, he says, companies need to be comfortable with a globalized workforce and have universal values that are effective in all cultures, while still benefiting from local best practice. "You need to be very open-minded to adapt to and leverage other cultures. At Infosys, we've practiced these values from the day we founded the company. For me, globalization is about sourcing capital where it is cheapest, sourcing talent where it is best available, producing where it is most efficient, and selling where the markets are. It's about operating without being constrained by national boundaries."

Lord Browne agrees. "Easy globalization is planting a flag because you have an easy advantage, such as technology," he says. "Hard globalization is when everyone's competing. It's when you hear: 'I'm Chinese and I know what to do. I can buy the technology.' The right view is the truly international one. It's only very recently that I've thought of

Britain as my home. I've only really lived here since the late 1980s."

In Shenyang, China, Liu Jiren, CEO of software company Neusoft, concurs: "Business is now conducted on a global stage. More and more Chinese business leaders are going to the US. In the world today, all business leaders need to work more closely to create an ecosystem to share resources worldwide. Now, no one is independent. All the resources, even human resources, are dispersed. Cooperation and open innovation are the future way. How to open, to communicate, to improve self are the challenge to Eastern and Western worlds."

A global mindset attacks every question from the perspective of a citizen of the globe, not a territorial national. Every problem is solved by reference to global best practice and through the application of globally sourced resources.

Ben Verwaayen says that the second vital component of a truly global mindset is a laser-like focus from the CEO on fostering deep-seated and far-reaching collaboration. He says, "Language is important. Americans talk about international business. The word 'international' is okay but 'global' is a threat. In the UK it's the other way around. Global is a state of mind, and that's why London is doing so much better than New York.

"'Global' is interesting because it depends literally on where you sit. We have 26,000 people in India, so at BT when I sat in Delhi and I talked about being 'global', the UK was part of 'global' but Delhi was local. When I talked to our colleagues in Spain, Madrid was local and India global. Most people reason from where they sit and that's in headquarters. And most chief executives talk about their domestic feeling and describe that as the core. But the art of a global company is to accept that it is multilocal. You have to challenge everybody. I needed to make sure that those 26,000 folks in India understood that it wasn't good enough just to be Indian in their thinking; they had to be global. I had to say to the people in London that this is not the center of the world for BT. We have to be global. And I had to go to the US and say to my US colleagues: 'Hey guys, the world is bigger than the US.' You have to work together in a seamless fashion regardless of

location. You have to be able to think as the leader without the
national colors in your head. You cannot raise the national flag in
your head every single day."

Cris Conde, chief executive of Sungard of California, agrees: "To
run a global business, you either run it as a series of very independent businesses, as old multinationals did, or you do something much
more interesting: you run it so that different members of teams are
in different locations. The latter is a truly global business. An off-
shored team is where the workers are offshore and the bosses are at
the center. A global team is one where some of the bosses are far from
the center. None of my direct team sit with me – and they haven't for
12 years. People talk about globalization but really they are talking
about treating countries or markets separately or offshoring their
business model. Until you integrate the teams and integrate management, you have not globalized."

Lenovo has also built its business around true globalization, as
president and CEO Bill Amelio relates. "I know this has become a
cliché," he says, "but the differences among geographies and markets
have shrunk enormously in the past decade due to open trade and
technology, enabling companies like Lenovo to apply competitive
analyses and cost of capital models consistently across the world. We
operate under a unique business model we call 'worldsourcing',
where we bring together our best people, ideas, and processes into
operational centers of excellence around the world and sell wherever
profitable markets exist. At the same time, we encourage our operational leaders to identify and utilize the best ideas
and diverse skill sets wherever they reside internally at Lenovo."

Senior vice-president of human resources,
Kenneth DiPietro, adds: "Worldsourcing is putting aside conventional
wisdom, not letting accounting and finance people do a traditional
cost–benefit analysis of each decision. In a one-timezone world, sourcing needs to be of the best, not the lowest cost. On the talent side, we
find the most talented and gifted people where they are and put the
infrastructure in that makes sense."

In a one-timezone world, sourcing needs
to be of the best, not the lowest cost

Of course, global collaboration also requires a superb understanding of the cultural differences within global organizations. Harriet Green, chief executive of distribution group Premier Farnell, observes: "There's a speed and a pace in Asia: a sense that anything could happen. The stretch goal is achievable. There is a bit of a sense of being the parent of teenagers. People don't know what they can't do but boy will they reach for the potentially unachievable."

In Europe, she says there is much more of a "sense of infrastructure and entitlement". "In Europe," she adds, "people spend all this time talking about work–life balance but just contrast the attitudes in Asia. I did a survey of employees in Asia and asked what their hobbies were – the question was treated as amazing and irrelevant. In the US it's all about money and you can incentivize almost any behavior."

Bernd Scheifele, chairman of the managing board of Germany's Heidelberg Cement, agrees that different management sensitivities are required depending on national territories. "If you run Germans like you would Mexicans, you will have big problems," he says. "Similarly, we too have to learn to run firms in India or China. In India and China, if you are always the nice guy and super-polite, they will not obey. They are used to being instructed very precisely and to following the horse."

So hard globalization requires you to adopt an entrepreneurial mindset to understand the local customer's problem and find the best global solution using the best people drawn from anywhere in the world, working together seamlessly to a 24/7 timetable.

Create a proper global strategy and operate a global business model

Your strategy for competing globally has to be in your corporate bloodstream. It has to affect the structure of the business and the manner in which it functions. Unless it does, you will fail to think globally, while acting locally.

In essence, your business consists of a globally applicable business insight – your way of doing business. The challenge is to understand how that insight is to be nuanced, translated, and applied to each individual market. It's the challenge you've always faced at home, but is multiplied by the number of alien markets in which you operate. Fundamentally, a new link has to be drawn between which operations are retained centrally and how much more power should be devolved locally. Establishing this from the outset gives clear direction on how local managers in a vast number of the markets you are trying to conquer can influence implementation and ensure that your business is thinking locally in every location, while following a general global plan that's being set centrally. We'll return to this in Chapter 12 when we lay out a new model for business leadership, but the headlines are below. The formulation of a proper global business strategy and of a global operating model composed of these five elements will be critical to success in the coming decade.

Set the core global proposition and give more freedom to localize
Rahul Bajaj sums up the consensus of our globalization leaders: "Give the customer what he wants at the price he wants. Where it is manufactured does not concern the customer at all; that's the concern of governments, not customers. You have to act locally but think globally."

But what does that actually mean? Daniels highlights consistency and simplicity. "You win in your core by being very clear on how you outcompete," he says. "When you have a strong core and you can outcompete in home markets, then you can take those skills abroad. You have to know how you're going to beat the locals."

What is the core of a global organization and how can it think and act beyond the nationality of its head office location? An example comes from Todd Stitzer, chief executive of Cadbury, the world's biggest confectionery group: "We try to have global platforms but customize locally. For example, our chewing gum pellets are generally the same size and generally packaged in between one and three types of packages. But we have local brands or flavors customized to local tastes using our flavor banks. For example, Stimorol is virtually the same as Trident. You have to seek scale in those things you can get scale in but customize locally where customer tastes demand."

At Singapore's Tiger Airways, chief executive Tony Davis says it's key to understand the relative importance of different elements of your company. For instance ground operations are core to the low-cost airline model, so he advises executives to be "ruthless" in making sure they are working optimally. "Understand which sensitivities matter and which don't," he notes. "Some are very important. Some are relevant and may represent business opportunity. Some are unimportant." One example he gives is the strong preference of families in Asia not to be split up on flights. Whereas this can cause operational difficulties for ground crews, it's also an opportunity to offer fixed seating at an extra cost: a good example of adding value for both customers and shareholders.

Tesco chief executive Sir Terry Leahy agrees. "Tesco's view of globalization is essentially industry related because the economics of retail are very much local," he says. "Because of the economics, we've had to develop our own approach to international development. Adopt very local business models, be very focused, and don't enter too many countries. We're flexible in our investments in each country, use multiple formats for new countries, and we concentrate a lot on transforming capability, not relying on scale as there's little international scale in our business. In time, build brands."

Joint ventures and partnerships can also help in this process. Bringing in local partners with detailed knowledge of their markets can give you the expertise you need at grass-roots level. It's not a question of what you need to own but of what structure you need to procure the most leverage and influence in the markets you are targeting.

Thras Moraitis, head of group strategy and corporate affairs at mining group Xstrata, advises: "No man is an island, so construct joint ventures and ecosystems to help you achieve what you want to achieve. Control will not be at such a premium in the future so do it now. This requires a high level of creativity." Tan Pheng Hock, president and CEO of Singapore Technologies Engineering, goes further, arguing that we've entered the age of "co-opetition", the ability to cooperate across company borders with sometime competitors in order for both to win.

Dealing with non-competing local partners is a huge supply chain issue in its own right. David Walton says that it's vital to understand local customs and sensitivities: "The key thing in dealing with the Chinese is to build trust with your partner. You need to have a relationship of trust and commitment. The problem is that the government is mistrustful and may then not sign off your deal, despite the good relationship you have built with your partner."

Sir Terry Leahy emphasizes the care that overcoming such difficulties requires of a globalizing business: "As a rule of thumb, it takes 10 years to build a physical network and 10 years to build a brand. The great global firms have needed decades. It took Nestlé 100 years to go from Switzerland to a truly global business. Therefore a sense of timing is important. You need a sense of natural timing. Lots of retailers have gone too fast.

"Of course, timing is not always in your hands. You are hedged in by government and regulation. The real trick is to avoid setbacks because they cost time, which is more important than financing. [Dutch retailer] Ahold rushed its expansion and made some poor acquisitions and is now probably out of the game for good, or certainly a generation. Sainsbury was a decade ahead of Tesco and is not yet in sight of doing it again – they will have lost 20 years if they do it again. The time you need to become global is amazing, even though things move faster now."

Fix strong global values
Narayana Murthy advises chief executives to institute strong universal values that are modeled on and celebrated in every culture in which you operate, while still leveraging unique local conditions. Azim Premji agrees. "We are very focused on our culture... keeping it alive and vibrant and anchored in our values," he says. "We are focused on never losing sight that applying innovation to help make our customers successful is what makes us successful, never losing our sense of humility and fairness and being unyielding on integrity. Globalization doesn't change, but only accentuates the importance of these basics."

We'll come back to the importance and development of values in Chapter 12.

The devolved power principle
Letting go, resisting the temptation to micro-manage, is one of the hardest management skills to learn when running a global business. But it is absolutely vital to devolve power to ground operations, in order to stimulate enterprise *Trust the team and let go. This is what* and creativity and to ensure that you get an *I found hardest* authentic local feel and character to what you are doing in each locality. "Trust the team and let go," urges Mike Turner, chairman of Babcock International and former CEO of BAE Systems, adding: "This is what I found hardest."

Ben Verwaayen believes that getting this balance between local and central operations right, developing the trust needed for this to run well, and making sure discipline is there to sort out problems are all part of the globalization journey. "You have to distribute power," he says. "You have to distribute intelligence. You have to distribute opinions. You have to distribute the ability to influence. You have to distribute the definition of success. These are all things that historically have a home at the center. The definition of success is probably the most important thing to change."

Narayana Murthy agrees. "It's very important to decentralize operations," he says. "In decentralizing, you must articulate your vision, lay out the norms for reporting and the delegating of authority, and formulate a clear escalation mechanism. In other words, you need a protocol which is understood and practiced by various cultures."

How does this work in practice? Verwaayen gives an example. "At BT it's done differently," he says. "The guy in charge of South-East Asia would come to me and say: 'I've decided to go to Vietnam. I have taken us there. Why don't you come and see what we've done?' He wouldn't come and ask permission to do it. He would take certain responsibility in the region, on the ground, knowing what to do. I would take the decision to go there and see how we've done."

In this instance Verwaayen's visit would form the beginning of the headquarters governance process. The earlier permission stage that might normally have existed in a corporate structure has been replaced with a trust in local area management, coupled with the steeliness to sort things out if they go wrong. This kind of devolution of real authority will be even more critical as global competitors increase the speed of innovation and imitation, making the window of competitive advantage ever narrower.

Keith Butler-Wheelhouse, former chief executive of engineering business Smiths Group, had a similar system. "My job was to identify blockages in the pipe and to clear them," he recalls. "Until then, I assumed that everything was going well, set timetables and targets, such as margins and sales for each country, and monitored for disruptions to the system."

Set global minimal standards on finance and business-critical processes
Devolution of power needs to be accompanied by complete transparency so that head office can see what local operations are doing. And you need strong central decision-making capabilities to sort out any problems that emerge from actions that have gone wrong.

"You need to have highly autonomous business units because you should make the decision at the point where the most information is," says Moraitis. "We devolve power from the group in exchange for transparency. At group level we raise money, manage shareholders, conduct transformational acquisitions, and assist in incremental acquisitions at the request of business leaders. The business units are left alone to run businesses but give total transparency on results and operational data."

Thus global businesses set global minimum standards on essential issues, such as health and safety, and make sure that they have a system for enforcing them, while allowing a devolved structure that takes local decisions about business opportunities and operations.

Bernd Scheifele adds: "The challenge is in reaching global technical standards globally, whether it is in production or with our sustainability program. So for production we use global best practices, but sales and marketing are managed locally because cement is a local market business. The group owns financial control."

Create a global company clock
Globalized companies need to learn to cope with working 24 hours a day, 7 days a week. Western call centers for internet banking are already running 24-hour operations, using offshore labor in the Far East to allow customers to call up at any time of day or night. But working on a 24/7 basis requires management too. The fact that there is always a light on in some part of your global operation brings opportunities for productivity and heightened customer service never before dreamt of. It also creates potential problems. One is that time and location can no longer be used as buffers.

Ben Verwaayen recalls an era when a customer wrote a letter and regarded a reply that arrived within a week as timely. Now customers shoot him emails and are not surprised when he answers them within an hour. "Time is disappearing," he says. "We all live in real time. Something happens now in India, bang, the share price in London goes down. So management today has lost time as a buffer. The second thing they've lost is location as a buffer. As a new leader you need to learn without the barrier of protection of location and time. You need to travel more, so you have to spend less time in the office. You have to work with that, feel comfortable with that. You have to communicate on different levels. You have to therefore organize your time differently, and you have to be comfortable in trusting your intuition."

Live globally

To lead a global organization requires travel – a lot of travel. Many of the CEOs we interviewed said that they spent 40–50 percent of their time on the road. At GE, chief executive Jeff Immelt operates a "swing" system, swinging into a country for a week to speak to local customers, top management, and politicians. The swing gives him a level, rather than corporate, view of a nation and allows him to understand market challenges, test his vision, and see how management is responding. GE's view is that the chief executive needs to get around the world and see people face to face once a year. After that, he or she can do things by telephone.

Bernd Scheifele agrees that frequent travel is essential. "You need to travel a lot and to talk to your people and to see them regularly," he says. "You have to understand different cultures without losing your line." As Tan Pheng Hock says, "You cannot be hands on but you have to breathe the air." Thras Moraitis believes that this means you have to be effective straight after your flight lands in another country; something that's a lot easier if you have learnt Mervyn Davies's lesson about being able to sleep on an aeroplane.

Being there, and alert, is not enough. Narayana Murthy adds: "You must also ensure that people from all cultures understand, so your communications must be simple and direct and you must lay out clear roles and responsibilities. Leave local nuances to local leaders: how to encourage employees, how to build the brand, compliance with local laws."

Getting yourself to overseas locations in a fresh and agile state is only the beginning. Communication is about much more than just being there. Language ability helps enormously. Harriet Green recalls once delivering a speech in Finnish and on another occasion giving a 16-minute address in Mandarin. She believes it gave her an edge in getting her message across. Chief executives should also make the most of new technologies to communicate with all parts of their businesses.

"Employee engagement is key as we all fight the war for talent," she says. "We want the best people working for us and they have choices. I communicate regularly with our worldwide team by email, DVD message, podcasts, satellite broadcasts, video conferences, twice-weekly blogs, and twice a year I go on my global 'road show' connecting with every employee across our business, using translators to make sure that the important messages do not get lost through language barriers."

Don't think this is a lesson only for big companies. Peter Warry, the former CEO of British Energy who now chairs polymer manufacturing group Victrex, says, "The board at Victrex operates remotely – it's practically a virtual board. You don't have to be a big company to be global – you can disperse the top team and work effectively even in a relatively small company."

Timing is critical

Reading the business press, you'd think that any business that has no position in emerging markets is doomed. This is clearly wrong, as is the suggestion that any who do are bound to be successful. The truth is, of course, somewhere in between. In essence, as in any market entry decision, you have to be measured on your timing. In some industries it's not appropriate even to use a go-out strategy. Equally, the answer is not merely to move every function to a low-cost economy.

Smiths Industries illustrates the point, as Keith Butler-Wheelhouse notes. "We tend not to produce products where labor is a high percentage of costs," he says. "Therefore the pressure to be in low-cost markets is less pressing than in many manufacturing businesses. The combination of research and development and parts manufacture in developed markets and assembly in developing markets gives us competitive prices in developing economies, but minimizes the risk of leakage into key markets. That said, you can be smart in using global operations. For example, our US design operations do send packets of engineering work to Eastern operations to be completed during the night in the US."

He is firm on how he prioritized markets for expansion. "We moved into new geographies on a customer demand basis," he says. "We needed to be in the markets that our customers were in, but we didn't need complete end-to-end operations there. We spread crumbs on the water. For example, we identified countries with high hospital infection rates and made a case to the health authorities for single-use products. You need to take a granular view of markets. We have a small but profitable Russian private health business, but we don't make any sales in the Russian general hospital market. Those hospitals just aren't ready for single-use instruments yet."

Eric Daniels has also had a similar experience. "At the moment the financial sector in emerging markets is mostly about microfinance, or loans equivalent to about £10," he says. "To do this you have to be deeply embedded in the community, because you cannot have complicated credit scoring systems. But the emerging middle-class market will change banking over the next 20–30 years. Also there are prerequisites for entry, such as rule of law and secured loans laws. China doesn't have a chattel mortgage so there are no secured consumer loans."

Kevin Beeston, chairman of outsourced services provider Serco, notes: "In the services we provide, the nature of the services and the amount of government liaison lead to a reluctance to have visible entry of foreign firms. There's a lack of trust and an aversion to risk. For Serco, India will require an acquisition or a partnership. Indeed in India, our product, managed services, doesn't really exist yet because of the limited infrastructure."

SECRETS OF CEOs: GLOBALIZATION

❏ The global economy will shift on a scale not seen for 200 years. For example, China
   and India will be 49 percent of world GDP by 2025 – as they were in 1819.
❏ The era of flag-planting, easy globalization is over. Companies can no longer open a
   few subsidiaries in far-flung places and sell unmodified products across the world.
❏ We have entered the age of hard globalization where everyone is competing globally.
❏ It is essential that all CEOs adopt a global mindset, whether they currently have global
   operations or not.

The Acid Test: Are you ready for hard globalization?
❏ Do you know exactly how your business outcompetes globally today?
❏ Are you certain that your company's purpose and values are lived globally?
❏ Can you devolve more power locally?
❏ Are your products and services completely localized in all markets?
❏ Do you "world-source" and share best practice on all the core elements of your
   business model right across the world?
❏ Do your metrics focus on siloed regions or on driving global business
   outperformance?
❏ Are your management team truly global? Are they making full use of the 24-hour
   clock?

The shift to hard globalization underpins all the following twenty-first-century business
realities and sets the context for the evolution of businesses that we suggest in Part III. It
is vital that all CEOs fully understand the true implications of globalization.

3

DECODING SUSTAINABILITY

"Climate change will be the single biggest business issue of the next decade. You've got to be on the right side of that."
James Murdoch, chairman and chief executive, News Corporation
Europe and Asia and chairman, BSkyB

"We must not forget that this should be about economic and social sustainability as well as the environmental agenda."
John Richards, chief executive, Hammerson

"We really need to rebalance the world economy. We need to address global warming, water supply, food supply, and migration."
Sir Bill Castell, former chief executive, GE Healthcare

Five years ago, sustainability was just an awkward six-syllable word beloved by academics; now it is one of the corporate buzzwords of our time. Like globalization, however, sustainability is not well understood. We found that asking CEOs to define sustainability produced a long list of vague answers and we heard more than a dozen definitions. Then we asked what constituted the biggest threat to their companies' own sustainability and we received nearly as many answers.

Of course, this variance in definition reflects the reality that sustainability is not defined by just one issue. The challenge is probably best captured by the United Nations' 1987 Brundtland Commission report, which defined it as "development that meets the needs of the present without compromising the needs of future generations to meet their own needs". From these broad roots, sustainability has come to be defined principally by climate change, as scientific evidence for the phenomenon has become widely accepted and fears of its effects have grown in consumers. A landmark was the signing of the Kyoto Protocol in 1998. Ten years later, 177 countries responsible for 64 percent of global greenhouse gas emissions had pledged to reduce their emissions of carbon dioxide and five other greenhouse gases or to engage in emissions trading.[1]

The debate about climate change still rages, with environmentalists warning that the world is acting too slowly and half-heartedly and skeptics claiming that the issue is being blown out of all proportion. However, sustainability is also about social responsibility and the role that companies play in their communities, which are demanding more from big business. The question is whether businesses can successfully both sustain themselves and maintain and enhance their license to operate globally. That is going to require changes in the social contract that they have with governments, communities, and society.

For some businesses, especially those operating in developing markets, ensuring a continuing license to operate is a very real concern. Brad Mills, at South Africa-based Lonmin, for example, sees "a fundamental threat to what has otherwise been a pretty sustainable market economy". He says, "There's an increasing backlash between this thing called capitalism and this thing called community. We do not understand the environmental effects and long-range problems that communities face; they don't understand business pressures of cost pressures and competition. This is not a good thing and could be very damaging. The challenge is to try and change the world by creating a different model which is much more life-affirming to people. You can support both corporations and communities and see them both thrive. What drives me is trying to transform that fundamental societal relationship in the name of long-term sustainability."

There's an increasing backlash between this thing called capitalism and this thing called community

"Sustainability" increasingly features in companies' corporate and social responsibility manuals and chief executives' speeches, though what it refers to ranges from mild social policing such as encouraging employees to cycle to work and only stocking fair-trade coffee in the staff canteen to the much more comprehensive environmental and social programs of the likes of Marks & Spencer, Cadbury, and Tata.

In short, sustainability has become an all-embracing term covering efforts to solve the world's social, environmental, and economic problems. And the solutions to such problems are now being put at the door of the business community. So how did this happen and what should businesses do about it?

Corporate environmentalism is growing around the world. However, it is in the UK that it is perhaps most entrenched. For example, BP in its Beyond Petroleum rebranding in 2000 was the first major oil group to focus effort on developing alternative fuels. In the public sphere, the UK government went further than most countries in publishing the *Stern Review on the Economics of Climate Change.*[2] Let's take a look at what's happening in the UK, as it is at the forefront of the corporate environmentalism agenda and likely to signpost developments around the world.

BATTLEGROUNDS OF CORPORATE ENVIRONMENTALISM

In the UK there are three key battlegrounds for the new corporate environmentalism: supermarkets, airlines, and natural resources.

The green supermarket trolley

Given the consumer focus on the environment, planet retail is a natural battleground for large-scale green programs. Landfill, recycling, and energy consumption increasingly top the consumer agenda and customers are voting with their feet for companies that show they care.

At Marks & Spencer, for example, chief executive Sir Stuart Rose has indelibly linked the retailer to action on both environmental and social sustainability, through Plan A, a campaign that is unashamedly evangelical and didactic, using the slogan "Plan A... because there is no Plan B". M&S has addressed climate change with 29 of Plan A's 100 sustainability commitments. The company aims to eradicate its 500,000 tonnes of direct emissions by 2012 by becoming more energy efficient, embracing green electricity, and using carbon offsetting. It has also pledged to make a difference by "breaking society's addiction to the plastic carrier bag", promising to reduce carrier bag usage by a third and send no waste to landfill by 2012.[3]

Marks & Spencer's head of corporate social responsibility, Mike Barry, says that when formulating the strategy, the company considered data showing that 39 percent of UK consumers wanted definite action on the issue, another 36 percent felt helpless to make a difference, and the remaining 25 percent didn't care. Marks & Spencer detected a genuine wish for leadership, he says, and decided it should respond to customers while also seeking to lead and educate them. It is therefore also encouraging its shoppers to wash their clothes at lower temperatures to save energy; labeling all its air-freighted products so that customers can make educated decisions about what to buy; and assisting in development of a carbon calculator to help the Women's Institute's 250,000 members understand and reduce their carbon footprints.[4] States Barry, "Customers were basically saying: 'If you take the first steps to do as much as you can, that would start to give us an idea of what to do.' They would start to come on the journey."

Tesco is also targeting the plastic bag. The supermarkets group, whose attention to changing consumer desires is legendary, has pledged to halve the average energy used in its buildings by 2010 compared with 2000, make all carrier bags biodegradable, and take 1m carrier bags a year out of use. It has piloted stores with a carbon footprint 60 percent lower than that of its conventional supermarket and set up a £100m environmental fund for initiatives including powering stores with wind turbines, solar panels, and geothermal power, and producing energy from waste food. The company has committed to stating the carbon footprint on the labels of all of its products and has

halved the price of low-energy light bulbs, with the aim of quadru-
pling annual sales from 2.5m to 10m.[5]

"Tesco has identified three key points that customers want us to
help them on," says community and government director David
North. "They want us to explain to them what they can do in their
own lives to make a difference on climate change. They want us to
ensure that a greener alternative economy is not a more expensive
economy. And they want businesses like Tesco to provide them with
information to make a greener choice."

Many commentators question the motives of such retailers.
However, it is clear that these businesses are now actively focusing on
the environment and making real changes. Action on climate change
has become a new dimension of competition.

In the skies

Aviation and travel are classic examples of industries caught out
by the rapid development of the sustainability movement. Despite
travel industry stocks plummeting after the terrorist attack on the
World Trade Center on 9/11, debt burdens driving major US airlines into Chapter 11 bankruptcy protection, and fuel prices sky-
rocketing, record numbers of people are flying. However, the
industry is under attack from environmental campaigners, media,
politicians, and also churchmen who preach against flying because
of its carbon emissions. Even evangelists of foreign travel are turning on the companies that made it possible, with Mark Ellingham,
founder of the Rough Guides travel book series, publicly deploring
what he refers to as "binge flying". "If the travel industry rosily
goes ahead as it is doing, ignoring the effect that carbon emissions
from flying are having on climate change, we are putting ourselves
in a very similar position to the tobacco industry," he argues.[6]
Indeed, the industry has become a public whipping boy, with
Gordon Brown doubling Britain's air passenger duty in 2007 and
planning in 2008 to impose increased taxes on planes rather than
passengers.

The pace of this debate undoubtedly caught airlines out, but they are coming out fighting with industry campaigns aimed at putting aviation's carbon footprint into context by comparison with other sectors. Budget airline easyJet published *Towards Greener Skies: The Surprising Truth about Flying and the Environment*, a report pointing out that air travel accounts for just 1.7 percent of global greenhouse gas emissions. The anticipated growth in air travel is expected to increase this to 6 percent by 2050, but that is still well below the emissions from cars, which account for about 9 percent. Longhaul planes, the report says, emit 110g of carbon dioxide per passenger kilometer – about the same as a medium-sized car with two occupants.[7]

"Much of the political debate has been characterized by gesture politics and discriminatory, often contradictory, proposals," says easyJet's chief executive Andy Harrison, "and it's time for consumers to tell the politicians that we won't be 'green-rolled' into accepting higher air taxes for a spurious green rationale. Politicians of all colors recognize that different cars have different emissions, but do not seem to see the same distinction within air travel. The critical thing is to get people flying in new aircraft. The way air passenger duty works at the moment is that people pay the same whether they are flying in an old aircraft, a new aircraft, a half-empty aircraft, or a full aircraft."

The airline industry realized that it was paying the price for underestimating environmental campaigners and easyJet, British Airways, Monarch, FlyBe, and Virgin Atlantic airlines joined manufacturers Boeing and Airbus and tour operators such as Thomas Cook to form air travel lobbying group Flying Matters. The organization seeks to counteract negative messages and promote the economic benefits of the airline industry. "What we need from politicians," says Flying Matters campaign director Michelle Di Leo, "are policies which recognize the work being done by the industry to reduce its impact on the environment and which balance this with the economic and social contribution made by aviation. Economic sustainability needs to go hand in hand with environmental sustainability."[8]

Natural resources

Energy companies are highly vulnerable to sustainability campaigners, both for their environmental footprints and for their impact on
the societies in the locations where their natural resources are found.
Disasters like the *Exxon Valdez*, in which 11m gallons of oil were
spilled into one of the world's most protected sites of natural beauty
off Alaska, have had a profound effect on the reputations of oil
companies.[9]

BP was an early pioneer in the industry's attempts to clean up its
act, investing in solar, wind, hydrogen, and gas power and playing a
part in reducing the environmental impacts of transport by developing biofuels and cleaner petrol and lubricants. Lord Browne says that
the sustainability debate caused him to make major structural
changes to the company. "Sustainability is fundamental," he says,
"and it's why I created two structures, a structure for conventional
growth and another for alternative energy. If we can create a sustainable planet that depends less on oil, then we may achieve a more sustainable balance between nations."

As BP has realized, climate change threatens energy companies'
core business and they are having to explore how to clean up their
operations, diversify into alternative energy sources, and communicate their environmental zeal effectively to their customers.

PAST THE ENVIRONMENTAL TIPPING POINT

These three battlegrounds alone demonstrate that corporate environmentalism is now a vital competitive battlefield for many companies.
Juhi Shareef, consultant sustainable management at Arup, sees corporate environmentalism moving front of mind in mainstream businesses and believes that carbon-reduction efforts are rapidly raising
general social standards. While retail, energy, and aviation are the
main industries under attack from carbon lobbyists at present, she
says that carbon reduction will very quickly become a major issue for

the shipping and information technology industries. "If anyone worked out the carbon footprint of identity cards, it would make them even more controversial," she observes.

Regulation will play a major part. The UK government, for example, has pledged to reduce the country's carbon emissions by 60 percent by 2050 and many experts believe it will go further and aim to reduce them by up to 80 percent. Tom Delay, chief executive of the Carbon Trust, says that no one should underestimate the magnitude of this task or the effort needed to achieve it. "Unless we take the right actions in the next five to ten years, we will never get anywhere near the 2050 targets," he says. "The next five to ten years are going to be enormous in the efforts to reduce carbon. Companies and individuals are going to come to realize that there are some incredibly difficult decisions to take if we are to get anywhere near the government's target." The UK and the EU have taken a lead in setting regulatory standards, but most observers expect the US in particular to follow over the next decade.

Cautious voices do exist. John Richards, chief executive of property group Hammerson, gets "worried by the eco-warrior mindset that says that if anyone does not have a zealot-style enthusiasm for it or dares question the science of the environmental lobby, they have to be shouted down". However, the corporate environmental agenda is here to stay. Says Mervyn Davies, "Sustainability has passed the tipping point in the UK. Most FTSE CEOs and politicians get it."

"Environmental sustainability is now core to a business," adds Samir Brikho, chief executive of engineering group AMEC. "There is no way out: you like it or you don't but you cannot ignore it. Sustainability is the way of the world – otherwise move to another planet. Do you want to live in a world where your children do not have the possibilities you've had? We have to go beyond our company to get society to get its pollution figures down. Business leaders in previous generations felt that they had unlimited resources. It's a new discovery of the last 20 years to find that it's not merely a question of well-intentioned conservation but of an imperative to conserve."

INITIATIVES IN CORPORATE ENVIRONMENTALISM

It may now be near essential to address corporate environmentalism, but CEOs' responses differ widely. Some take part in the agenda with "greenwash", spinning initiatives they would engage in anyway as examples of their environmental commitment. Our interviews indicate that the number in this group is shrinking, because most CEOs are coming to accept the arguments for action; and the risks of being caught out and being shown to be insincere are becoming unacceptably high. At the other end of the scale, some businesses are making significant commitments to embed sustainability metrics and concerns deeply within their business and achieve real improvements in their environmental footprint. For example, Ben Verwaayen chairs the Confederation for British Industry's climate change taskforce, within which 18 businesses with international footprints are working to share best practice on corporate environmentalism and develop metrics for the performance of their operations. Under his leadership, the group's members have committed to reduce their collective footprint by 1m tonnes of carbon dioxide within three years, and to create products that will halve emissions at work and home by 2020.[10] CBI director-general Richard Lambert says, "Moving to a low carbon emission economy is the biggest challenge for our generation and business must be part of the solution."

In between these two extremes, many CEOs are keen to address this area but, caught up in their other daily challenges, are struggling to execute against their aspirations to do the right thing. This has provoked skepticism in the press. John Waples, business editor of the *Sunday Times*, is "not convinced that chief executives see the environment and CSR as little more than a way to get a quick headline". He adds: "Most companies do have a lot of green initiatives under way but they don't cut deep enough." However, while some CEOs are settling for quick wins like carbon offsetting rather than genuinely reducing their carbon footprints, the more ambitious are making deeper changes.

Governments have targeted company supply chains as effective mechanisms for corporate compliance. Policing of new carbon standards and the global nature of such chains is likely to drive meaningful change across the world.

It seems clear that global businesses will follow the path the UK's businesses have set out on. Government encouragement will help and so will the traction gained by European corporate environmentalism and the response from customers and staff. Progress will also occur naturally as the international supply chains of enlightened businesses are greened from the center.

Although Western observers are cynical about the likely response of governments in emerging markets given their focus on growth and local issues, the environment is rising up the agenda with corporations there too. Says Rahul Bajaj, "The environment is getting more and more important around the world, even in India." Frank Tang, founder of Fountainvest, a prominent private equity investor in China, adds, "The Chinese government has made environmental action core in its five-year plan and is increasingly making this a very high priority. I expect to see continued policies rolling out from the Chinese government in this area." Indeed, alternative energy was the third largest sector for private equity investment in China in 2007.

While there is a long way to go, 77 percent of companies in the Fortune 500 index now respond to the Carbon Disclosure Project,[11] which seeks to hold companies to account on carbon change by annually quizzing them in detail about their actions and publishing their full responses. Such initiatives have created new metrics for measurement and comparison of company performance that are scrutinized closely by governments, corporate environmentalists, and other businesses. Theo Schoenmaker, head of sustainability at Dutch electronics group Philips, believes that this is the true meaning of "triple bottom line" – a term that has unfortunately become rather clichéd.

"The way companies are measured is now about people, it's about the planet, and it's also about profits," he says.

Of course, there is a fundamental question here: Are we moving fast enough on the green agenda? The Bali Accord looks to have set the process in motion for a successor treaty to Kyoto, but good intentions need to become effective action and the accord needs to be rigorous enough to prod recalcitrant corporates.

James Berrien, president and publisher of Forbes Magazine Group, sees a continued skepticism about whether climate change is a legitimate issue and whether anything can be done about it. "Most CEOs in the USA see it as important from an image and branding point of view but I'm not sure that people see it as core to their business," he says. There is also understandable doubt in many developing markets, where improving the standard of living is seen as a more pressing priority than meeting the green agenda.

Even where global business leaders understand that they need to act, it is unclear to them how they should change their core business operations, define projects, and develop metrics for the effective rollout of meaningful international initiatives. There's a lot of work to be done, but as Unipart Group chief executive John Neill says, some progress has already been made. "For the first time I can think of, we can have alignment between all the players," he says, "Governments, corporates, and individuals; the world has a common enemy to fight against."

THE NEXT PHASE: BROADLY DEFINED SUSTAINABILITY

Enlightened companies around the world are moving on to define sustainability much more broadly. Mervyn Davies puts it succinctly. "As a CEO, get on the sustainability train or you will go out of date," he warns. "I think the train left a couple of years ago, really. The agenda has moved much faster than people realize. Tomorrow's story is that what you are doing to help the planet be a better place will be part of your brand promise. Sustainability

What you are doing to help the planet be a better place will be part of your brand promise

is gathering pace at the international level and companies will have a very, very big role to play. This will mean there is pressure on boards of directors to squeeze sustainability into what is already a packed agenda." In the future, being "green" will only be the start.

Again, countries like the UK, where corporate environmentalism is already mainstream, are leading the way in understanding the value of a broad definition of sustainability. However, our research suggests that CEOs in visionary companies across the globe are discovering that broadly defined sustainability matters for the following reasons, and that these reasons mean that corporate sustainability will globalize much as corporate environmentalism already is.

It can boost sales with consumers

James Murdoch is clear on his primary motivation. "Sustainability for our business is first and foremost about being customer driven," he says. "It's about understanding customers' needs and caring about what they care about and not being caught out." Sir Terry Leahy expands the point. "The battle to win customers in the twenty-first century will increasingly be fought not just on value, choice, and convenience," he says, "but on being good neighbors, being active in communities, seizing the environmental challenges, and on behaving responsibly, fairly, and honestly."

Similarly, Michael Dell, chairman and CEO of Dell Computer, states: "We are seeing an increased need for greater energy efficiency across all product lines. Our customers are asking for it more and more in the data center as well as in their desktops and notebooks. On top of that, customers are increasingly aware of a product's environmental impact not just while it is being used, but before it was plugged in and after it is boxed up again for disposal."

These views do not represent soft thinking. An Environics study showed that at least two-thirds of 25,000 consumers surveyed in the US, Canada, and Western Europe form impressions based partly on a company's ethics, environmental impact, and social responsibility. In the US, 60 percent of the adults polled said that knowing a company is mindful of its impact on the environment and society makes them more likely to buy its products and services; 40 percent stated that they would avoid buying products if they thought the disposal of their packaging presented a potential threat to wildlife.[12]

At BT Group, surveys indicate that customers who rate the company highly for its corporate and social responsibility work are 70 percent more likely to come back with repeat business than those who don't.[13] James Murdoch was also an early convert to such evidence, making BSkyB the second company in the FTSE100 index to go carbon neutral. The company takes its social responsibilities seriously too, offering audio description for blind and visually impaired people and a remote control that makes life easier for those with manual dexterity problems. It claims it has pioneered new ways for parents to control the programs their children watch, and promotes the educational value of its programming in bringing the UK national curriculum to life on screen to help students study at home.

It helps attract and retain staff

Somebody's customers are often someone else's employees, so it shouldn't be surprising that if consumers are demanding sustainable business practices, staff are pretty keen on them too. Therefore embracing sustainability is more than merely good public and customer relations. "Talking about profit is a complete waste of time if you want to motivate people," declares John Varley, chief executive of banking group Barclays. "Am I am able to motivate 120,000 people here by telling them I want them to make more profit? You can forget it. You might as well go and talk to the birds. You have to have an emotional motivation. Our people are motivated by something very deep – the human instinct to help."

Our people are motivated by something very deep – the human instinct to help

Richard Baker adds that one of the reasons Alliance Boots started giving its old products to hospitals was the reaction of its staff. "Taking lots of stuff to landfill upsets the lorry drivers who drive it there," he says. "They hate to see all this waste, so we give our old products to hospitals and hospices." Philip Green agrees, saying he filled a 500-seat cinema with United Utilities staff to watch *An Inconvenient Truth.* "Employees love an effective sustainability agenda and yet it costs almost nothing," he says.

At the Financial Times, CEO Rona Fairhead notes: "Our concern for the environment: that's driven by today's customers and tomorrow's employees. Both want to know that you're doing the right thing."

This matters to CEOs in the US too. States James Berrien: "For CEOs, acquiring and retaining talent is at the top of the list. Generation Y cares a lot about sustainability so it is becoming a talent acquisition issue in the US."

It typically saves cost

BT Group has cut its carbon emissions by 60 percent since 1996[14] and now has 70,000 flexible workers, including 11,500 who are full-time home workers without any office at the company. It says using video and telephone conferencing technology saved it 97,000 tonnes of CO_2 and accounted for £141m of the £229m group savings from environmental improvements in 2007.[15]

Richard Baker agrees that CSR can save money. "Being responsible corporate people is doing the right thing," he says, "But in eliminating waste sent to landfill and helping energy conservation you can also be more efficient and have less waste." Philip Green has also found that going carbon neutral is good value for money. "We're investing £37m in our carbon policy but it's paying back," he states.

Wider socially responsible activities can save money too. John Neill is vehement. "It's much better and less expensive to train people well in the basics at school," he says. "We can then develop, train, and inspire them to achieve world-class performance at work."

Some investors view sustainability initiatives favorably

In addition to the efficiency, brand, and commercial benefits of embracing sustainability initiatives, there may be a correlation between good sustainability practice and better stock market performance.

A report published by US investment bank Goldman Sachs when it launched the Goldman Sachs Energy Environmental and Social (GSEES) Index states: "The bulk of the value of any company is determined by its long-run or sustainable returns, the next 20 percent by secular or cyclical change observed in the coming 12 months and the remainder by longer-term growth or other issues. One-off issues have a limited impact on share prices. In our opinion, environmental and social issues will have an impact on share prices if they affect the long-term return profile of a company." A later report observed that companies ranking as leaders in the GSEES and in the top 50 of Goldman's Environment, Social and Government Index had outperformed their peers by an average of 24 percent in the previous 20 months. Laggards on both measures had underperformed by an average of 5 percent.[16]

Moreover, many funds have sprung up with the specific aim of making investments in sustainable and socially responsible businesses. Indeed, there are now more than 300 specific socially responsible investment funds in Europe, while sustainability research is offered by a wide range of major broking houses. Rating agencies Standard & Poor's and Fitch have launched corporate governance ratings, while the Carbon Disclosure Project is backed by more than 315 major institutional investors who together speak for $41 trillion in assets.[17]

Private equity believes it too, says Martin Halusa, chief executive of private equity firm Apax Partners. "We need to build sustainable value," he says. "It is absolutely true that there is a

We see ensuring sustainability as premium for good corporate sustainability.

absolutely core to the value we create Therefore, we see ensuring sustainability, ensuring CSR, ensuring employee health, safety, and protection as absolutely core to the value we create. Corporate sustainability is now at the core of our portfolio evaluation process and forms a separate section in our twice-yearly assessment of the entire portfolio. Our team members are tasked with bringing these issues up so sustainability is a core part of our business today."

Frank Tang agrees, "I'm a big fan of sustainable development. It's one of Fountainvest's key themes," he says. "We think it will be extremely important for China going forward. It represents opportunities and also pressure on companies to incur additional expense in the short term, but in the long run if they do not do that they will suffer. So, firms need to budget the cost to do it."

Businesses are coming under pressure to justify their position in society

Fundamentally, businesses have to earn the right to operate in society. "If you become divorced from your communities, it is potentially quite dangerous and threatening because corporations have no sense of loyalty any more and communities have become increasingly hostile to business," points out Brad Mills.

"Our customers have said they want us to be a good retailer, a good neighbor, and to be fair and honest in our dealings," adds Sir Terry Leahy. Ben Verwaayen also sees the issue clearly: "Your relationship with the societies in which you operate is what we call corporate social responsibility," he says. "That's the respect you give to society as a license to operate. So, I think corporate social responsibility is not charity. It's not nice to have; it's a must-do if you want to be a global company. You need to give society the reason to accept your presence in their midst by being a responsible company, by looking to climate change, by looking to diversity, to education, and to other things. It's about what you do with shareholders, customers, and the societies in which you operate."

One extremely senior UK chairman and former chief executive goes so far as to worry whether this will threaten Western capitalism itself. "I worry about the sustainability of the economic model I grew up with," he says. "I think there's a real threat to capitalism. Only about a billion people in the world participate in free markets. The other six billion are excluded from them. Capitalism has to prove that it's the best way to run an economy. People think the battle was won when communism fell in the Eastern bloc, but I think the jury is still out."

Capitalism has to prove that it's the best way to run an economy

Leigh Clifford has a similar set of beliefs. "You've got to make sure you don't create a land of prosperity in a sea of poverty," he stresses. "The community has got to get something out of it as well. The balance between profits and sustainability is a bit like the balance between profits and safety. You need to have both. Companies cannot have double standards about this."

Similarly, the chief executive of one major British high street retailer admits that his business is "very vulnerable" to the child labor issue. "There are 4,000 garment factories in Bangladesh; you cannot check them all," he says. "At a macro level, it's great because they're highly productive and efficient. At a micro level, there's the worry that we cannot know what's going on there all the time. We really do have obligations. We try to leave as small a footprint as we can. The impact on the human population of Africa is such that if you do things wrongly out there, that can kill people. I do not want to go to bed one night thinking we have made money out of some sort of abuse. I like to know I'm part of the solution."

Sometimes leaders embrace sustainability solutions for religious reasons. Life insurer Friends Provident, for example, has strong ethical values, having been founded to provide savings products for Quakers. "Sustainability has become a bit of a bandwagon but our values are not an accident," says former chief executive Philip Moore. "We've been talking about sustainability for 175 years."

However, leaders don't need a religious bent to think that sustainability is the right thing to do. "We do this stuff because our role in society is something that's multifaceted and very important," says James Murdoch. "I just think that businesses can be better."

Businesses can make an enormous difference

The imbalance in living standards in the world is well documented: more than 1 billion people live on less than $1 a day. What is less frequently observed is the capacity for good that companies can have. Businesses are in a better position than government ministers to act as they are global, typically have little patriotism, are not prey to election fever, are not mortal, and have fewer employees than states have citizens, so each person should be easier to mobilize. Employees are also paid to listen to their CEO's views – something that can't be said for the public and politicians. Sir Bill Castell, now chairman of the Wellcome Trust, stresses that "companies can be more effective in solving some of the world's problems than politicians. Politicians are elected by a national vote; corporations have an interest in global success. The best CEOs have a vision for their company's impact on the world for 20 or 30 years ahead."

At Business in the Community, a forum for business engagement with sustainability issues led by Prince Charles, CEO Stephen Howard argues that business's ability to innovate will be key to pursuing the sustainability agenda. "Businesses and their leaders have a critical role in society because, unlike governments, they now have to think beyond geographical boundaries, ministerial systems and election terms, and short-term headline-grabbing press releases," he says. "Global businesses are not the problem; they're actually the solution. Key to making things work is the enterprise of corporations. The key to sustainability is not regulation but business innovation. Enterprise is key to unlocking the talent and some of these more difficult issues."

Many senior figures agree. For Mervyn Davies, "The role of companies is increasingly important because they cross borders more easily than politicians. Therefore, they need a sustainability agenda." Management professor Michael Porter and Mark Kramer, managing director of social impact advisers FSG, stated in the *Harvard Business Review*: "Companies are not responsible for all the world's problems, nor do they have the resources to solve them all. But each company can identify the particular set of societal problems that it is best equipped to resolve and

When a well-run business applies its vast resources to problems, it can have a greater impact on social good than any other institution

from which it can gain the greatest competitive benefit. Addressing social issues by creating shared value will lead to self-sustaining solutions that do not depend on private or government subsidies. When a well-run business applies its vast resources, expertise and management talent to problems that it understands and in which it has a stake, it can have a greater impact on social good than any other institution or philanthropic institution."[18]

So what can you do?

The experience of working on corporate environmental issues has led businesses and stakeholders to take a fresh look at the broader CSR agenda. Tomorrow's Company, a thinktank on global business, summarized the way leading companies can take action on the sustainability agenda in a report compiled in collaboration with leaders from companies including ABB, Anglo-American, Ford, Infosys, KPMG, McKinsey, and Standard Chartered:[19]

❏ Tomorrow's global company should expand its view of success and redefine it in terms of lasting positive impacts for business, society, and the environment.
❏ Having redefined success, tomorrow's global business leaders should stand firmly behind their convictions and use them as a basis for their business strategy and decision making.
❏ Internal processes, especially measurement and reporting and external communications with all stakeholders, need to be consistent with this view of success.

Embed CSR in the core of your business

Tony Manwaring, CEO of Tomorrow's Company, says that business "needs to move beyond a focus on inputs and resources to thinking through the role of business and work in ensuring that we fulfill our potential as human beings now and in the future: as individuals, as communities, and as a species in balance with nature."

Nandan Nilekani, co-chairman of Infosys Technologies, says that "truly global companies will need to develop a compelling vision which enables sustainable, profitable development of their business whilst benefiting the society at large". Bill Amelio reports that when

Lenovo merged with IBM's personal computer division in 2005, the company's emphasis on social responsibility dovetailed perfectly with IBM's legacy in sustainable global business practices. "The result today is a culture in which sustainability is embedded in Lenovo's core values," he says. "It's a big part of who we are as a company and who we are as people and represents a guiding light in our decision-making process."

Lessons can also be learnt from family companies which, without short-term pressure from public shareholders, have had this as a fundamental way of doing business for many years. At The Timberland Company, for example, chief executive Jeff Swartz says, "We believe in our guts that commerce and justice are not separate ideas; that doing well and doing good are not antithetical notions; that being cognisant of this quarter's earnings is part of what we are responsible for – just as being our brother's and sister's keeper is part of what we are responsible for, every business day."[20]

Explore CSR metrics appropriate to your business

The question of how to quantify the value of sustainability measures precisely is still a thorny one. The consensus among CEOs seems to be that most initiatives are highly value accretive, but at present require companies to act on beliefs often without a fully proven financial case. Mark Armitage, president US of The CarbonNeutral Company, says, "Smart businesses get sustainability and realize that it's simply the right way to do business. They act on these beliefs while other companies that are more financially orientated and more cost-conscious still need a detailed business case. Unfortunately, they may have to wait three to four years before a really rigorous case will be available."

At present, there are no generally accepted set of non-financial metrics for success in pursuing the overall corporate sustainability agenda. However, some leading companies are now starting to develop financial and non-financial metrics around this broader agenda. Tesco has added "community" metrics to the "growth wheel" that drives all its store managers' work. At Cadbury, moreover, Todd

Stitzer notes: "It is specifically included in each of the senior leaders' objectives that their businesses must invest in education and health in their communities. It's their choice what they do, but they have to come and tell us what they've done."

Get your investors on side

Businesses should be run in a sustainable way. However, we are not dreamy-eyed here. As Rahul Bajaj warns: "There can be a trade-off between CSR and maximizing shareholder value. To my mind, you cannot be a good corporate citizen by limiting supply, mistreating employees, and so forth. You cannot just make donations and cover issues up. So, there is a compromise here. But you have to recognize that there is a trade-off."

Long-term value will only be built by sustainable businesses in the coming decade. Sir Martin Sorrell says, "If you want to build a business for the long term, you'll take into account the interests of all your stakeholders, so you're not going to foul up the environment, you're not going to annoy governments, non-governmental organizations, or employees. If you're interested in making a quick buck, you're probably not going to do it. But if you are interested in building a business for the long term, it's a no-brainer."

A trade-off between long-term value and short-term profits entails a need to convince today's fickle financial institutions of the intelligence of your sustainability plan. We'll come back to the challenge of managing your capital base in Chapter 5.

Engage and motivate staff

CEOs report that CSR can galvanize and motivate staff. One popular path is to make use of not-for-profit organizations in this arena. Says Ben Verwaayen, "There are already enough forums on the environment and broader corporate sustainability. We don't need to create any more but we do need companies to actively get involved and make things happen at the forums that already exist."

Business in the Community's "Seeing is Believing" is an example of a program that brings home to leaders how businesses can effectively address deep social issues. Senior managers visit community projects and meet people whose lives have been transformed for the better. One experience reported in the organization's 2007 annual review relates to the testimony of a man called Eddie, who had been a shepherd until the UK's foot-and-mouth epidemic robbed him of his flock. He then spent four years sleeping rough, latterly in a graveyard, before eventually finding a job as a temp at a law firm through BITC. He is now working full-time and has integrated back into normal life. "If everybody takes and nobody gives back, there'll be nothing left," he told chief executives at the event. Some were moved to tears. Prince Charles believes that "Seeing is Believing" is one of the most powerful experiences many people have had in their business careers.

Charlie Mayfield, chairman of the John Lewis Partnership, recommends that business leaders go on Seeing is Believing visits. "It's by doing that you see the real power of it," he says. "It's not just about one individual. It's about bringing groups together to do community initiatives that will work and have staying power."

John Studzinski, senior managing director at private equity group Blackstone who is also involved with Seeing is Believing, adds that the visits involve a lot of readjustment. "I advise executives that these people are homeless," he told the *Daily Telegraph*.[21] "They are very suspicious of business people. They will wonder why you are there but they will also regard you with great promise and great hope. A lot of people will tell you about yourself and ask why you are there. What happens then is something magical," according to Studzinski. "Homeless people tell you their stories and they are so compelling. Where Seeing Is Believing is very precious is in the one-on-one interaction that you get. Something clicks. People have terrible stereotypes. The only way to break the stereotypes is putting humans together. It's transforming. Executives come away feeling that it is sad and there must be a solution. People start the day sceptical and end it full of hope. It does have a profound effect on individuals. It makes them very conscious of how to engage with society."

Engage more widely and collaborate

All sustainability initiatives are inherently collaborative, as they relate to supporting the community and future generations. Bob Harrison, CEO of the Clinton Global Initiative, says, "To solve some of the big world problems, the agenda shouldn't be dominated by any one stakeholder. As many as possible should be as fully engaged as possible in taking collaborative action. It will be increasingly important that key global business leaders connect with other stakeholders to have a real impact and make a difference."

Recognizing this, visionary CEOs are increasingly championing this agenda through organizations such as the World Economic Forum at Davos, the Clinton Global Initiative, the

I see a world where we have much   Global Reporting Initiative, and other non-govern-
more three-way cooperation between   mental organizations. These organizations are
industry, government, and NGOs   building very strong networks and Sir Bill Castell
                                     only sees this trend increasing. "I see a world
where we have much more three-way cooperation between industry, government, and NGOs," he says. "I want all three to work together, to increase accountability, increase success, and mean that society becomes more trusting."

This need not be apple pie and motherhood. For example, 70 percent of the cocoa required for Cadbury's chocolate comes from Ghana. However, Cadbury noticed that the average production for a cocoa farmer had dropped to only 40 percent of potential yield and that cocoa farming had become less attractive to the next potential generation of farmers.[22] Consequently, it has partnered with the United Nations and other NGOs to pump £50m into the cocoa industry to protect its supplies. The Cadbury Cocoa Partnership aims to improve farmers' incomes, introduce new sources of rural income, through microfinance for example, and invest in community-led development. Farmers, governments, NGOs, and international agencies will work together to decide how the funding is spent and connect with local organizations to turn plans into action.

One final network effect is worthy of comment. The huge and very public philanthropy by mega-rich executives like Bill Gates and Warren Buffett marks a change in the giving of rich donors, especially in the US. The mega-wealthy are no longer simply endowing their former universities but realizing that they need to do more for the wider world. They are using existing networks and developing new ones. They are setting powerful leads and establishing paths that other executives and corporations can follow.

Decide where to draw the line

Despite all this, chief executives must not lose sight of the requirement to turn a competitive profit. As Rahul Bajaj says, "Of course, we cannot decide for India or the world so we have to fix limits as a CEO and as a board." Chief executives need to draw up internal guidelines for their company's actions in this space. Speaking at Davos in 2008, Peter Sands, chief executive of Standard Chartered, stated: "Clearly, we don't forget that our core role is to run a business that serves customers well and generates shareholder returns. We also recognize we have a broader responsibility and you have to make choices – you can't do everything. We apply four tests to what we do.

You have to make choices – you can't do everything

"Firstly, is it relevant to the markets we operate in? Secondly, it should leverage our capabilities and infrastructure. Ideally, it can also become a business for us so we can embed it and make it a success and scale it. Lastly, we think it should be something where we can make a distinct difference."

Ultimately, it's for each company to decide whether it simply does what it must to earn its license to operate, or whether it goes further and seeks to be a force for good beyond the geographies and communities in which it works directly. However, making an effort to go beyond immediate necessity can produce unpredictable but direct business benefits in future years. Cisco Systems CEO John Chambers argues that "the most successful people and businesses in life have an obligation to give back because it is the right thing to do, but because it is also plain good business. We were early into Jordan along with a number of other companies in a joint initiative with the World Economic Forum. Years later, we have had a number of significant wins from the government because they recognize that we give back to society."[23]

CONCLUSION

A tipping point has been reached on sustainability. Chief executives must now address the corporate environmentalism agenda; those that don't will be caught out in the coming years. Top CEOs are already looking beyond "green" to the commercial benefits of doing business responsibly in a wider sense. CEOs in the future will embrace sustainability and prioritize the raft of initiatives required to demonstrate that their companies are responsible and care about the societies in which they operate.

Top leaders believe that doing "the right thing" is also great business in the long term and that all stakeholders will eventually call for businesses to embrace a role in society beyond respect for the environment. The good news is that the proliferation of best practice, and of fora in which to learn it, as well as the increasing level of concern among the wider population, mean that CEOs will be swimming with the tide in addressing the sustainability agenda.

Overall, the outlook for improved sustainability efforts from business looks quite promising at present, but the recent downturn in developed economies will undoubtedly be a sharp test of the commitment of every company.

Secrets of CEOs: Sustainability

❑ Environmental sustainability is becoming a new battleground, especially in the West. Companies will have to adapt their business models to be environmentally responsible. Key constituencies will force the issue in the West, while there will also be increased pressure on this front in developing markets.

❑ Global CEOs will have to develop and apply a broader definition of success – for shareholders, society, and the environment – to earn the right to operate.

❑ Visionary companies are increasingly adopting a mindset of collaboration to work with other corporates, governments, and NGOs to make things happen.

❑ CEOs must take a long-term view and build momentum by energizing and motivating their employees while ensuring that the business continues to succeed.

❑ Shareholders are increasingly supporting sustainability measures that will build and protect businesses.

❑ These broad CSR initiatives will need to be embedded in the way a company delivers its core business and creates rigorous milestones and planning. Recognized metrics will take time to formulate.

❑ Above all, the decision on where to draw the line with sustainability initiatives is up to you. Only you can decide whether your sustainability efforts stop after you have earned your license to operate or whether you carry on, undertaking wider initiatives for the good of society.

4

SURFING THE THIRD WAVE OF THE WEB

"The next five years will see a faster rate of change in consumer behavior than ever before. What took 50 years will take 5."

Mark Clare, chief executive, Barratt Developments

"Virtual worlds are at the same point of development today as the web was in 1994."

Philip Rosedale, founder and chairman, Linden Lab

The internet, widely dismissed in corporate boardrooms as a passing fad 15 years ago, is in its second phase and about to enter its third. The ramifications of the relentless progress of the internet into new areas of life will touch all businesses – and yet 61 percent of CEOs admit that they do not know enough about emerging technologies.[1] A recent Heidrick & Struggles poll found that 56 percent of senior business people had never logged on to Facebook, the website that symbolizes the latest flourishing of the web.[2]

Clearly there is a generation gap issue, as most CEOs are in their 40s or older. CEOs who got burnt in the financial fallout of the dotcom bubble in 2001 or overinvested in preparing for the damp squib that the Y2K computer bug turned out to be a year earlier also typically have deep reservations about investments in technology. In addition, most chief executives don't come from technological backgrounds, so don't understand the internet or other key developments.

One CEO coach is scathing, reckoning that there are two types of CEO in this regard: those who get conned and those who don't want to talk about the issue. Caterina Fake, co-founder of Flickr, the photo sharing and social networking website that was arguably the world's first high-profile Web 2.0 business, is equally blunt. "I found at Davos, again and again, that companies would say: 'We've crossed the chasm. We've gone digital. We get it'," she recalls. "But going online is not going to suffice. The new religion is you cannot sleep and rest on that. I've been working at Yahoo!, a ten-year-old company born on the web, and it needs to be disrupted. When corporate leaders say to me: 'We've done that', I say: 'Wait until you see what's coming around the bend.' It's tiring. You can't rest."

Meeting the challenge of the third wave of the internet is the twenty-first-century business reality that is least understood by today's CEOs; it's vital that this changes. This chapter aims to give a quick overview of the web's recent development, set out the business implications, indicate the likely direction of future changes, and offer some suggestions on how to get up to date from CEOs of Web 2.0 businesses, as well as those at the cutting edge of adoption of the web in traditional industries.

THE THREE WAVES OF THE INTERNET

Wave One: Late 1990s to 2001

In the 1990s computing left the desktop and local area network and hit the internet. The start of mass adoption of its possibilities was accompanied by a great deal of hype and financial markets speculated wildly on web businesses that were often loss making but were considered early pace setters. The model of the time was the internet portal such as Yahoo! and AOL, a supposed gateway to a world of entertainment and e-commerce that would benefit from the traffic attracted by the world's first major internet brands.

Websites pushed information out to passive consumers, but access across clunky dial-up connections was slow and while the internet was loved by technology geeks, many of the consumers exhorted to

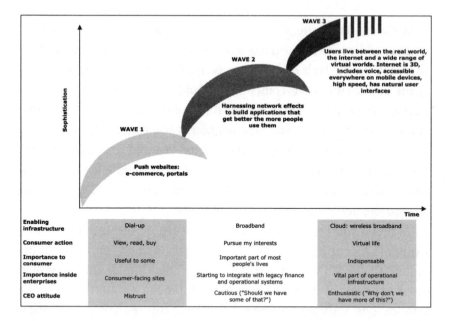

	Dial-up	Broadband	Cloud: wireless broadband
Enabling infrastructure	Dial-up	Broadband	Cloud: wireless broadband
Consumer action	View, read, buy	Pursue my interests	Virtual life
Importance to consumer	Useful to some	Important part of most people's lives	Indispensable
Importance inside enterprises	Consumer-facing sites	Starting to integrate with legacy finance and operational systems	Vital part of operational infrastructure
CEO attitude	Mistrust	Cautious ("Should we have some of that?")	Enthusiastic ("Why don't we have more of this?")

view, read, or buy online ignored it. Certainly, the attitude of most CEOs at the time was mistrustful – and with some cause, as the constraints on adoption seemed immense. Internet programming was difficult, bandwidth was expensive, and many core technologies were not proven.

The common refrain then was that few experts could see a way for the internet to make any serious money. Organizations might like to create websites to disseminate information and telecoms companies would make money from hosting them, but these businesses were not going to make fortunes and certainly not for "old-economy" activities. Despite this, lots of investors did make – and lose – a great deal of money as technology stock prices were driven up. However, the boom was short-lived and after 2001 many of the start-ups ended up out of business without ever having turned a penny in profit. Financial markets crashed and many chief executives who had eventually embraced the internet revolution felt duped.

Since 2001, internet penetration and computer sales have nevertheless continued to rocket and "bricks-and-mortar" companies have opened up "bricks-and-clicks" operations to take on the dot-coms at their own game. Marksandspencer.com and Neimanmarcus.com have become huge successes, while Boo.com, the internet darling of clothes retail a decade ago, went down in flames and has been termed one of the greatest defunct websites in history.[3] It's a similar story in food stores, with Tesco.com and Walmart.com building profitable online business in contrast to the swift demise of dot-coms such as Webvan. "Old world" companies have quietly been creating new digital channels that are integrated into physical operations. Now they've become the new internet kings, and this is not just happening in retail. From Reed Elsevier, which is transforming itself into an internet business-to-business publisher, to high-street banks that now offer online banking as part of their basic accounts, websites that not only inform but transact business are now the norm.

Wave Two: From around 2004

Web 2.0, or the second wave of the internet, has harnessed social networks to build applications such as MySpace, Wikipedia, and YouTube that get better as users load them with information ever more relevant to them. These social networks have flourished as broadband penetration has expanded; as many consumers have learnt to pursue their personal interests online, networking sites have become an important part of their lives. Facebook, which allows users to keep up to date with groups of friends in real time and to share a vast range of information including photos, videos, and games, has grown to span more than 58m active users. Software developers have built more than 7,000 new applications onto the platform and the phenomenon has given birth to a new demographic description, the "Facebook generation".[4]

Chief executives are now increasingly interested in the potential of communities with millions of the sort of young consumers that advertisers love – but they are also cautious. What if they blunder in like a dad at a school disco? How can they make the most of a medium they don't really understand?

Key elements of Web 2.0

It connects people and is easy to use
Web 2.0 websites are easy to use and you don't have to be a geek to take full advantage of the services they offer. Says Caterina Fake: "Web 2.0 is taking what the web has always done well and making it available to millions and millions of people. At the outset, the thing I loved about the web was having fruitful conversations with people around the world. The web was contributory and freewheeling and everyone had a voice. But you had to be a power user. You had to be able to code and to do command line stuff in Unix. With Web 2.0, everyone can do what they want. This is changing the way people can interact and participate in culture. It's not that traditional media has lost its value: editorial judgment and fact checking will never do that. But the change is that these two now have to be seen as the opening salvo in a debate. Good software allows you to find what's meaningful out of the cacophony."

Chad Hurley, co-founder and chief executive of YouTube, shares Fake's excitement about where this will lead: "Web 2.0 definitely is a buzzword and I think it has been overused," he says. "But the movement itself is just getting started. And that movement is just leveraging the power of people, leveraging the power of a community, giving everyone the chance to participate and that's the nature of the internet, so I think you're going to see this trend continue."[5]

The dispersed user network is in charge, not the corporation
There's a fresh illustration of a well-understood principle here: Networks are more valuable than the sum of their individual participants. But harnessing that power requires a fundamental shift in the power relationship between the business and its service users. A social network relies on the business giving the users tools and complete freedom to create content and connections themselves, entirely independently. Contrast that with a traditional media business such as distribution of feature films for screening to a passive audience receiving the director's vision. Hurley stresses that his business puts

the user at the center: "We've not only allowed peo-
ple to participate but also listened to them," he says.   We allowed the users to dictate how we
"We left our platform open and allowed the users to   developed our service and that has
dictate how we developed our service and that has   helped us grow as a company
helped us grow as a company."[6]

David Sifry, founder and chairman of blog search engine
Technorati, believes that the "artificial distinction" between a consumer and a producer is dissolving. "I like to call it the idea of the par-
ticipant economy as opposed to just the consumer economy," he
says.[7] Stephen Taylor, former vice-president of Yahoo! Search and current CEO of online energy supplier BizzEnergy, observes that in looking to engage with the internet user rather than push products and
services to them, and in populating the web with tools rather than
just sales pitches, embracers of Wave Two are flipping Wave One on
its head and saying, "This is a platform, this is a tool: do what *you*
want."

The fundamental lesson is that businesses have a valuable way of
getting nearer to achieving one of their age-old objectives: to develop
a much closer relationship with their customers. However, Hurley,
Sifry, and Taylor believe that reaping the benefits of this will require
a radically different relationship with customers than is traditional.

It is underpinned by a new generation of global consumers
The internet is accessible to everyone online all over the world, providing them with the tools to communicate with each other. Web 2.0
caters to a new segment of global individuals: people who are net
savvy and actively manage their lives, interests, and experiences
online, sharing them with other users. In this way, social networkers
have become defined more by their activity than their nationality.

The number of heavy users who have access to the full range of
networking technologies, whether it be blogs, podcasts, or vodcasts,
is rocketing. According to Morgan Stanley, internet user growth was
up 16 percent in 2007 and broadband penetration increased by 28
percent. This is a global phenomenon: Asia accounts for over 40 percent of internet users.[8]

What are the consequences of this new demographic? For one thing, connected consumers are more demanding of service levels. Increasingly accustomed to participating in the creation of bespoke entertainment or personal portals, they want traditional products and services to be personalized and are prepared to switch, not least because the cost is often vastly lower online. And they are not afraid to be vocal about their experiences at the hands of large corporates.

Rupert Murdoch, chairman of News Corporation, told *Forbes* magazine: "Everyone knows that networking, once a face-to-face affair, sometimes captured in a Rolodex, is now worldwide, instant, and impervious to constraints of distance, time or cost. Those of us in so-called old media have also learned the hard way what this new meaning of networking spells for our businesses. People want content more than ever, and there is a role for companies that can provide good stuff. Quality is more important than ever, because the marketplace is more ruthlessly competitive. Options are not merely one click of the remote away; devices undreamed of a few short decades ago are at least as tempting as a change of the channel. Companies that take advantage of this new meaning of network and adapt to the expectations of the networked consumer can look forward to a new golden age of media."[9]

The internet has not changed the fundamentals of Murdoch's business. However, it has widened his competitor set and further complicated the challenge of satisfying the desires of his customers. All consumer businesses now have to consider how best to serve the connected consumer.

To understand more about the possibilities of Web 2.0, take a look at sites such as the following:[10]

- ❏ del.icio.us – social bookmarks
- ❏ www.demandmedia.com – social media company, owner of sites such as eHow.com and Airliners.net
- ❏ digg.com – sharing user-submitted content from all over the web
- ❏ www.facebook.com – social networking
- ❏ www.flickr.com – photo management and sharing

- ❏ flock.com – free web browser incorporating Web 2.0 features
- ❏ maps.google.com – directions, interactive maps, and satellite imagery
- ❏ www.joost.com – free on-demand television using peer-to-peer technology
- ❏ www.ponoko.com – marketplace for product plans
- ❏ www.slide.com – social entertainment applications
- ❏ www.tripit.com – trip planner and travel itinerary
- ❏ www.youtube.com – user-generated videos
- ❏ www.wikipedia.org – free collaborative encyclopedia

Implications of Web 2.0 for businesses

As Stephen Taylor observes, "Web 2.0 is real for consumers and start-ups but not for the companies that existed yesterday." So what are the key implications of Web 2.0 for business?

It creates new business opportunities and massive disruption
Jean-Marc Frangos, head of innovation at BT, identifies three fundamental Wave Two business models: "making possible communication and collaboration, attention and its monetization, and aiding the achievement of a purpose. Today such purposes are quite limited, such as the weekly grocery shop. But in the future the web will seamlessly support the planning of complicated tasks."

MySpace and Facebook are just the two best-known examples of companies successfully monetizing the attention of people drawn to sites that increase their ability to communicate and collaborate with people. The key way to do this is by charging for adverts on the sites from companies that want to access these demographics.

However, traditional industries are also seeing new models develop thanks to Web 2.0. A good example of how Frangos's elements can be harnessed in a traditional industry is the rise of peer-to-peer lending platforms. Companies such as Zopa in the UK, Prosper in the US, Boober in the Netherlands, and Smava in Germany are allowing individuals to nibble at the retail banks' loan businesses by matching people who need a small loan with others who have extra cash to lend online. These businesses constitute web-based community approaches to collaborative achievement of an important purpose with effective monetization in an industry that has previously relied heavily on huge intermediaries. They are therefore a scary prospect for traditional CEOs unwilling to explore the possibilities raised by the web.

Brent Hoberman, co-founder of Lastminute.com who's now set up Web 3.0 site mydeco.com, offers such CEOs little comfort: "The web will continue to disrupt more and more industries and the major corporates will be faced with a choice to cannibalize themselves or wait for a start-up to do it to them," he says. "Very few have the bold, courageous leadership to do this. Some believe they get it, but in fact most don't as they struggle to act on instinct, experiment, or respond to dynamic customers' reactions, so are unlikely to get to critical mass first and gain those advantages through experience.

"I know one board that only adopts technology when enough of the board members' grandchildren buy in to and start using it. For corporates like this, it is probably better to buy in rather than build."

Fortunately, some CEOs in very traditional industries are on to this.
What took 50 years will take 5 years.   Mark Clare, chief executive of Barratt Developments,
Ignore the web at your peril   says: "The next five years will see a faster rate of
change in consumer behavior than ever before. What took 50 years will take 5 years. During the past 50 years, information passed by word of mouth and that was slow. The younger generation is increasingly going to use Facebook. Ignore the web at your peril."

Wave Two of the web can make traditional businesses much more efficient
Traditional as well as dot-com businesses can use the internet to coordinate, streamline, and augment their core functions. At Lloyds TSB, for example, Eric Daniels says the bank has built more than 200 decision models about customers and their propensity to buy or not buy particular products.

At Tesco, Sir Terry Leahy highlights the breadth of internet applications. "The Web never stopped being important," he says. "We were early innovators with Tesco.com, which we've grown from £1 to £2bn. The role of the internet as a medium for creating new retail businesses is growing in significance. Its role in enabling efficient operations is gathering pace. And its role as a place for developing relationships with business is growing rapidly. Most of our research now goes online because it's instant, easier to recruit panels, and the panels feel that they're shaping policy, that it's a two-way thing and they can co-create."

Tesco's experience is instructive. Every business should give serious consideration to where in its operations internet technology can be applied to best effect.

But retail is not the only "traditional" industry shaking from the effects of the web. It's going to permeate everywhere. Take healthcare, a business with large public-sector customers, huge infrastructure assets, and a sometimes conservative and ponderous attitude to technology. Liu Jiren says, "Web 2.0 is a very good opportunity and a very important technology. When we design hospital IT solutions now, for example, we're seeking to get all parties to collaborate: doctors, families, hospitals, our systems. Web 2.0 will be vital to that." Sir Bill Castell is even blunter. "The internet and information are going to fundamentally transform lots of industries in the next decade, especially healthcare," he says. "The ability to engage patients in their own health will lead to a change in medicine from an art to a proper science and allow true personalized treatment."

Or take publishing. Says Rona Fairhead, "The web itself is very interesting for Pearson. It will allow us to reach a lot more people more effectively. For example, we set up a virtual classroom with Cisco and Nokia to help educate people in poorer parts of the world where it was not economic to ship books to them."

The message is clear: Consider adopting Web 2.0 in every business in almost every sector.

Businesses can forge much closer relationships with their customers
Most large traditional retailers have now launched an online store and it's become commonplace for companies to send out viral marketing games and videos by email. It's also now *de rigueur* to use the

web as a channel, a brand-building tool, and an advertising board. However, trail-blazing consumer businesses are going far beyond this. Recognizing that Web 2.0 is about giving users tools, they are inviting their customers to design the products they want.

Nike is a good example. Mark Parker, president and chief executive of Nike USA, says, "Web 2.0 is enabling a fundamental shift in power... that really is giving the power to the consumer to engage, connect, and create and to do so on a scale never seen before. That's going to have so much ripple effect or so much change in ways we don't even know." He gives the example of the www.nikeid.nike.com website where consumers create their own shoes. "Sometimes when you create product like this you create communities," he says, "and they make it into something we can't even imagine."

Businesses are only starting to understand how to harness the potential of the web and the latent creativity of its users – but they know they're on to something. "We certainly don't have this figured out, and nor does anybody to my mind," says Parker. "It's an exploration for us, but one of the things that we're learning is how to create more of a two-way dialogue. It used to be that companies or organizations were putting a one-way message out there but not really getting much back. Now there's an interaction and that's really creating a whole new dynamic in how we and other businesses and organizations operate. We're getting actionable insights that really drive new products and new experiences and for us that's really exciting. Our ability to tap into that collective intelligence is incredibly powerful and exciting."[11]

Russ Shaw, director of innovation at Spanish telecoms group Telefonica, concurs. "We need to go and co-create with the consumer. We're pushing bundles, but are they the right thing? In mobile telecoms, if you get churn down, your earnings and cashflow rocket. That's one place co-creation can help us."

It's not just consumer organizations that can revolutionize their business model with smart use of the web. Take Premier Farnell, a global distribution group whose main products are electrical components for design engineers at major industrial conglomerates. Harriet Green's team are asking their customers what they need in a very sophisticated online exchange and co-design forum: "We can already see our electronic design engineer customers customizing our online tools and creating new ones once they trust our services," she says. "The web enables us to share what engineers want to have; to build products around known needs, requirements, and thoughts. Rather than simply delivering orders from a catalog, we now help engineers make real the world they're imagining. We give them information, a product range, and an ability to chat to other engineers." Using the web, Green says that Premier Farnell is evolving from a paper catalog mail-order business into a much more interactive, value-added twenty-first-century distribution business.

Businesses can evolve their structures and refresh relationships with employees
Web 2.0 will allow companies to minimize inappropriate command-and-control structures and enable more sophisticated, flat structures. John Chambers believes that collaboration technology and other Web 2.0-related innovations will increase productivity by between 1 and 5 percent by 2012, just as the first wave of the internet did between 1997 and 2002. "We see the next wave of productivity re-accelerating around the world," he explained at a recent conference. "It's an instant replay of over a decade ago. It's not phase one, which took 12–15 years in terms of self-service and ordering online. It's the power of us. Our world's ability to collaborate will determine the future of companies or countries."[12]

Subrah Iyar, CEO of web conferencing company WebEx, adds: "Previously, in vertically integrated businesses, the problem was how to get internal interaction: how to tighten tight coupling. Now, the problem is how to create loose coupling across dispersed businesses and joint ventures and partnerships. In twenty-first-century businesses, no one dictates solely and there's agreement on the fly. All individuals have communities, so all businesses have communities."

Philip Rosedale, founder of Linden Lab, owner of virtual world phenomenon Second Life, is as forceful as Chambers: "Effective decentralized models for decision making and governance, as they are accelerated by technology like Second Life, are very likely to be competitively superior to what's being done today," he says. "The technology gives you the ability to rule corporates with a looser hand and make a better and more aggressive environment. It's very important for CEOs to realize that if they maintain a rigid, top-down, command-and-control structure in the future, they will probably fail. Improved technology leads to radically greater transparency, which leads to looser management and lower cost. At Linden Labs we have an extremely high level of transparency in our business. Everyone has to submit what they've done to benefit the company each week. We also use an internal economy to drive performance management and remuneration. Everyone gets to pay people for services. This means we run a market economy inside our own business."

If you maintain a rigid, top-down, command-and-control structure in the future, you will probably fail

Lenovo and Dell are living this advice. Says Bill Amelio, "Our intranet is a critical forum to communicate with employees on a regular basis. It's also very efficient. We're getting better at building interactivity to ensure the free flow of ideas internally across borders and timezones. The intranet is also a key tool to unify our culture. Additionally, we have initiated social networks inside the company to help technical teams and other functions better communicate and socialize ideas." Lenovo has set up an online "cultural compass" blog to allow greater dialogue between all levels of the company. "I was very impressed to see the number of so called 'undiscussables' raised on the compass," says Amelio. "This is a clear demonstration that we're improving our trust among all colleagues."

Michael Dell adds: "We commit the same resources to listening to our teams as we do to our customers. Soon after we introduced IdeaStorm as a blog service for customer comments for the external Dell community, we introduced EmployeeStorm internally. We've gotten great feedback from our teams about how to improve Dell as a workplace, and also for our customers."

Amelio and Dell are not alone in noticing the ability of Web 2.0 tools to surface difficult issues, unlock innovative ideas, and reduce the impediments of a conventional hierarchy. Google's president, EMEA operations Nikesh Arora also acknowledges that the development of consumer web tools has forever changed the face of business technology. "Employees now expect – and in many cases demand – the same ease of use at work and flexibility of access as they have with applications in their personal lives," he says. "This means sharing information and collaborating on projects in the same way as they share their photos, chat on social networks, and invite people to comment on their blogs. Information sharing is as important, if not more important, within organizations as it is to individuals, but many businesses don't have the time, money, or infrastructure to provide this experience for employees."

Embracing the web will help businesses develop and sustain the flatter, more dispersed, and less hierarchical structures that will be favored in the coming decade (see Chapter 12). It also provides tools to encourage knowledge workers' creativity and collaboration.

Web 2.0 challenges

Web 2.0 presents all businesses with vast opportunities. However, capturing them involves challenges. For instance, Zopa may be an exciting new business model in the banking industry, but not only do CEOs today find it difficult to dream up such disruptive opportunities, they can also find that their conventional structures are challenging environments in which to execute them, which can create a tension with core businesses. Similarly, it can be very difficult to get sufficient cross-functional collaboration between functions such as IT, marketing, and the line businesses to implement the technical and institutional changes required to profit from Web 2.0 technical innovations and reap their efficiency gains in a mature business.

In addition, as Caterina Fake observes, "Corporations find it very difficult to relinquish control and authority and engage in collaboration and be humble." It is hard for companies to modify their traditional structures to create a business that effectively harnesses the energy and initiative of workers from the bottom up. We'll come back to this challenge in detail in Part III. Finally, loosely coupled businesses that engage in open collaboration with customers and other stakeholders, like Premier Farnell is attempting, may present challenges of intellectual property rights management and revenue sharing.

None of these challenges is insuperable and the rewards are immense, so it's well worth CEOs overcoming their self-professed ignorance, educating themselves, and embedding the web in their businesses. At Wipro, Azim Premji has done just that. "We use the web widely," he states. "We use it for training, employee self-service, asset management, collaborative team-work, risk management, and as an internal marketplace for jobs. The list is endless. Every function, every business, every group; everyone uses it. It's just completely integrated into our operations. It's a driver of efficiency, immediacy, and collaboration. And it continues to present big business opportunities that we pursue."

Every function, every business, every group: everyone uses the web. It's completely integrated into our operations

WAVE THREE: WHAT NEXT?

Another change is coming and will be as transforming as the original web was to the pre-internet world. In Wave Three, or Web 3.0, users will live between the real world and a wide range of virtual worlds. The internet will be three-dimensional, will include voice command, and will be accessible from everywhere on mobile devices. It will operate at high speed and have natural user interfaces. The key entry point will be wireless broadband and the web will, at last, be compelling and indispensable to most consumers. Will chief executives get the point quickly enough?

Watch out for the following elements of Wave Three.

Web 3.0 will be vital to the fabric of life

Tomorrow's adults will take the internet and mobile telecoms for granted. For them, the world has always been connected. In the developing world millions of people are coming online. Often they are leapfrogging technologies and moving straight to mobile broadband. Thus users around the world will increasingly become accustomed to accessing the internet at any time and in any place.

This development in infrastructure will be matched by a step change in software use. Nikesh Arora explains: "Cloud computing is how we talk about something called web-native software. The key feature of cloud computing is that both the software and the information accessed through the software live on centrally located servers rather than on a single user's computer, which means that users can access the information they need from any web-enabled device, which changes the way we use the web. In practice this means that if your laptop breaks when you're on a business trip you don't also lose all your work, because it's stored in a data center and you can access it from any device."

Jean-Marc Frangos puts it another way, predicting the luxury of seamless communication through the ultimate personal communication dashboard. "On all devices, PC or mobile, you can permanently refer back to your standard environment," he says. "We're not quite there but we are getting close to true unified communications."

Enterprise collaboration as well as consumer-facing applications

Many visionary business leaders hope that Wave Three will include business waking up to and fully embracing the true potential of the internet. Narayana Murthy states: "Web 2.0 has been focused on social communities, on individual relationships; things not focused on the office. I would like Web 3.0 to be about more interaction between customers and vendors and competitors, on making life better for the customer. And I would like to extend the functionality of Web 2.0 to the corporate world to provide better collaboration on business problems. There needs to be a shift in mindset."

The challenge is communicating to chief executives just how much further transformation Web 3.0 can bring. John Chambers says, "I think it will be dramatically bigger than the first wave both in terms of network volumes as well as productivity and business model changes. It's going to change business models in a way that will make the first phase of the internet look small. That's what this next decade is about."[13]

Vastly more compelling and enjoyable

It takes imagination to see what the web is likely to become, but it's already a forum for some of life's most important interactions. "Flickr is hosting pictures of events of world significance," observes Caterina Fake. "Social networking sites are seeing great connections being forged. Totally different groups are coming into contact. In the short term this increases tensions, but they reduce as they get exposed to each other. I never knew what it was like to be a 20 year old in Dubai before."

The high degree of personalization that Wave Three will encompass will also make it a core channel for content consumption. Frangos predicts: "Web 3.0 will be a rich personality repository; it's a window on your true interests. I can see a future where you log on to a personal page and it is a combination of Facebook, Netvibes, Pageflakes, My Yahoo!, Google, and lots of other things. We've only seen the beginning of personalization for online consumers and we'll see it in enterprise applications too. The old model was a broadcast model. Now you can communicate to a segment of one."

A glimpse of the future

All this may sound like a nice vision that's totally impractical. In fact, today's online games and virtual worlds provide exciting signposts to the future. Many CEOs we interviewed had no idea of the current state of development of Web 2.0 technologies like video and voice communication and how much of an impact further development is going to make on the internet. Two case studies observable today show the level of penetration of everyday life the internet may come to achieve globally.

Korea: Addicted to broadband and social networking

As Caterina Fake remarked to us, South Korea and its Cyworld phenomenon provide a live example of just how embedded in the fabric of life the web and virtual lives may become in the future.

Today, South Korea has the world's highest penetration of broadband: 94 percent of households had access to broadband in 2006, compared with a mere 44 percent of UK households.[14] At that piont, half of the nation's 3 to 5 year olds were online.[15]

The South Korean experience is startling. In recent years the country has been swept by enthusiasm for Cyworld, a social networking website that offers functionality similar to Facebook but includes 3D avatars and a virtual room as a home page that users purchase items to decorate. Remarkably, in 2005 a third of Korea's population – 15m people – and 90 percent of people in their teens and twenties were signed up to Cyworld, which launched around the turn of the century and only took off after it was bought by SK Telecom in 2003.[16] In March 2007 users were still spending an average of nearly five hours per month on the site, down from a peak of nearly seven hours in July 2004.[17]

Young Koreans are now so accustomed to running their lives via the internet that they find it difficult to conceive of how life would work if the technology wasn't there. Notwithstanding recent falls in Cyworld's usage times, the web and social networks are deeply embedded in South Korean society and offer an indication of how much potential for broadband and social networking penetration there is in other nations, even those without such a strong sense of community.

Virtual worlds burgeoning

Virtual worlds are 3D realities created online. Users design an "avatar", a 3D representation of themselves however they would like to be seen. Typically, users can buy land, build artefacts, and trade. Virtual worlds are different from games. In a game characters, rules, and artefacts are tightly controlled; in a virtual world, just as on a social networking site, the users create the content within a framework designed by the host company. The best known and by far the largest is Second Life.

Second Life estimated in December 2007 that it had 11m regis-
tered users, of whom about 1m had logged in during the previous
month. Its users are "spending" $1m a day and there is an active
exchange between the virtual Linden dollar and the real-world US dollar. Some very high-profile brands have been attracted by the allure of
these customers. Adidas, Toyota, and Mazda have started selling virtual products to their consumers in Second Life, while Reuters, Sky
News, and BBC have set up virtual offices to manage media.

People appear to use virtual worlds for three main reasons, argues
Philip Rosedale. First, they relish the imaginative possibilities. "The
core argument for the appeal of virtual worlds is that we can imagine
a world better than the one we live in," he states. "If the real world
represented a real and infinite palate for our minds, then virtual
worlds would have no appeal. Interestingly, our lowest take-up in the
USA is in New York and Los Angeles. Our sense is that you can already
be whoever you want to be in these big cities. Compare that with
being in a small town in the Midwest."

Second, virtual worlds give a sense of presence to the internet
experience. "You will see and experience other people's presence,"
says Rosedale. "You will sense you are with them in some manner.
Amazon.com would be a vastly better experience if you could turn
left and right and see and talk with the people there with you.
Extending the backbone of the internet so that we can be in each
other's presence will be transformational."

Rosedale also argues that Second Life and its peers make communication substantially easier. "Some real-world businesses are using
Second Life for collaborative meetings," he says, "because our voice
technology allows you to hear people in 3D, as in the real world. All
the voices of the people on the call do not appear to come from the
phone on your desk. For example, Cisco and IBM
are having meetings in Second Life."

*Virtual worlds will soon be larger in
their daily use than the web*

Unsurprisingly, he has high hopes for the technology. "Virtual worlds will soon be larger in their
daily use than the web because you are there with other people," he
says. "That makes a lot of things extraordinarily easier and their

semantics are understood by everyone. Compare a wander through Tokyo on the web and in a virtual world. You don't need to speak Japanese to walk around the streets."

Rosedale's enthusiasm may be more than good PR. Forecasters Gartner are predicting that by the end of 2011, 80 percent of active internet users and Fortune 500 enterprises will have a "second life", without necessarily being involved in Second Life itself, although the company does "not expect [corporations] to undertake profitable commercial activities inside most virtual worlds in the next three years".[18] In fact, Rosedale considers that this take-up will have dramatic implications for retailers. "I believe that ecommerce will be profoundly affected by virtual worlds in years to come," he says. "We don't shop in empty stores. We like shopping with people. To invest in the future, as a corporate, I'd be trying to build shopping experiences. For example, IBM has been helping electronics retailer Circuit City to try to build a shopping experience which uses the unique capabilities of Second Life."

Two key assumptions on the development of virtual worlds underpin Rosedale's confidence. He expects the penetration of virtual worlds to follow the same development path as the web, with heavier business use, substantial applications in education, and their spread across the globe over the next ten years. He also predicts that very significant technology advances will render virtual worlds hugely more realistic representations of reality. "It takes about ten years for the best movie technology to be usable on PCs," he says. "Today, computer-generated forests go beyond reality. That technology will be running on your PC and on your phone in ten years. Within a decade, you'll be flying through an artist's dream of the Swiss Alps. It'll be better than reality. Surreal person-to-person experiences will be possible. In addition, we'll see quality doubling every couple of years because network effects will drive content and grow the economy, while technology will drop barriers to entry and gesture and input technologies will improve."

However, Rosedale is a pioneer and self-interested in this area; skeptics do certainly exist. Caterina Fake argues that virtual worlds add back complications the web removed and will not reach the level of trust required for such high growth. "The great thing about the web is that you don't have to walk down the street to shop," she says. "The thing the web does so well is remove the friction of the world. Until you would file your taxes on Second Life, I'm not a believer. You need to have 100 percent confidence in it. John Chambers did an analyst call in Second Life and it got interrupted by a streaker!" (Just in case you were worried, you can't see the genitals on an avatar.)

Both Wipro and Neusoft are excited about the prospects raised by virtual worlds, though Jiren adds a note of caution. "We will see virtual worlds. That's happening already," he says. "These worlds present challenges to legal systems. People may be hurt. People like to live in both worlds, real and virtual. I don't know if that's good or bad. This may be a new crisis for our society, but I don't think anyone can control these developments."

Over time, many CEOs will come to embrace the powerful stimulative capabilities of virtual worlds, though few will become devotees of the wild fantasy worlds that consumers will increasingly create online.

The world may not follow Korea's adoption rate or grow virtual worlds as fast as Rosedale claims. However, these case studies illustrate the massive uptake that some Wave Three internet business have had, as well as some of the real-world consequences of that uptake to date and the technical possibilities that will be with us in abundance.

Words of caution

Technology flattens the world but doesn't solve the core problems
Companies should still focus on what they have to do to win and figure out how to do that using the best available methods, including the web. "Fundamental business principles have not changed. You need to understand the consumer," says Martina King, former managing director of country operations for Europe, Yahoo!. "You have to ask what your core proposition is," adds Russ Shaw. "What will the customer pay for? Then, you need to create a seamless experience."

Remember to focus on the customer rather than being bewitched by new technology. Citibank once brought out a new generation of ATMs that had color touch screens. Customers loved them in the laboratory but hated them in practice, because they required a new card with a clever algorithm that did not work in other banks' machines. NCR's lower-tech ATMs, at one-fifth of the price of Citibank's, were the volume success.

"Citibank also invested gazillions in automated mortgage advisers in Australia and they didn't work," recalls Eric Daniels. "People need to understand that technology for banks is only ever an enabler and if you try to use it as a product, it will almost certainly fail. When you get too far ahead of the market, things won't work. In banking, it's much better to be a fast follower. It's very hard to cause consumer behavior to change; behavior will change because of things you can't even imagine. It's much better to listen carefully to your customer." Such advice applies way beyond banking.

Web 3.0 will increase the price of operational mistakes
Reputational damage in the Web 3.0 environment will be swift for companies that are caught out, because of the speed with which information can spread around the world. Security of company internet protocol is also a big issue. Val Gooding, former chief executive at health insurer BUPA, says, "I would urge caution, as putting out personal information can lead to people hounding you. I see a lot of violence and intrusion of privacy if more information is opened up." National Grid chairman Sir John Parker agrees. "Privacy is an issue," he says. "Companies have to install the right protections." There are also huge risks regarding the protection of consumer data, a point that Barbara Judge, chairman of the UK Atomic Energy Authority, underlines: "There is a huge amount of information on the web and there's no doubt that this will create worrying opportunities for fraud against all of us."

Technology adoption always takes longer than you think
"When I worked at Intel in the 1980s, there were posters on the wall reading: 'Have you emailed today?'" remembers Subrah Iyar. "I also

recall a friend at Bell Laboratories telling me that it took 15 years for people to adopt the push-button telephone over the radial dial! Remember: Adoption always takes longer than you expect."

CONCLUSION

Web 2.0 has been a consumer-driven phenomenon, but it's clear that businesses will catch up in using the web to relate to employees, suppliers, customers, and the media. While CEOs should obviously not embrace every fad, the web is increasingly becoming the core global platform for businesses as well as for individuals. Although its development is difficult to predict, companies must be speedy fast followers. They must quickly adopt external and internal Web 2.0 principles and implement key initiatives to make these a reality, at the same time scanning the horizon for Web 3.0's early ripples. As Bill Gates warned CEOs at the World Economic Forum in Davos in 2007: "In coming years you're going to look at what we have today and think it's kind of a joke."

Secrets of CEOs: Technology
- ❏ Your business must understand how best to serve customers physically, digitally, and virtually and know how to compete in a rapidly evolving multidimensional world.
- ❏ All businesses can adopt Web 2.0 principles and should fully consider what new business opportunities these open up.
- ❏ CEOs must create better conditions for collaboration and innovation both internally and with external partners, drawing on all appropriate technologies.
- ❏ Businesses today must be quick and flexible enough to get in and out of new technology ventures or partnerships speedily and painlessly, not missing great opportunities but also not getting stuck in misfiring ones.
- ❏ There should be someone within your executive line-up who really understands the connected consumer and can act as a radar for Web 3.0 initiatives; you may need to skip a generation to find them.
- ❏ The corporate CEO has a choice. Just like Neo in *The Matrix*, CEOs can choose to take the red pill and enter "a world without rules and controls, borders and boundaries; a world where anything is possible". Or CEOs can take the blue pill and retain the status quo. Where you go from here is up to you.

5

COPING WITH THE CAPITAL CRUNCH

"Of course you have to get the costs down… but if you cut too hard and too fast and too near the bone, you cannot come out of the crunch fast enough."
Carolyn McCall, chief executive, Guardian Media Group

"A manager's job is to manage in the good times and the bad times. Great managers use difficult times to position for competitive advantage."
Archie Norman, former CEO, Asda

In mid-2007 Western capital markets effectively closed to many companies as a result of the US sub-prime mortgage crisis infecting the wider debt markets and causing a chronic Western liquidity shortage. Global investment and commercial banks subsequently suffered huge writedowns in profits and, in many cases, the near collapse of their share prices. Some, like Bear Stearns, were taken over at a massive discount to their pre-crisis valuations. Thereafter, the financial crisis spread to pose the risks of a wider recession across Western markets and of depressing emerging markets. The result is an enormous capital challenge. The higher cost of finance and the weakening of consumer markets that Western-focused businesses now face is in sharp contrast with the preceding five years, which were typified by cheap debt and solid growth.

However, that is only half of the capital story. Prior to the credit crunch, CEOs were already wrestling with a rapid transformation in their sources of funding. The "capital" in capitalism has become more complex and globally diverse than ever before. Significant inflows of capital can now be gathered not only from institutional and private investors but also from private equity firms, sovereign wealth funds from Asia and the Middle East, and hedge funds. Some of these capital sources can be vital lifelines; others are a new form of predator. CEOs must work out how to choose between the various forms of capital available to them.

In wrestling with this changing nature of capital, CEOs are finding themselves asking:

- ❑ How long and deep is the credit crunch likely to be? What will the impact be globally?
- ❑ How do I ensure that my business survives the downturn?
- ❑ How do I best lead in an environment of extreme turbulence?
- ❑ How do I understand and perhaps draw on alternative capital sources?

A PROLONGED DOWNTURN WITH GLOBAL IMPLICATIONS

Global CEOs agree that the current credit crisis will last at least until the end of 2009. They also agree that the credit crisis will cause an economic slowdown – many say full-blown recession – in those countries that have seen a property boom over the last 10 years or so, in particular the US and UK. Take Andy Hornby, chief executive of HBOS, the banking group that owns Halifax, Britain's biggest mortgage lender. "This is not a blip," he told us in July 2008. "The credit markets will stay closed for at least 12–18 months."

This slowdown seems certain to lead to weakening Western consumer demand and the failure of overleveraged businesses and will last at least as long as the credit crisis, if not considerably longer. John Neill told us, "It's pretty awful at the moment – it's the kind of thing you only see a few times in your lifetime." Some commentators are extremely bearish. Roger Bootle, managing director of Capital Economics and economic adviser to Deloitte, forecast in June 2008 that "it could be five years before things return to normal".[1]

One big question is the extent to which the problems in the US and UK will infect the rest of the world, notably the Asian growth engines of India and China. Most of the CEOs we interviewed believed there would be significant knock-on effects in all markets and a global slowdown, although few believe Asian growth markets will slow dramatically.

Alan Rosling points out that the credit crunch triggered by the US mortgage crisis is now intertwined with an inflationary spurt caused by high food and commodity prices, a price correction in the stock markets, and a weak dollar. "It's hard to predict how long these trends will take to work through," he says. "Much of the real economy has remained robust, and much of the world continues to grow well, despite issues in the US, but markets are so interconnected that this cannot continue for long."

Mark Tucker's view is that the Asian economies, while connected to those of the West, are also "self-sustaining growth stories with rapidly expanding middle classes, urbanization, and changing demographics". He adds: "It's likely that the economic motor that's been firing on all cylinders – with growth rates at 10 percent in some countries – will ease back somewhat, and this will actually be helpful in countering inflationary pressures, but I don't see the Asian regional economy stalling."

SURVIVE FIRST, OPPORTUNITY SECOND

Whatever their view on the economic prospects, CEOs agree that the survival of their businesses is the first priority in a downturn. For most, this means ensuring that the balance sheet is strong: that the business is adequately capitalized and that the company is generating the cash needed to meet debt covenants. Here are top CEOs' tips on ensuring that your business is operating efficiently.

Capital and cash are king

In a growth economy, businesses perceived as lazy and inefficient face pressure to return capital to shareholders. In a downturn, share buybacks and special dividends swiftly dry up as companies ensure that they have sufficient capital to support their operations.

"Cash is king so keep the balance sheet strong,"
advises Ian Coull, CEO of property group Segro. He adds, "You will then have the fire power to take advantage when things settle down."

Barclays CEO John Varley, however, believes in keeping the balance sheet as efficient as possible, even in a downturn. Barclays' £4.5bn fundraising in 2008 was criticized by some analysts who believed it would be insufficient, but Varley told us: "As an organization, you have to form a point of view about how much capital you need to run your business. You have to be prudent in that and you have to be analytical. You have to determine that number and that's what you've got to have."

Critical to operating within capital constraints is efficient cash generation, as Rahul Bajaj explains. "In a downturn, cash in particular is king and a tight focus on operating efficiency and working capital is necessary," he says. "In a growing business, sometimes operating efficiency (costs, productivity) and working capital take a back seat and businesses bloat up. This can hurt in a downturn. However, if the business is always run lean with continuous focus on increasing efficiency, then no special effort is required in a downturn."

In tough times the temptation, exaggerated by the feverous sentiment of the markets, is to cut deep and early, a move often presented as "decisive and brave". However, CEOs need to take great care not to be short-sighted. Philip Green thinks that "leadership is about the tough prioritization calls. Yes, you have to cut costs but what you consciously do not cut is just as important," he says. "We will continue to invest in our priorities – especially talent, training, and climate change."

Overall, you are best placed to exploit the recovery when it happens by keeping focused on the long term, even while addressing the immediate, as Alan Rosling summarizes. "Leaders need to balance the immediate issues, which will lead to greater caution, cost reduction and a more careful risk profile, with the need to maintain the long term," he says. Investment in brands, training and development of people, technology and innovation, and the opening of new markets needs to continue even while the immediate performance of the business is maintained."

Focus more intensely on organizational performance and talent

Archie Norman, the former Asda chief executive who now runs private equity firm Aurigo Management, believes it's critical to clear the decks straight away. "You must try to avoid continuous surprise," he says, referring to the multiple   It's much better to try to "panic early" attempts at emergency capital by some banks. "It's much better to try to 'panic early': declare your losses, get any luggage over board, and get your people facing the bad news."

Andy Hornby also says that ensuring operations are really slick is critical during turbulent times. CEOs should "surround themselves with people who don't mind having to take tough decisions," he states. "From the finance director to divisional chief executives, people should be comfortable with saying 'no'. You need to get people around you who have the strength to say no when things are not right."

Equally, some of your high-fliers will need more attention in a downturn. Warns Ian Coull: "There needs to be more hands-on activity as many of the high fliers will not have experienced it before and they could panic." Archie Norman agrees: "You have to get people motivated and facing the recession. They must not feel bad that there's a global recession – it's not their fault!"

You need a highly capable company coming out of the recession so it is vital, despite short-term pressure, to continue to develop your people. "Smart guys' careers can't stop just because there's a recession," states one prominent former CEO.

Have radar and act fast

Speed is of the essence in fast-changing markets: a long delay can mean missing a crucial opportunity that could make or break the company. A great example of this is the rights issues that several major banks have been forced to make.

"I'm not a sailor," says Andy Hornby, "but one of the things that everybody has said to me is that capital markets are like the tide. You have got to catch the tide. Once it has gone out, you are left high and dry." For HBOS, that meant organizing a £4bn rights issue to give the group the capital it needed to repair balance sheets and meet liabilities. The HBOS rights issue was fraught, but it was fully underwritten and raised the money the company required. Moreover, Hornby is certain that if he had delayed even by six weeks, that window could have closed. Managing capital in a constrained market requires CEOs to take advantage of limited opportunities.

Pulling off such deals requires a very responsive business. "It is really important when doing something like this that your lines of communication are short and effective," says John Varley. He has been on the bank's management committee with Barclays' chief executive of investment banking Bob Diamond for more than ten years and says that they had "continuous and effective" contact with each other during the company's global capital-raising activities. "Bob and I know how each other work," he says. "That kind of shorthand that you get from knowing each other and trusting each other is very valuable in the intense period of activity around a big transaction like this."

Good market and customer intelligence and a dynamic response are also vital. Cable and Wireless's John Pluthero says that in January 2008 his team cut the plan for the year again so that the company could hit its targets through cost management alone. They also put in place extra early warning systems, looking into the business's pipeline to see if customers were canceling or deferring projects. "Every week we review whether we need to execute our back-up plan," he says. "It's about managing in real time and having the real systems in place to be getting a real steer on the dynamics all the time."

The credit crunch is an opportunity too

Mark Tucker is insistent that "often a downturn brings opportunity – that's why boldness becomes vital". He adds: "There needs to be a preparedness to take these opportunities. The difference at this juncture between good and mediocre is that the mediocre will tend to be overcautious or reckless, rather than bold and decisive." Of course, leading through a downturn does not feel like business as usual after a long period of broadly benign economic conditions. However, many CEOs believe you have to just accept the economic reality as a fact for the foreseeable future and look to grow market share and competitive advantage with the same intensity as pre-downturn, and that economic turmoil will create unique opportunities.

This assertion is powerfully illustrated in the financial services industry – even while many players are reeling. Says Bob Diamond at Barclays: "Most foreign banks have not succeeded when they've entered the US market. However, we entered 2008 with six or seven of the key players in the US domestic capital markets pulling back. It's counter-trend to be investing in the US, but we see an opportunity to move into the top three or top five in all the areas that are important to us and we're already seeing progress."

Liu Jiren advocates a careful review of how you can take advantage of the change in circumstances across your organization, saying companies should consider their ways of operating and search for new business models that may help them focus on exploring long-term industry possibilities. "During any economic recession, it is much easier to complete a buyout or merger at a lower price than usual," he says. "Consequently, in addition to cost-effective possession of the brands, customers, and technical resources of the companies that are purchased, buyers can beat their competitors and move up in the industry rankings through resource restructuring. In a sense, we may say that any economic downturn could be a strategic time for enterprises to invest for the future."

Even as the recession appears to globalize, it seems clear that there will be great opportunities for organic growth, in particular in emerging markets. In Alan Rosling's view: "The emerging world will become relatively more influential as a result of a slowing in the developed world. Good Western companies will continue to grow their businesses in emerging markets, while emerging-market companies will gain relative position."

LEADING THROUGH TURBULENCE: THE MOMENT OF TRUTH FOR CEOS

As in the event of any major shock to the business, downturns put the CEO right in the spotlight. Experienced CEOs offer the following advice.

Be visible and have a roadmap

It is very easy to be knocked by a tough economic climate. Carolyn McCall is clear: "For me, the most important thing is the posture and language of my top team. It's very easy for directors to seem beleaguered in a downturn and that is very dangerous. Leaders need to bring energy and belief to their teams."

The bottom line is that all your people need reassurance during tough times. CEOs stressed to us the paramount importance of communicating clearly and frequently with your people, so that they are reassured and can reassure your customers. One leading CEO sent an email to his whole business explaining the need for a rights issue and by lunchtime he had had 2,000 responses! Another confided: "People will follow you through almost any troubles if they know the business is facing reality and has a roadmap ultimately to get to a good place in the future."

Believe in yourself

It's in times of downturn that you can make the right decision for the medium or long term and still watch your stock price plummet by 60 percent. This is where it is a lonely personal burden to keep an eye on the long term. Being CEO at these times is not a popularity contest and analysts and commentators have little idea of what's going to happen to the economy. "The reality is you have to go more with your gut," one FTSE100 CEO told us, "because the markets and analysts don't give you credit for doing the right things for business in the long term at this stage of the cycle."

Stick by your convictions about the business

In tough times, you must be flexible and avoid dogmatically sticking to out-of-date plans. Equally, however, you come under harsh financial performance pressures and it can be tempting to do business that does not fit with your long-term strategy. You must resist. "During tough market conditions we need to make sure we stick to our principles of not writing business for a short-term gain and maintain our longer-term view and financial discipline, and do not succumb to the temptation to please the market with robust sales growth at the expense of profitability," underlined Mark Tucker. Ultimately, you must not be distracted by the market and must continue to grind out great business every day.

Do not succumb to the temptation to please the market with robust sales growth at the expense of profitability

Discipline also requires you to safeguard the assets you will need to capitalize on during the economic recovery. "Of course you have to get the costs down… but if you cut too hard and too fast and too near the bone, you cannot come out of the crunch fast enough," says Carolyn McCall. "When palpable opportunities reappear, you won't have the resource to take advantage."

THE NEW CAPITAL REALITY

Even before the credit crisis, CEOs were having to adapt to the new capital reality. While the diagram below illustrates that institutional investors still provide the lion's share of equity to businesses, conventional equity sources are today supplemented more frequently and more deeply by other important sources, notably sovereign wealth funds, hedge funds, and private equity.[2]

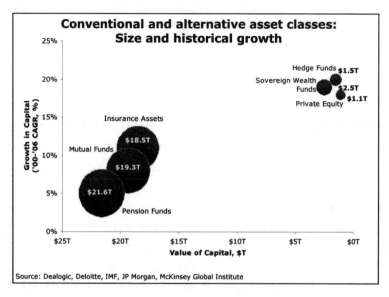

In our interviews, CEOs emphasized that it is imperative to understand the particular handling that each of the new investors requires and their special significance in the current economic climate.

Sovereign wealth funds: Long-term capital

In early 2008, sovereign wealth funds were attracting most of the attention given by the media to alternative capital. Broadly speaking, such funds are investment vehicles for surplus funds raised through tax revenues, typically generated by Middle Eastern or Far Eastern governments (although Norway has a massive fund that invests the proceeds of North Sea oil revenues).

Sovereign funds are not new. However, their recent activism is a relatively new development because for much of their 50-plus years of existence, sovereign funds have been conservative investors, content to hold investments in secure assets such as US treasury bonds. With most sovereign fund money generated from oil revenues, the tremendous growth in the oil price has created a huge glut of funds on which managers are seeking to make a higher return, and in so doing they have created a stir on international capital markets. As Brian Larcombe, former CEO of 3i, states: "You only have to look at the sheer size of these funds to realize that they will be a serious investor and have a significant impact on US and European countries going forward."

Public company CEOs have had to sit up and take notice of sovereign wealth funds as potential investors. "If Citibank, Merrill Lynch, and Morgan Stanley had not been recapitalized so quickly, we'd be in a global meltdown," says David Giampaolo. "We should be sending sovereign wealth funds the equivalent of champagne." Archie Norman adds, "I think they're great sources of capital. It's not a piece of sovereign imperialism. They're not there to achieve some political agenda. They're there to maximize and grow the stored wealth of their country and their systems, and therefore they're going to be driven by investment criteria first and foremost. It's happening with the credit crunch and the banking crisis. They are providing the new capital."

Investments such as the China Investment Company's $5bn stake in Morgan Stanley and the Abu Dhabi Investment Authority's $7.5bn injection to Citigroup have brought both the benefits of and concerns about sovereign wealth funds out into the open. For CEOs, the huge stakes taken in major financial players have illustrated that sovereign funds can provide massive injections of capital at short notice – something that's indispensable at times. More significantly, once the investments have been made, CEOs talk warmly of sovereign investors' long-term horizons and willingness to ride out periods of volatility in their portfolio's share price. For example, the Kuwait

Investment Authority has been a shareholder in Daimler since 1969 and in BP since 1986 and is one of the most stable investors in these businesses, despite the turbulence both companies have suffered. The Norwegian Pension Fund is another long-term investor that talks about being "an investor forever".

Ultimately, chief executives want stable, knowledgeable shareholders – and preferably few of them, especially at times of economic hardship. Indeed, long-term investors like sovereign wealth funds can have an anchoring effect on shareholder bases because smaller shareholders may be reassured by their presence. Management, they may think, will be prudent in their treatment of shareholders with such a significant investor on the books. While you will always have some short-term punters trading in and out of your stocks, these shareholders are not your priority as CEO. Sir John Parker, who as P&O chairman had direct experience of takeover bids from Temasek and Dubai Ports World, says, "Frankly, it's refreshing in a world of short-term capital like hedge funds to have major long-term investors out there."

There are concerns, particularly among protectionist elements in the US, that sovereign wealth funds in China and the Middle East will suffer political interference in their investments. On Capitol Hill, notably in the Committee for Foreign Investment in the US, politicians fret about purchases of assets in "strategic" industries like finance. Indeed, notwithstanding the rescue funds they've recently provided, most pundits agree with Guy Weldon, partner in Bridgepoint Capital, who expects "American protectionism will increase as the US economy weakens". However, so far this has not been backed up by what investors have done. In most cases sovereign wealth funds have not sought to control their financial investments. For example, China Investment Corporation bought a 9.4 percent interest in private equity group Blackstone and was the largest shareholder to decline voting rights when offered them. In fact, CIC does not even put a representative on the Blackstone board.

Notwithstanding the rights and wrongs, in an attempt to allay political concerns several sovereign wealth funds are drafting a voluntary code of conduct. One area they might do well in would be to commit to publishing reports on fund investments and performance. This is something Norway does and it could go a long way to allay many concerns; transparency could really help to relieve fears of protectionism.

For CEOs, then, sovereign wealth funds will continue to represent potentially hugely valuable and sophisticated long-term investment partners and, in the short term, are potential sources of equity at a time when it is in short supply. However, if you operate in an industry that your government might consider to be "strategic", negotiations with sovereign wealth funds are likely to be subject to government scrutiny and perhaps interference, bringing with them the risk of delay or failure.

Hedge funds: Mostly a danger

At the highest level, where private equity funds seek a change in ownership and governance to drive operating change at their targets and, at the other end of the spectrum, mutual funds seek to capture market growth ("beta"), hedge funds encompass a wide range of investment vehicles that, broadly, seek to produce returns uncorrelated to the market ("alpha"). These could be vastly higher than index-tracking funds can produce; equally they may be designed to offset other positions in a client's portfolio.

In 2008, some hedge funds were actively betting against troubled public companies, putting their share prices under significant pressure. Indeed, most hedge funds are short-term investors who can do a lot of damage to your business, so you need to understand where they are coming from rather than simply dismiss them. If they are highlighting an area of weakness in your strategy or a pressing imperative for action, you would do well to heed their calls. Ultimately, however, it's unlikely that you will be able to do much to control their impact. Sir John Parker states: "You need to understand their objective motive. It's very difficult to serve someone who only invests over three months. At National Grid we are securing the energy supply for the nation; our strategy can't bend to the three-month strategy of a hedge fund. However, of course, hedge funds can exert a lot of influence on a deal."

Ultimately, you must understand the motives of hedge funds, but you're likely to be better rewarded by spending most of your time with longer-term investors.

Private equity: Good operational lessons and perhaps a new relationship

Private equity firms typically have investment horizons longer than those of hedge funds but shorter than sovereign wealth funds. The current downturn presents them with a quandary: their portfolios are heavily exposed to the economy and valuations are slipping, while the industry has vast amounts of committed but not invested capital – and investors to please. Consequently, funds are reassessing their approaches. Even in mid-2008, we saw funds look at taking strategic equity stakes in banks, rather than attempting full-blown LBOs. David Giampaolo, head of Pi Capital, says, "Private equity won't just be about buy and build; firms will have to look to take assets into new areas. They will also have to look at minority stakes and taking non-controlling positions given debt markets are effectively closed."

Stephen Murphy, CEO of Virgin Group, agrees that CEOs should no longer only think of private equity funds as predators: "CEOs should reappraise their sources of capital given the changes in the capital markets. In the current environment there are different risk profiles and alternative sources – be they sovereign wealth funds or private equity – can increasingly meet these needs." Professor Andrew Kakabadse of Cranfield School of Management agrees that "many CEOs, and for that matter chairmen, do not seem to have realized the strength and wealth of the capital options available to them through private equity and sovereign wealth funds". That said, predatory PE is not dead. Paul Thompson told us, "As a private equity buyer focused on financial services, the credit crunch will create significant value opportunities and an opportunity to buy distressed but fundamentally sound businesses."

Well before the 2008 downturn when the need for operating efficiencies became pressing, many public company chief executives in our study were telling us that they were eager to learn from their much-maligned rivals in the private equity sector. CEOs now see such learning as even more valuable.

Praise was most commonly given to the focus that private equity houses bring to their investments and the greater efficiency they have been able to generate. Gareth Davies is not alone in disliking the vilification of private equity. "At the end of the day, the economic world is about the efficient allocation of resources," he says, "and if private equity can do it more efficiently than any other corporate business model, fair enough. It's just an extension of the free market." Consequently, the lessons these public company CEOs are drawing from private equity are directly and immediately applicable to the tough times ahead.

After all, the top-quartile private equity firms make a lot of money for their investors. Their annual internal rate of return, at 36 percent, outstrips the average annual shareholder return of top-quartile S&P500 companies by an impressive 8 percentage points. David Rubenstein, co-founder of private equity giant Carlyle Group, observes: "It's obvious we're getting money because we give spectacular rates of return. People recognize that if you are in a top-quartile buyout firm you are likely to get a higher rate of return than almost anything you can legally do with your money."[3]

So at times when the spotlight really is on streamlining operations, what lessons can CEOs learn from private equity?

Ambition, rigor, and speed
Private equity comes in with a clean sheet of paper and is looking to realize the full potential of the business, not just incremental year-on-year improvements. Because the private equity model requires rapid growth and excellent cashflows to generate the best returns, acquired companies are typically given three- or five-year plans to catalyze change. Implemented properly, these plans instill focus and urgency in the acquired business, massively accelerating its development.

Tony Froggatt thinks that quoted companies need to learn from the rigor of this approach. "Private equity firms like it simple; they like it clean," he says. "The smart chief executives are now beginning to think how they can apply some of its urgency and mentality."

Heavy and ruthless incentivization

Paul Pindar believes that the pay structure in most public companies has got out of hand and that lessons can be learnt from private equity. "You have a reward culture that's abstract from the performance of businesses," he states. "I think you have to look very hard at how you're structuring these companies, because some of the management teams of public companies are lazy and average."

In a time of cost discipline, a careful examination of value for money on pay is called for. Equally, CEOs warn that you must continue to be fair, not mean, not least because the high rewards in private equity will continue to present a retention risk to quoted companies, as a former FTSE100 chief executive who has joined a private equity firm observed: "I think the biggest challenge for public companies is retention opposite private equity companies."

Shareholder focus on value

As shareholders, private equity firms offer focused ownership with a single shareholder providing a single vision, a detailed knowledge of the business, a strong conviction of the value in the business, and a single cost base. This conviction can be invaluable in times of economic difficulty; although, admittedly, the high leverage of many deals is putting some portfolio firms under pressure.

Cris Conde says, "We have been private for two-and-a-half years. In that time we have grown more than three times faster than we did previously as a public company. Why were the public markets so intolerant of what we did? I spend more time with the PE firms than I did with the public shareholders, but the amount of value added is marvelous."

In addition, private equity houses, without the public markets' stringency of regulation, offer CEOs a lower regulatory burden. "Some of the private equity firms have taken corporate governance out of the boardroom," observes Paul Walker. "Corporate governance can stifle a company if you are not very careful." Jim Sutcliffe, chief executive of financial services group Old Mutual, adds: "The amount of time you spend on public company governance is ridiculous, so there's going to be more private equity in the future than there has been in the past."

Dwight Poler, managing director, Bain Capital Europe, says that portfolio companies value the firm's input "as a highly informed and aligned strategic sounding board", adding, "We are often asked if we might stay on the board even after we've sold our financial stake."

CONCLUSION

Cycles are a fundamental part of economic life and the disciplines of good management apply in both up and down cycles. The very best CEOs prove themselves through recessions as well as capitalizing on periods of high growth; their businesses come through recessions leaner, stronger, and better positioned to power ahead of their competitors. In a downturn, where a business is not being flattered by a growing market, only the best leadership can achieve results.

Day to day, top leaders are convinced that good leadership in tough markets requires them to tread a difficult line between keeping their businesses afloat in the short term and positioning for long-term growth. They are focusing on keeping their businesses lean, often consciously taking lessons from the private equity textbook, summoning all their self-belief to make tough decisions without the likelihood of near-term reward from the markets, and examining novel sources of long-term capital to supplement their capital bases. These techniques are applicable to any cyclical downturn.

We'll bear these lessons in mind in Chapter 12 as we explore how visionary leaders think businesses will be best structured to be nimble and responsive in the coming years.

Secrets of CEOs: Coping with the capital crunch
❑ Survive first but keep scanning for opportunity.
❑ Cash and capital are king.
❑ Act fast to trim any fat from the business and take heed of top-quartile private equity firms' best practices.
❑ Do not cut out muscle required to take the business forward in the inevitable upturn. After a downturn, the early bird gets the worm.
❑ Step up during your CEO moment of truth: face reality, be visible, and stick with your business convictions.
❑ Be open to a range of capital beyond conventional institutional sources, e.g. sovereign wealth funds for the long term and private equity as a potential strategic investor.

6

WAGING THE
FIRST WORLD WAR
FOR TALENT

"Human capital is more important than financial capital."
Sir Bill Castell, chairman, The Wellcome Trust

"My ideal people have Ivy League brains and blue-collar brawn."
Andy Haste, chief executive, RSA (formerly Royal & Sun Alliance)

In our survey of FTSE100 CEOs, 68 percent put the talent and human capital agenda as their number one priority. Strategy was the top priority for a mere 9 percent and execution for only 25 percent. This is not a phenomenon confined to the UK. In 2007, 74 percent of 600 US CEOs told *Forbes* that staffing and human capital issues amounted to a "very significant challenge" for their company.[1] CEOs are right to be concerned, because the workforce is going to get a lot more unstable and complicated to manage. Research by Heidrick & Struggles and the Economist Intelligence Unit suggests that graduates entering the workforce today will have 13 jobs by the age of 38.[2]

This chapter explores why the first world war for talent is now upon us, the inadequacy of the typical corporate response to date, and how companies need to adopt a fundamentally different approach to the new world of work and leadership.

TALENT TOPS THE CEO AGENDA

CEOs are clear that talent is front of mind. Even those who did not tell us that talent was their number one priority put it in their top three. Sir Martin Sorrell marvels at the power of making the right appointments. "One of the biggest issues is attracting talent," he says. "If you have the right people running the business units, it works magically. It's like turning up the volume. We invest $8bn in people a year on revenues of $12bn. Our business is about people. We are better than others if we have better people and we are worse than others if we have worse people." Why, Sorrell ponders, do analysts fret about capital investment when two-thirds of WPP's turnover goes straight into the pockets of what he genuinely does feel are his company's greatest assets?

If you have the right people running the business units, it works magically. It's like turning up the volume

Keith Butler-Wheelhouse is also a believer in the benefits that talent can bring. "It's all about the team and the correct choice of people," he says. "I cannot overstate how important that is. It's not what people do; it's how they do it. Because everyone has come up the same way, they predictably come up with the same solutions and that does not work. You have to bring in individuals who think differently when no one else can understand what to do." Sir Michael Rake, chairman of BT, agrees. "The biggest challenge for global companies is to unleash the power of our people," he says. "It's not easy to do as cultural issues get in the way and it needs common values as a platform, but the more diverse the employees the more innovative, richer, and the more likely you are to find a global solution that will succeed."

Kevin Whiteman, chief executive at utility Kelda Group, has seen the damage that a poor team can do to a business. "You have to understand what makes people tick," he says. "We've all seen dysfunctional teams at the top. They destroy organizations. The biggest keystone is the unity and clarity and purpose and togetherness of the top team."

It's clear that recruiting and managing the right talent is critical. Even in a solidly performing business, says Richard Pym, "If you look at a senior team of, say, 50 people, you normally only have to change two or three of them to make a difference." But it's in a turnaround, transformation, or new initiative that fresh blood can really super-charge performance like no other lever available to management. For Archie Norman, "Changing means changing the people and therefore recruitment is a chief objective of the mission; you are what you recruit. Your success depends on it." Mike Roney agrees. "The man-agement team is key," he says. "In a turnaround situation, the quick-est way to turn things around is to change people. The more difficult thing is to change behaviors."

TALENT: THE CRITICAL NEW BATTLEGROUND

The first world war for talent will be a central battleground for busi-nesses because it's the result of powerful global demographic forces that will persist far beyond the next decade. Global operations leave businesses prey to four critical forces: poor Western demographics, the skills shortage in the East, the lack of global leaders, and the fre-quency with which employees are now shifting jobs.

Western populations are ageing. According to consultants BCG, 75m US managers and leaders from the postwar "baby boomer" gen-eration will retire over the next five years, to be replaced by only 30m "Generation X" people born in the 1960s and 1970s.[3] Put another way,

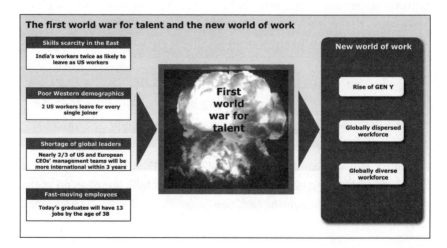

The first world war for talent and the new world of work

Skills scarcity in the East
India's workers twice as likely to leave as US workers

Poor Western demographics
2 US workers leave for every single joiner

Shortage of global leaders
Nearly 2/3 of US and European CEOs' management teams will be more international within 3 years

Fast-moving employees
Today's graduates will have 13 jobs by the age of 38

First world war for talent

New world of work

Rise of GEN Y

Globally dispersed workforce

Globally diverse workforce

in the US two workers left the workforce for every one that entered in 2006.[4] To cope, the US Bureau of Labor Statistics announced that by 2012 two-thirds of all 55 year olds and over will still need to work and will comprise a quarter of the total US workforce; that's quite a shift when in New York in 2006 this demographic comprised only 13 percent. Indeed, a *Harvard Business Review* study showed that by 2011, 50 percent of the workforce of RWE Power will be over 50 and that by 2018, 80 percent of the workers will be over 50.[5]

This chronic labor shortage will force global businesses operating in the West to be imaginative in sourcing talent. They will look cross-border more often. Some 200m people now live in a country that's not the one they grew up in and that number is expected to continue to grow exponentially.[6] This will enrich the cultural, racial, and linguistic mixes inside companies, but increase the risk of conflict. Top businesses have already started to tap wider talent pools, including older workers, returning mothers, job sharers, and part-timers.

Most businesses will also have to have operations in the East, where there's not so much an ageing population as a lack of vital skills. One legacy of not operating a market economy in China and India is that the current generation lacks a deep pool of skilled managers ready to lead complicated commercial entities. Economic growth in these nations is also outstripping the supply of young people trained to internationally competitive standards. Each year, India produces about 450,000 engineering graduates, between 600,000 and 700,000 computer science Master's degree and computer applications graduates, and perhaps 90,000 with MBAs,[7] while China turns out about 600,000 engineering graduates.[8] However, very few of these graduates are yet suitable for developing modern businesses. Quoting data from a McKinsey survey of HR professionals, Narayana Murthy believes that about 25 percent of the engineers and 20–25 percent of the MBA graduates in India are "easily employable", but in 2006 only 1 out of every 125 applicants was suitable for Wipro.[9] Indeed, China has declared that it has a deficit of nearly 100,000 executives against its business industrial needs for the next five years in the telecommunications and technology sectors. The shortage of talent at all levels is creating huge competition for what talent there is in the East.

The third element of this conundrum is a global leadership vacuum. In recent decades businesses have tended to breed technical managers: executives trained to operate to linear, rigid plans within siloed and hierarchical businesses. This is a skill set ill-suited to leading organizations characterized by global operations and highly diverse workforces, as we will explain in detail in Chapter 12. To compound this problem, few executives around the world have experience of leading teams in both the East and West and even fewer are really good at it. Kevin Kelly, CEO of Heidrick & Struggles who has led businesses in Europe, the Far East, and the US, states, "Attracting talent capable of accelerating national or regional businesses has been a tremendous challenge for CEOs for years; there's a very limited number of top-flight twenty-first-century leaders who are truly global in outlook and can take a global profit-and-loss account to another level. They're gold dust."

> There's a very limited number of top-flight leaders who are truly global in outlook. They're gold dust

So the coming decade opens with a demographic crunch in the West, a skills shortage in the East, and a global hunt for the top 1 percent of leaders who can really take global organizations through a step change in performance. What McKinsey called the "war for talent" has to date been about bargaining for the best resources available in local markets, reflecting most businesses' historical focus on regional, national, or export-oriented internationalization. The first world war for talent shifts this to a truly global battlefield. Leading companies will harvest talent from wherever it is found and invest equal resources in keeping their star performers out of the clutches of predatory competitors.

THE NEW WORLD OF WORK

The fruit of the search for global leaders will be exhilarating new workforces characterized by dispersion and striking differences between workers. In an Economist Intellience Unit survey of US and European CEOs, 60 percent of respondents said that their senior management teams will become more international over the next three years.[10]

Harvesting global talent will force businesses to truly adopt technology that supports remote working and collaboration. Asian, American, or European superstars no longer need to relocate to work together at a single location; members of senior leadership teams can be scattered across the globe. Philip Rosedale says, "Today's technology is fundamentally lowering the cost of communication. So now it's very easy to connect people remotely at low cost. Therefore businesses will increasingly focus on the output of their workers, rather than measuring whether they spend eight or nine hours in a fixed location."

Moreover, corporations' teams, whether co-located or globally dispersed, will be composed of vastly different people. Steven Langton, managing partner for Heidrick & Struggles' Asia Pacific leadership consulting practice, says, "Teams will be composed of people of widely differing ages, ethnicities, nationalities, native tongues, religions, health, and physical abilities. Working mothers will rub shoulders with lifestyle part-timers, the semi-retired, and the thrusting career-hungry. Recent immigrants will adjust to their latest home alongside twentieth-generation natives."

Let's unpack one facet of the leadership challenge: leading a multi-generational workforce.

A number of CEOs express deep concerns about this, worries that have gained traction. At a World at Work consortium, 88 percent of 3,000 workers stated that ongoing management of this kind of workforce posed a major risk to company growth and success. But should we be so concerned?

The workforce will certainly be multigenerational. By about 2013, the US workforce will include significant percentages from five generations as retirement is pushed further back. Different generations have experienced different situations and tend to work in contrasting ways, as the snapshot of generational characteristics overleaf outlines.

SNAPSHOT OF GENERATIONAL CHARACTERISTICS

	VETS	BABY BOOMERS	GENERATION X	GENERATION Y
AGE in 2008	64–83	44–63	24–43	4–23
% US WORKFORCE	5%	37%	40%	18%
INFLUENCES	• Rationing, guilt, community stoicism and 'be grateful for what you have' • Korean War, Second World War, Depression • Pre-Cultural Revolution China	• Competition • Nostalgia • 1960s revolutions • Martin Luther King, Cold War, Chinese Cultural Revolution • "Fed-on-demand" babies, Dr. Spock	• End of Cold War, recessions • Split families, working parents • Fear of Aids, global war, terrorism • Tiananmen Square • Parented by proxy	• Social and fictional heroes • Post 9/11 society • Commercial reforms of Asia • War in Iraq, Columbine high school massacre, only saw Berlin Wall torn down • Fearless about future because don't have experience of feared past
ATTITUDE	• "Let's just do the job we've been given" • Work is an obligation, a duty, and a privilege	• "Let's have a meeting and talk about it together" • Work is an exciting adventure	• "I'll do my part, you do yours, we can meet up later" • Work is a challenge, a contract	• "I can and I will, just let me" • Work is a means to an end
RESONANT THEMES AND CHARACTERISTICS	• Conformity, stability • Sacrifice, dedication • "Ours is not to reason why, ours is but to do or die" • Duty, patience, formality over informality, dress codes as discipline • Make work and gender roles • Respect for authority, law and order	• Invented the 60-hour week • Level playing fields • Group achievement and competition • Belief they can and will change the world • Hard working, workaholic • Optimistic about future • Success and achievement are visible	• Best educated and trained • 50–70% divorce rate • Loyal to colleagues not companies • Indifferent to authority • Work ethic, self-reliance • Not natural team players • Skeptical, worried about future	• "Why?" • Streetwise better than qualified • Volunteers in the community • Highly spiritual • Individualism • Adultolescent: immature and selfish • Want authority of adulthood without accountability • Non-linear career • Isolationist
MONEY	• Save money for children's inheritance	• Minimize debt • Leave children secure	• Maximize debt • Leave children insurance advice	• Spend it as they earn it • Already largest consumer group in history of US

Source: Talkin' 'bout my generation: The economic impact of aging US baby boomers, McKinsey Global Institute, June 2008; US Bureau of Labor Statistucs, 2007 Household Survey, assuming working age of 16–69.

	VETS	BABY BOOMERS	GENERATION X	GENERATION Y
HOW THEY CONNECT WITH THE WORLD	• Letters, newspapers, family • Low technical acumen	• Associations, networking, conventions	• Television, travel, sophisticated socialization, events, Web 1.0	• Technology, internet, mobiles, Web 2.0
MOTIVATORS	• Thank-you letters • Socialization • Honor with relics and artifacts • Face to face • Valuing their wisdom and experience	• Balance and personal growth • Autonomy • Public recognition, perks, status • Rewarding their work ethic and long hours • Showing them they are valued and needed	• Wealth, money, materialism, balance, fun, development, career, flexibility as long as upward • Lots of projects and challenges • Praise from boss's boss • Technical gadgets • Measuring on results not longevity	• Including them in all decisions • Listening to and hearing them • Mentoring them • Not boring them • Not trivializing their contribution • Being rich and famous
STRESSORS	• Slang • Swearing • Poor grammar and spelling • Disrespect	• Aggression • One-upmanship • Prima donnas	• Wasting time • Corporate speak • Resistance to change • Low performance drive	• Cynicism, sarcasm • Condescension, patronization
PERCEPTION BY OTHER GENERATIONS	Rigid, judgmental, wary, distant, set in their ways	Self-absorbed, workaholic, fickle, hypocritical	Cynical, ungrateful, disloyal, casual, not team players	Inexperienced, immature, selfish, greedy, over-confident, lazy, naive
MANAGING THEM	• Keep them plugged in, retain and harvest their knowledge, use them as mentors and ambassadors • Ask for their wisdom and experience • Appreciate and respect them	• Offer balance and time flexibility • Give them autonomy • Communicate a sense of meaning • Appreciate and respect them, "we need you" • They don't want to retire – purpose, energy, financial health, health	• Develop them and resource them for early growth • Appreciate and respect them, "do it your way" • Helping them manage other priorities	• Involve, value, and appreciate them • Allow them to challenge and ask why • Forgive them, their intent is not their impact • Help them build their CVs – "I want it and I will get it"

It's clear that on the basis of age alone, tomorrow's workforce will be a true melting pot. For example, James Berrien says that baby boomers' backs tend to fly up when Generation Y recruits (those born between 1985 and 2004) rush into the workplace expecting instant wealth. "Folks coming into the workforce have read about the dot-com millionaires," he says, "and so their expectations on career path and remuneration are dramatically accelerated against those of ten years ago. CEOs are struggling with this." Emma Reynolds, co-founder of Ask Gen Y, a specialist Gen Y consultancy, adds, "My generation [Gen Y] have been brought up to believe we can change the world. Growing up with the psychological theory that the child is the center of the family, we are naturally optimistic, passionate, and filled with a sense of empowerment. We would rather be measured on outputs than inputs. We are constantly connected 24/7, so working Monday–Friday 9 a.m.–5 p.m. just doesn't make sense to us. It's not about work–life balance, it's about work–life integration."

It's not about work–life balance, it's about work–life integration

In fact, Generation Y will create particular problems because twentieth-century thinking, focused as it is on homogenization to suit command-and-control businesses, sees in all this a risk of a workplace characterized by conflict, discord, and inefficiency. Managers worry about how they will get all these people to conform to a single approach. However, it's this outdated thinking that represents the main risk, not the multigenerational workforce itself. Friction can be creative and difference is power: multigenerational brainstorming is far more powerful than having a homogenous group and most companies' customers span the generations.

The challenge is twofold. First, you have to attract the right generational mix for your situation. People from Generation Y and the so-called dream generation will be especially important in growth industries that rely on new skills and the latest expertise in IT, professional services, consulting, and finance. Facebook founder Mark Zuckerberg, for example, is a member of Generation Y, born in 1984,[11] and the average age of employees at Wipro is only 26.[12]

Secondly, CEOs should recognize that they will have two key constituents in their leadership cadres. Generation X and Y employees, having grown up in an increasingly global and connected world, are well placed to transition quickly into true global leaders. However, older executives comprise the preponderance of today's leadership teams and occupy roles that younger executives aspire to fill right now. Many of these older executives have valuable skills, contacts, and irreplaceable experience, especially of difficult times such as recession, that are needed to balance, form, and develop youngsters. Top companies will create meritocracies that allow younger leaders into key roles as soon as they are ready. At the same time, they will also find creative ways of retaining access to the experience of their older employees.

There are also tricky practical management issues in building a multigenerational workforce that are tremendously more challenging than those presented in the past. Tomorrow's workplaces will require the balancing of multispeed demands for career advancement, flexible working, transnational and multilocational working, differing work–life balance expectations, and varying feedback structures.

Philip Green puts it all together. "Leading a multigenerational workforce is one of the biggest challenges of leadership for CEOs today," he says. "CEOs clearly need to run meritoracies and actively fast track younger talent, but at the same time be smart in not losing experience and corporate memory. One way of doing that is to invest actively in knowledge management and creative ways of keeping potential retirees engaged in special projects and also adviser roles, which they will enjoy and which will give them the opportunity to contribute. I don't worry about age – indeed, in my business, we have a director who is only just in his 30s – but there does need to be a balance of youth and experience, as well as gender, industry background, and psychological type."

> Leading a multigenerational workforce is one of the biggest challenges of leadership

While it will be hard to gel teams and benefit from, rather than suffer from, a multigenerational workforce, it will not require superhuman effort. Let's try a quick experiment. What do you make of the following values statement?

❑ "Help me be productive, do great things, and be the best I can be.
❑ Let me know where I stand and how I'm doing.
❑ Invest in me to help me grow fast.
❑ Pay me fairly and recognize my contributions.
❑ Make me an integral part of the team.
❑ Create a positive work environment."

Do you think there's a generation that would not be enthused by these values? In fact these are the values of American IT firm Intuit, the business behind the Quicken finance package, and they were derived after a lengthy analysis of what would most appeal to Generation Y.[13] The way these values resonate across all generations shows that leaders should focus on what is common to the generations and then tailor their interactions, such as communications and feedback, for each particular need, rather than helplessly watching the impending battle.

To provide support to the variously experienced teams he or she will be faced with, the CEO should first foster respect for the contributions of others, even when they are radically different to an individual employee's own contribution. Strong values and incentive systems are essential here. Likewise, to ensure that the value of individuals' skills is always recognized, the CEO should aim, over time, to create a true global meritocracy within which skills are efficiently channeled to where they are best used. The internal marketplace for skills at Linden Lab, whereby colleagues have notional money that they use to "pay" each other to solve problems thereby focusing company resources on the most pressing issues, is an example of a radical approach here.

Great leaders will embrace, encourage, and deploy difference

At the core, great leaders in the coming decade must embrace, encourage, and deploy difference to ensure that the workforce is balanced. They must then provide the values, cultural glue, and leadership required to overcome the natural tensions.

EQUIPPING BUSINESSES FOR THE TALENT WAR

Our research suggests that most companies have underinvested in talent development. So CEOs who say they see talent as the number one success factor have not been matching their rhetoric with their management time and resources. Three problems persist in most of the organizations with which Heidrick & Struggles works. CEOs do not invest sufficient time in talent to fully exploit its potential to supercharge business and to signal its priority to the team. They also tend not to regard the human resources department as a strategic partner in their talent-development efforts. Finally, search firms tend to provide a transactional, role-filling service rather than being a valued business partner.

Walking the talk

"CEOs don't make time to put talent on the agenda," says one senior HR director at a major consumer brand. "We ask the right questions, we really want to drive it. And they believe it and buy it, but don't give it time. It comes back to us, and it stays an HR initiative. They get it but are not executing."

Despite this, there are CEOs who make sure they do address this issue. Steve Holliday, chief executive at National Grid, is unusually rigorous. He aims to allot 20 percent of his time to talent development and has his personal administrator calculate his performance against the target every two months. "Everyone thought I would never do it, but I am at 25 percent so far," he says. Moreover, he feels that the results are worth the effort. "If you get really good people," he explains, "it's amazing the difference they can make."

Martin Halusa is similar: "At Apax Partners, global talent development is the primary function of the CEO. I spend more than 50 percent of my time managing our talent – recruiting, firing, coaching, and making sure the compensation is fair. We are a partnership of extremely talented, insecure over-achievers. Keeping all these people motivated and working at full capacity is my job."

Michael Dell is emphatic about the importance of talent. "One of the questions I was asked recently was why we hadn't articulated 'people' as one of our five priorities," he says. "The answer is a simple one – they are the ultimate priority. They are a given. I spend a good portion of my time on talent."

Sir Martin Sorrell also says that he is careful to go a long way down into his organization, looking at all hires of more than $150,000 a year. "I don't do it to stop hires," he says. "I do it because I am interested whether we are hiring good people." Eric Daniels goes further and tracks his hit rate. "You cannot hire someone to engage all the staff and make sure you have the talent that you need throughout the organization," he says. "That's something the CEO must do. We have eight layers in our organization and I get involved in recruitment, compensation, and promotions in four of them. Hiring in general is a pretty random walk, but a person who is a bad fit has a very profound negative effect on the company. I spend a lot of time researching and trying to figure out how people are going to add value. I think my hiring success rate is a little over 70 percent. I'm very conscious of the cost of a miss."

A step change in HR performance

Many CEOs are scathing about the HR profession. Philip Green is typical. "Few HR departments are able to deliver HR's potential," he complains. "The low appetite within businesses for HR is depressing – as is the scarcity of excellent HR professionals. For me, HR is a critical function: it should be an enabler for the general managers in the heart of the business." Brent Hoberman is worried for the future. "Most corporate HR teams are not great as they are inflexible and can't respond to the packages required for the new world of work," he says.

John Boudreau of the Center for Advanced Human Resource Studies at Cornell University explains: "The HR professional provides sophisticated control frameworks, but rarely provides sophisticated decision support... This is one reason that HR is seen as administrative or even obstructive by many line managers and employees... Human resource leaders (except for the rare handful) have been focusing on designing and gaining support for HR programs."[14]

Command-and-control businesses required only a mechanistic service from HR: an efficient compensation and benefits system and a slick hiring and firing process. In many instances this created a strong process orientation in HR directors. Says Archie Norman, "I think the trouble is that there's an HR profession which is a menace. They bring with them a process. They flaunt at you regulation all the time. That's their trump card. When you find they've won every other argument, they say 'Ha, ha, but you've got to have a consultation', and when you have a consultation they manage to make a great meal of it which is designed to make everybody miserable. And because everybody is miserable, they want to reinforce the process and spend even longer on it, and it's distrusted further by the people."

Former Granada CEO Sir Gerry Robinson agrees: "I'm not a great fan of human resources because I believe that the key to success is getting the right people. There is a tendency in HR to try to do more than that. My experience is that HR has a tendency to get involved in things that do not contribute as they should at the sharp end."

Some HR directors share Norman's concerns. Harriet Kemp, former vice-president human resources excellence at ICI, says, "The comfort zone of HR people is doing and delivering. Today, almost all of them feel uncomfortable to step up; there are only a few examples that have managed to break out."

About 60 percent of line managers think that HR lacks the capability to develop talent strategies aligned with business objectives and the same percentage think that HR is an administrative department, not a strategic business partner.[15] Indeed, data from 1,400 HR directors bears this out, as the graph overleaf shows. Unfortunately this is reflected at the pay level: one survey showed that senior sales, finance, marketing, and IT managers earn up to 50 percent more than their HR counterparts.[16]

The first world war for talent requires a much more substantial strategic contribution from HR. At present there are only are a small

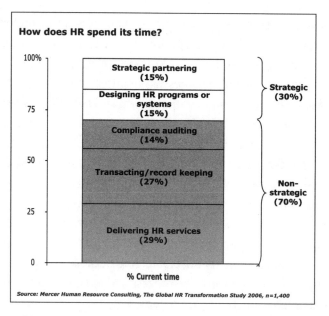

How does HR spend its time?

Source: Mercer Human Resource Consulting, The Global HR Transformation Study 2006, n=1,400

number of businesses where HR is regarded differently, as a strategic partner to a CEO truly committed to the talent agenda. At Cadbury, Todd Stitzer says that there has been an HR person on the board for the last 30 years and that talent development, succession, and the identification of external talent are given two prime hours at every monthly executive committee. In addition, when he does his five or six in-market reviews each year, he always has a talent breakfast with 20–30 people deemed to have high potential in the region he's visiting.

At self-storage group Public Storage, CEO Ron Havner has appointed his HR director to the executive committee. "She attends all business planning meetings and is my go-to person on all aspects of talent. She's also got the total respect of my leadership team – as demonstrated by the fact that she's one of the top five best-paid people in the company."

What are the top HR directors doing in businesses that are a magnet for talent? At such companies HR is regarded as a truly strategic function and people value the department's judgment in discussions of strategy and organizational design. Carolyn McCall, chief executive of Guardian Media Group, believes HR has to be an enabler and a facilitator at the strategic level. "I work with my human resources director in a discursive way," she says. "Once every six weeks we meet and understand issues and team coaching and support. She sees the business in a fresh way and suggests ways to do it. I ensure she has good operational HR people to deliver."

Interacting in this way enables McCall to work closely with her HR director to share the burden of owning the talent agenda. "I don't have to worry about talent targets and I maintain my inputs at the strategic level," she says. "HR is a perennial issue. The only way to deal is to have someone who understands human resources and business. Human resources specialists tend to have a narrow focus. You need someone who can be operational and strategic and fix business problems."

> You need someone who can be operational and strategic and fix business problems

HR professionals are under increasing pressure to raise their game and develop robust commercial and strategic judgment. Therefore, they need to be drawn from a commercial background, or rotated through line roles, so that they truly understand the reality of life on the ground. Rotations can serve more deeply to engage line managers in the talent agenda. Eric Daniels states, "Most banks have lousy HR departments, so none of the candidates for my head of HR position were from a bank. I looked for an extraordinary executive with a pattern of success."

HR must also be truly global. Globally dispersed leadership teams need an HR framework to support them. Mervyn Davies says, "As businesses go global, talent management by necessity becomes more bureaucratic. The leader cannot just walk down the corridor to see his people. Therefore HR becomes a strategic partner to the CEO instead of a 'nice-to-have'." You cannot fight a global war with a locally based army and no intelligence on developments outside your home market; HR has to be in the trenches in key countries fighting for the top 1 percent of talent globally.

Fortunately, some HR directors understand the challenge. Angela Smith at Virgin Management says, "It's important that we talk to CEOs in their language. We have to challenge them and be business orientated. As HR directors, we have to keep the dialogue going; share the responsibility with them and make sure it's not just an HR initiative. We struggle with challenging the CEO and board to hire great HR people who can drive the business." At Lenovo, Kenneth DiPietro pushes his team to "think differently, innovate differently, and conceive of different talent models".

Raising the game in search

Can chief executives simply go to external search consultants to bolster their internal HR function and deliver their talent agenda? Although the answer should be yes, a lot of CEOs don't feel that the search industry is particularly good either. They want a proactive talent partner, but many search firms are perceived to be too transaction based and unready to be a strategic partner. "I've never met a headhunter with in-depth knowledge of my sector," says Val Gooding. Krister Svensson, founder of CMi specializing in developing high-quality board directors, observes, "Headhunters rarely challenge perceived wisdom, instead they often seem to take orders like a *maître d'hôtel*."

Notwithstanding the difficulties, Richard Baker believes that chief executives need a talent partner from the search industry. "They need a radar on the industry and on perceptions of their company," he says. "The search partner should be like a deputy HR director. He or she should be in the CEO's diary every month." Jan Secher, CEO of chemicals company Clariant, says, "I decided I wanted a real talent partner because I wanted someone to really understand the business, the culture, the talent, and my team."

The search partner should be like a deputy HR director. He or she should be in the CEO's diary every month

Several CEOs feel that they are underserved by the headhunting industry. One says, "The search industry is still essentially a personal business. Most consultants have a narrow geographical or sector focus and are transactional; they drive you to do the highest number of searches possible as quickly as possible. Most senior guys are industry lifers and were mostly originally from non-commercial backgrounds, such as the army, politics, and journalism, so they don't really understand the business agenda. They're really farming their contacts rather than identifying the best global candidates using a rigorous process of talent identification that goes beyond their current assignments. I don't think any of them could give me a list of the top 1 percent of global talent." Another states, "Look, there are a bunch of large branded search firms that get closest. But I don't think any of them can consistently guarantee to find the best people globally."

From within the industry Kevin Kelly comments, "We're listening to CEOs and recognize that they've issued the industry with a challenge. We're developing global practices, continuing to hire people with real commercial skills and advisory backgrounds, and we're investing hard in developing our existing talent."

THE TALENT MINDSET

Talent-magnet companies will make it a critical objective to attract the top 1 percent of the best people globally. They will structure their businesses and growth to ensure that they provide attractive and stimulating routes for that talent.

Talent development will also be global. "You need a single, integrated approach to talent to succeed in a global, integrated world," says Sir Bill Castell. "You need to be global and give the opportunity to grow leaders outside the home market." Liu Jiren is equally emphatic. "There will be no difference between Eastern and Western leaders in the twenty-first century because the world is now a small village," he says. "Western and Eastern leaders have the same language and ability so will compete together. Although cultures will not merge, abilities will."

There will be no difference between Eastern and Western leaders because the world is now a small village

In acting globally, talent-magnet companies self-consciously aim to be talent scouts. Today most companies fill vacancies reactively, a resignation putting them on the back foot, scrambling to locate good enough candidates. While positions lie open, businesses hemorrhage momentum, morale, and the chance to align themselves decisively for long-term opportunities and even cash

TALENT MANAGEMENT THE ARSÈNE WENGER WAY

English soccer in the age of the Premier League is not renowned for talent management. The bigger clubs have the wallets to be able to buy the international stars they want. Occasionally, teams like Sir Alex Ferguson's "class of '92" come through the youth system and lower-league clubs like Crewe Alexandra have an excellent record of producing players that go on to be internationals.

In recent years, however, Arsenal manager Arsène Wenger has stood out from his peers for spotting global talent and fast-tracking it to his first-team squad. From formerly unknown quantities like Nicolas Anelka, Kolo Touré, Gaël Clichy, and Cesc Fàbregas to more mature players like Thierry Henry, whose career was transformed by joining Arsenal, Wenger excels at spotting young and gifted players from all over the world through a global network of scouts and contacts. He then hones and develops their skills, giving particular attention to players' diets and lifestyles and using statistics on performance to create health and fitness regimes tailored to each player. "We scout them, ask them to come here and we give them the guarantee that we will try to develop them," he says. "We are not successful with everybody and you can only pay for their education with the points which you lose. I think it is more a question of the right or wrong spirit rather than nationality. I have looked for players with the Arsenal spirit. I don't look at the passport. You are good enough or not good enough."[17]

and employees. In the next decade great businesses will proactively and continuously scout for talent that can form a semi-warm bench of potential recruits for when a succession question appears to be looming.

Business can adopt the same approach as soccer manager Arsène Wenger (see above). For example, one former FTSE100 CEO used to conduct "talent trawls through local markets looking for talent outside the company". Scouting for talent requires investment in customer relationship management-type systems to capture interactions with good people on a global basis.

Talent scouting will result in workforces characterized by difference. It is vital never to forget that talent is about individuals, whether you're trying to attract, retain, or develop people. Scouting for talent proactively will turn up irresistibly attractive, exceptional individuals who do not fit any particular predefined hole. So break the mold.

"Businesses are all about balance between control and innovation," says John Richards. "If you want to lead rather than follow, you have to make space for and tolerate the odd maverick. These characters don't always file their expenses on time; they can be easily coaxed into compliance but they are inevitably going to reoffend. I am prepared to tolerate that because we want this person's contribution to the success of our business."

Allan Leighton, chairman of the UK's Royal Mail, agrees. "You have to have a balance of 10 percent mavericks and 90 percent non-mavericks," he says. "You're not balancing that enough if a manager does not have the capability to have three or four people who don't fit the usual mold. Actually, I find it very easy to manage mavericks. You just go around telling everyone that someone is a complete maverick or a bit of a maverick. Everyone laughs and the mavericks quite like it. You make a big deal out of the fact that they are the exceptions."

This mindset is underpinned by a commitment to investment in human capital as though it were financial capital. Too many CEOs seem to treat talent acquisition and development as an area of discretionary spending, even when it comes to their top teams. They fret that overinvestment is a waste and also renders their high-fliers more attractive to others and therefore more likely to leave. In the coming decade, the reality will be that a failure to invest will probably lead to the flight of high-fliers to companies more interested in development, as well as the loss of the vital competitive edge that such top performers bring to your business.

Talent tactics

Talent-magnet companies will employ a number of distinctive tactics to attract, develop, and retain the top 1 percent of global talent.

Todd Stitzer says, "I want to surround myself with the smartest people I possibly can. People with the same value set in how they treat other people and people with a desire for accomplishment. Top people are highly motivated, value orientated, and are focused on high performance but doing things the right way."

Similarly, Richard Baker states, "I always look more for personal qualities and who's got an edge rather than technical competencies and when I do that I inevitably get it right." They are in effect warning against the slavish application of overly simplistic competency frameworks. Candidates must have the requisite technical competencies and experience, but what distinguishes the best are their personal characteristics and their fit with the culture and values of your organization.

Companies trumpet their training programs, but many of these schemes are overdue an overhaul. The trick for talent-magnet companies is the focus of their training. This means development programs designed at the collective level, such as courses at corporate universities, company-wide and functional training, and sharing best practice, but also coaching at a personal level on performance and leadership.

Initiatives should focus on developing a deep understanding of business realities to empower executives to be independent decision makers. They must, as far as possible, be explicitly global, providing participants with a chance to learn and lead together with truly international peers. While buying in training resources can be cost effective, all programs need to be carefully tailored to the precise requirements of your business environment. Day to day, it is typically the personal coaching that is poorly carried through. We'll dissect the kind of measures that are needed in detail in Chapter 13.

Businesses such as Wipro, Infosys, and Unipart stand out as examples of top-quality talent-development programs. Liu Jiren used inventive talent strategies to grow Neusoft. "When we started the company," he says, "we also started several courses at Northeastern University, where I was a professor, where we learnt a lot from professors from Japan, for example. We sent young people to set up new businesses. We had excellent people who learnt and succeeded very fast and these quality people meant we grew by 100 percent per year for the first six years. Today, to develop our talent we have our own private university, which has 22,000 students. The university is an HR tool and a driving force in growing fast. It very significantly reduces the cost when people join the company."

Because talent is about individuals, you have to know your people. Most CEOs do not know even their top 100 people in detail, but to

TOP GUN TALENT DEVELOPMENT

The US Navy has an elite academy for the top 1 percent of its pilots, officially called the Fighter Weapons School but known as Top Gun. It aims to train the best fighter pilots in the world.

Winning the first world war for talent means putting talent truly at the heart of business and creating Top Gun-like academies. CEOs need to recognize that talent is as critical to the business as serving the customer and that they must commit to a heavy investment of time and money in attracting, retaining, and developing talent.

have a true focus on individuals the CEO and HR must know the aspirations, motivations, morale, and capabilities of the business's talent. True individualization leads to flexible action. When an employee hits a personal crisis, for example a death in the family, the company's reaction will forever color his or her relationship with the organization and colleagues. HR and line managers must be close enough to employees to spot these issues and must also be empowered and bold enough to push through genuine short-term accommodations to help them.

This level of commitment to talent takes a huge amount of time. In response, some companies split HR systems maintenance from the talent function. Says Mervyn Davies, "People in HR have to be talent spotters and developers. The operational aspect of payroll, compensation, processing needs to be separated from talent development. In Standard Chartered, top managers do a stint in HR."

While you want to retain the true talent, it is important to recognize that you will not have a 100 percent success rate in hiring. Fire fast if you make a mistake. Archie Norman comments, "The ones that don't work out, you've got to get out of the business again and you do it fast, because otherwise you accumulate people who are halfway successful or no good at all, and because you've got investment in them, it takes you two years to figure out you made a mistake. My best performance was recruiting somebody and parting company with them the same day they arrived. I say that not because it's a great illustration of my own failure, and of course it was, but because it was the right thing to do. It was obvious it wasn't going to work for him and it wasn't going to work for us."

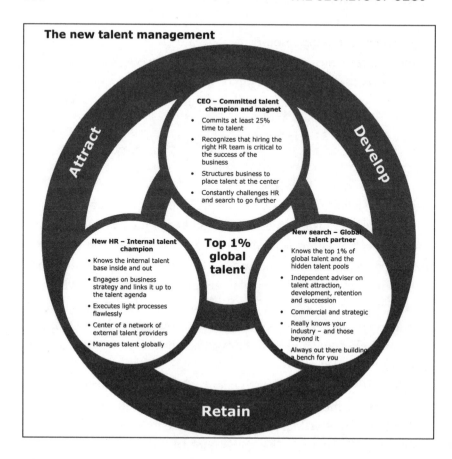

The new talent management

A CENTRAL ROLE FOR THE CEO

The CEO needs to drive the talent agenda. Ahmed Fahour, CEO Australia at National Australia Bank, "feels like the chief HR manager" in his business unit, while leadership expert René Carayol agrees that "the CEO at the back of house doesn't work any more. A CEO should be a talent magnet." Greg Dyke, former director-general of the BBC, points out, "If you want to change the culture of an organization, human resources cannot do it; HR can only do it if it has the chief executive with it."

The CEO must also make the talent agenda a priority for everyone in the business. Talent attraction, retention, and development must be made key responsibilities for all line managers and they must be incentivized on this. Companies should be just as ruthless about underperformance on talent as they are on growth and margin targets. As part of their ownership of the issue, the CEOs of many companies are likely to find that their HR function will need repositioning and upgrading. Whether the CEO decides to split HR processes from talent development or not, HR needs to be given real teeth, reach, and weight in the business at a global level so that it is a credible strategic partner. This will likely require upgrading the quality of some HR personnel, drawing on people with a stronger commercial background.

Winning on talent is hard. Matt Emmens, CEO of Shire Pharmaceuticals, states, "It's sort of like you're on the train and running the engine and changing the wheels. In some ways, it is controlled chaos. You're changing all the systems while they are in place."

> It's like you're on the train and running the engine and changing the wheels. In some ways, it is controlled chaos

Sir Terry Leahy at Tesco and Jeff Immelt at GE are good examples of CEOs who are fully engaged in the talent agenda. Leahy sits on five committees, the executive, property, and trade committees, and the people matters group, which he chairs. He says that people are managed as rigorously as commercial or financial assets. He and the committee examine Tesco's work levels four and five – about 400 people. He comments, "The lack of a global HR director is recognition that in a people-intensive business, managing people is core to being a good line manager. HR is core to what we do so we don't have a separate function, but have a lot of HR people integrated into the business. I and all the executive directors have our own HR directors without a team who work just for each one of us so their impact is direct. These HR people develop talent pools and run the Academy. We do lots on developing talent ourselves."

At GE, Immelt is actively involved with all 180 VPs and 450 senior executives. As CEO of GE Healthcare, Sir Bill Castell says that he was actively involved in the assessment, development, and succession of more than 460 people and spent 60 days a year on talent issues. Great CEOs are continually asking how they should set up the business to get the best from talent and develop talent effectively.

Talent is so important that non-executive boards' nomination committees are already starting to monitor talent development three levels below board level. The CEO will have to be on the front foot to meet the NomComm's questions.

THE TALENT PARTNERSHIP

The first world war for talent requires businesses to adopt a new partnership between the CEO, HR, and the search industry.

Historically there have been tensions in the relationship between HR and search firms because the broader relationship between search, HR, and the CEO was unclear. Businesses now need a new engagement between the three parties. CEOs are starting to recruit a new breed of HR director and search firm who will work together with them in a true partnership. HR will act as the internal talent champion but maintain a view on the external market, informed by its search partner. For its part, the search industry will continue to look for exceptional candidates for its partner's specific short-term hiring needs, but top firms will also invest heavily in specific talent-management initiatives that go beyond their client's live searches to ensure that they are constantly aware of all the top talent who could be relevant to their client in the medium term.

This partnership will rely on mutual respect for each party's contribution, trust that all parties are working in the best interests of the group, unshakeable commitment to finding the top 1 percent of global talent, and a proactive approach to talent acquisition. All these changes will need to be underpinned by a new economic arrangement between the three reflecting a deeper and more exclusive approach.

For the unprepared, the first world war for talent holds out the grim prospect of wage inflation, high turnover rates, and long periods of uncertainty while key posts lie empty. However, companies that bite the bullet and invest in talent will have the foundations to be leading businesses in their industry. As CEO, will you lead the way and put talent at the top of your agenda?

SECRETS OF CEOs: TOMORROW'S TALENT DEVELOPMENT

❑ We are at the outset of the first world war for talent, driven principally by unfavorable demographics in the West, skills scarcity in the East, a worldwide shortage of global leaders, and the frequency with which employees are now shifting jobs.

❑ The need to hire multigenerational, highly diverse workforces and the rise of the demanding Generation Y will create a new world of work that will place new leadership demands on global CEOs.

❑ Most CEOs talk a good game on talent, but top CEOs recognize that talent is as critical to their organization as are their customers and invest time and money to act as talent magnets and talent champions within their businesses.

❑ Winning the first world war for talent will require a deep and trusting partnership between CEOs, HR directors, and search. Rather than organizations being on the back foot and hiring reactively, developing a successful global partnership will position companies better to attract, nurture, and hold on to the top 1 percent of global talent.

The acid test: In your business
- Is talent as high a priority as serving customers?
- Are you committed to investing money and 25 percent of your time to talent development?
- Are your key executives drawn from the top 1 percent of global talent?
- Are your HR team and search firm proactively finding you the top global talent?
- Do you have premier league facilities – the squad, the scout network, the academies?

PART II

LEADING AT THE TOP TODAY

"There is not one answer to leadership: one is trying to find the keys to the answer for one point in time."

John Pluthero, Cable & Wireless

So there you have it: CEOs are worrying about a huge range of problems that affect their businesses, but five critical trends stand out in their minds. We think that many companies will struggle to cope with the trends we examined in Part I and so we spend Part III looking at how some of the best CEOs are reshaping their organizations to profit from these testing times.

Before we examine how businesses are likely to change, in Part II we think it's important to examine the way CEOs are actually leading their businesses today. What have the best leaders learnt about how to lead?

❏ How do top chief executives really run their businesses?
❏ Where have they come from?
❏ What motivates and drives them?

The first insight from our analysis is that most current CEOs are really professional managers. It seems clear that the start of the new century has been characterized by the replacement of the 1990s' publicity-hungry "celebrity" CEOs with professional managers. The latter are typically more risk averse and, wary of eye-catching ventures and personal publicity, may prefer to make incremental adjustments to their company's core businesses rather than seeking to promote dramatic change.

The second insight is more heartening. In contrast to professional managers, top CEOs are far-sighted leaders who are open to radical change but not set on it, and who paint a sophisticated and compelling picture of the future for their employees, customers, and shareholders. Not for them a bland three-year planning cycle: these CEOs are always impatient and looking to push the boundaries of their organizations.

The third crucial insight is that top-quartile CEOs fall into five distinct categories. In fact, we were surprised by quite how different the operating styles of our top CEOs were. In this part of the book we define these leadership types and illustrate how they work through detailed profiles of leading examples. While we feature UK leaders of global businesses, we have found that these types hold true wherever in the world leaders are from.

Note that we did not set out to "pigeonhole" CEOs' leadership styles. We have here identified the characteristics these top leaders have displayed up to this point in their careers, and in the leadership situations they have faced. It is not impossible that their leadership styles could evolve in the future, or that they have strengths that have yet to be brought out by their experience.

Equally, any classification brings clarity but risks simplification: it is clear that the individuals we profile are superb, broadly based leaders and will also exhibit characteristics that are associated with other leadership types. The truth is that great leaders outperform most of us on most elements of leadership, but also have particularly pronounced strengths that characterize their style. We have tried to focus on our profilees' most instructive clusters of strengths (and weaknesses) in the following chapters.

In outline, the five leadership types we've identified are as follows.

Commercial executors focus on how the business is trading: "What are our like-for-like store sales this week?"
Commercial executors have a driving focus on achieving the best results in their industry, combined with a relentless attention to detail in order to ensure that operational and strategic ambitions become a reality. Tesco chief executive Sir Terry Leahy is our prime example.

Financial value drivers *focus relentlessly on the financial worth of their business: "What's the business worth today?"*

Financial value drivers recognize that business metrics are essential, but what really keeps them awake is the group's valuation and where the next value-accretive deal might come from. They understand the metrics of their industry and are often highly skilled in identifying value-enhancing corporate transactions or realizing value from portfolio disposals. Xstrata chief executive Mick Davis illustrates this type.

Corporate entrepreneurs *live their business: "What's happened to my baby today?"*

Corporate entrepreneurs have something to prove. They disrupt industries because they believe in a better way of doing things. They excel in spotting breakthrough opportunities and making them a reality. We feature Sir Martin Sorrell, who founded WPP, now one of the world's largest advertising and marketing businesses, and describes the experience as "the closest that a man can get to giving birth".

Corporate ambassadors *worry about the global impact of their business: "How can I transform the geopolitical landscape of my industry?"*

Corporate ambassadors have a global vision that has a broader societal impact; they operate at a geopolitical level and often deliver transactions that transform industries. Lord Browne, the former CEO of BP who is now forging a new career in private equity, propelled BP from a mid-ranking European company into the third largest oil company in the western world.

Global missionaries *wake up every day and renew their personal mission: "How do I make my company and the world a fundamentally better place for all my stakeholders?"*

Global missionaries want to make a significant personal difference and at the same time make their companies great. They are typically customer champions and lead by inspiring people and energizing them to tap into their potential. One of the best examples is Ben Verwaayen, former chief executive of BT.

In the following chapters we set out the measures of success that most resonate with these leaders, the situations in which each type generally excels, the industries in which they are most commonly found, their particular strengths, and the risks with which they are most often associated.

We hope that this part of the book will help you gain a better understanding of how you lead, the likely gaps and shortfalls in your leadership approach, what skills to look for in potential team members, and whether the industry and situation you are in are the most appropriate for you.

7

COMMERCIAL EXECUTORS

Commercial executors are so named not for their skills in chopping heads or cutting costs, but for their ability to get things done. They combine a driving focus on achieving the best results in their industry with a relentless focus and attention to detail in order to ensure that operational and strategic ambitions become a reality.

There are two types of commercial executor: driving personal leaders and team marshals. Let's take the most common type first, the driving personal leader. One of the best examples is the man who, as chief executive of Tesco since 1997, has turned that company from a good business into a great one, making it Britain's biggest retailer and then taking its operating model to Asia, Eastern Europe, and the US.

When Sir Terry Leahy became chief executive of Tesco, the name of the game was still fierce rivalry with Sainsbury's for the position of Britain's top retailer. However, great driving personal leaders excel not only at pushing their companies to deliver but at spotting new battlegrounds to win in. When the City began to doubt whether Tesco could continue its UK growth story amidst a planning clampdown on new out-of-town superstores, Sir Terry took the battle to the high street, stunning the City with the acquisition of convenience stores group T&S Stores for £337m. In one swoop, the acquisition boosted Tesco's still fledgling high-street operations by 862 convenience stores.[1] Later, he surprised analysts again by buying a £100m majority stake in Dobbies Gardens Centres, a new area of business for Tesco.[2]

Acquisitions are just one tool in Sir Terry's kitbag. He has proved that he can grow Tesco organically in the UK, building its share of the nation's wallets to today's position where it accounts for £1 out of every £7 spent in the country.[3] He has also demonstrated that he can expand overseas, quietly amassing retail operations in more than ten countries in Eastern Europe and the Far East before embarking on Tesco's long-awaited push into the US. "We have more space outside the UK than within," he told the *Daily Telegraph*. "It's an extra-ordinary statistic. We're highly profitable outside the UK and growing rapidly, and yet the number of expatriates in our overseas operations in less than one in 1,000, so we have been able to achieve all these things with a relatively light investment in management."[4]

It's instructive that Tesco began its international expansion in 1995, two years before Sir Terry's appointment. Corporate executors don't always need to be the people who start trends or come up with innovation; their flair is for turning strategy into successful reality. Sir Terry did not lead on this initiative, though he was on the board that backed it. However, his eye for detail, organizational excellence, energy, and relentless focus on results have made the expansion a huge success. "It was a big decision for Tesco," he says. "Retailing is the most local of industries and it was far from certain there could be an international industry. But we felt that if we were to stay in the front rank of our industry we would have to be international, to seek out the best competitors and to learn from them. We knew that it would always take time to put down sufficiently deep roots in a market to provide a platform for long-term success."[5]

The international story is only one element of Tesco's transformation under Sir Terry's leadership. Other components include the power it has accumulated in "non-food" areas like consumer electronics and music retailing, the growth of its Tesco Extra hypermarkets, the astonishing success of its Clubcard in driving customer loyalty, and its successful diversification into financial services products such as home and car insurance.

All these strategic moves have been accomplished with little fanfare and without simply following fashion. Key is Tesco's focus on carefully chosen business metrics and peer comparisons against which to measure its performance and a constant opportunism for chances to extend the brand.

This opportunism is underpinned by a commitment to the values that Tesco has associated itself with: simplicity, economy, and excellent service, all the values that underpin the CEO himself. Rather than this being a case of an egocentric CEO putting his stamp on the company he leads, it seems that Sir Terry's 29-year career at Tesco has engrained the business in him. Indeed, it's hard to see where Tesco stops and Sir Terry starts. There's no doubt that his relatively low ego by CEO standards, strong family background, and dry wit, including his long-suffering support for Everton Football Club, keep him grounded in reality.

Sir Terry on being a driving personal leader
"In business, the important thing is the relationship between the firm and its customers. I've always had a very strong sense of what's important. It's what the business is for. It's its customers. All you can do is leave the business better than you found it. What else is there? That's enough. The radar comes from working with customers. What do they need in their lives? You're talking about where they are heading, what they want, what's changing. The talent radar is easier because retailers are managers of people. That's what you do. So through the process of managing people you're managing talent.

"What you don't do also matters. That is why we tend to be internally focused. That's what matters, not the cocktail circuit. It's not driven through the lash; it's driven through the culture. A lot is driven through giving people confidence to make decisions for themselves, for the customer. It's not to be driven by fashion. Our presentations to shareholders don't change over the years; we concentrate on the same things."

Formative roots and career
Terry Leahy grew up in a prefabricated maisonette on the Lee Park council estate in a working-class part of Liverpool, UK. The third of four brothers born to a greyhound trainer who worked as caretaker on the council-owned farm where they lived, he went to a Catholic grammar school before gaining a business science degree from Manchester

University. "My brothers all left school at 16 but my parents worked very hard so that I could stay on and do my A-levels," he says on his former university's website.

After university, he worked for the Co-op for a year and a half as a graduate trainee before quitting to move to London with Alison, now his wife. There he joined Tesco, initially as a casual worker stacking shelves, aged 23. He soon joined the marketing department and before he turned 30 had become Tesco's marketing director. Eight years later, in 1992, he was appointed to the board of directors, and by the time he was 40 he had worked his way up to become chief executive.

Sir Terry's family background has given him a down-to-earth approach with a solid connection to day-to-day life and "ordinary" people. He eschews a chauffeur-driven car, does not sit on other companies' boards, and prefers pacing his shop floors to networking at glitzy receptions.

"Being centered must come from your upbringing," he says. "I had loving parents and a very secure background. My Catholic education brought me up to serve, not to judge people, and to know that no one is better than you but you're not better than anyone else."

Core beliefs and values

Sir Terry's ordinariness is not a front or a stunt. He is obsessed with the company he runs and is committed to making sure that it stays in touch with its customers and with trading trends. His biggest motivation does appear to be helping people lead a better life, but he is no dewy-eyed bleeding heart; he knows that Tesco's resonance with value-focused shoppers is what gives the stores group its *raison d'être*.

This commitment is genuine. "Sir Terry is the sort of man who feels more at home discussing football in a Liverpool pub than among London's glitzy set and this is the root to his rapport with Tesco's customers and staff," said a BBC report.[6] "Coming from Liverpool hasn't given him airs and graces," added *Management Today*, "and it has equipped him to ignore them in others."[7]

Sir Terry is tough and during the early part of his career he was known for an aggressive management style. Although the aggression has long softened, he remains impassioned, believing in the importance of employees and customers, ensuring that Tesco is a company where people can succeed regardless of their background, and driving the business with consistency and relentless customer focus. And you still have the sense talking to Sir Terry that he is eyeing you just as he would a sample product from a new supplier – coolly and piercingly.

Sir Terry on managing business

"Intensity is to some extent harnessing the skills in the business because, as a retailer, Tesco has a lot of people. These people tend to be from ordinary backgrounds so they feel that they have to work hard to get on and so there has always been extraordinary energy. So we harness these assets: focus that energy and it can be tremendous. And with energy comes discipline. People work hard and don't obstruct action unnecessarily. At a senior level, you have to drive consensus; you need a lot of discipline at the top because then you need to project that out, in our case to 400,000 people. In two competing businesses, the one that projects the vision out furthest wins.

"[In making a strategy] you tend to start with where the growth will come from, perhaps not if it's a new business, but usually you take up a business with strengths and weaknesses. Before answering that, you look at the assets of the business. And what those two really lead to is the purpose, because it's necessary to answer what the business is for because you need to align everybody.

"Purpose is really for employees: this is what we get up every day to do. Then there is a secondary use of the purpose for explanation to people outside. Strategy then comes underneath the purpose and the values – it expresses how you make the growth. And you have to make it as stretching as possible. The objectives we have laid out are really about the vision (what are we here for?), the values (how do we behave?), and the strategy (what do we do for growth?)

"So that's the sequence. The great next thing was the balanced scorecard, because you need to connect these things to the complicated wiring of the business. Retail is about people, property, and products, so you need to structure your time to face these.

"In Tesco, people are managed as assets like property. Most of the top people have grown up in the business. There's tremendous loyalty and they have always been stretched so they don't feel held back. They've always had new opportunities when ready.

"There's quite a good culture. People feel stretched but valued. Generally, you feel your boss is on side, not your biggest problem. This is not Wonderland but generally people feel challenged, not judged. There's quite a lot of empowerment. People don't realize that Tesco tends to run on trust and confidence. We do a lot of work on motivation.

"The biggest challenge is maintaining the values of the business as you go to new countries and face new expectations. If the business stays close to customers and retains its values, it can go anywhere."

Work–life balance

Sir Terry lives a comfortable but unglamorous life with his wife, a medical doctor, and their three children. He cites his wife as a major support.

"You do have to have a work–life balance and an even keel, but it is not easy," he says. "There's often less pressure at the top than in the middle, because you have more control and an inner self-confidence so that you can leave things alone much more easily. For people in the middle, it is not their judgment. They're trying to work to the judgment of others.

"I think I have a work–life balance. The more difficult challenges are physical travel and external stakeholders who want the CEO in person. Managing £1m is much like managing £1bn and managing 100 stores is much like managing 1,000, within reason."

Life after Tesco

It is difficult to conceive of Sir Terry running a company other than Tesco. He said in an interview back in 2003 that he'd lost count of the calls he's taken from headhunters in his near three decades with the company. None was entertained. "Some people are stayers and some are movers," he told the *Financial Times*. "I'm obviously a stayer. I think it is partly in your personality. I make a joke about it: one wife, one football team, one firm. I remember saying to myself: 'What would make you move?' In the end, I concluded I would stay at Tesco up to the point that the business stopped me from contributing in the way I wanted to contribute. It never did."[8] Nor is it easy to imagine him "going plural" with a portfolio of non-executive directorships or spending all his time on a golf course. Barring a corporate disaster, Sir Terry looks likely to be inseparable from Tesco for some time to come.

He told us, "Professionally, Tesco means everything. No other job could compare because all my relationships and experience have been here in Tesco and it is important work – it matters to people. How long I do the job has never been an issue because it's genuinely not for me to decide. That's for the board, though I have some say. So don't worry about what you can't control.

"The best thing you can do is concentrate on the business. It's not necessarily decades for me but it is for the firm. You always think long term. The days and months take care of themselves."

From the Tesco perspective, this presents several challenges. One is ensuring that the company does not begin to believe its own publicity and loses track of reality. While there are millions of happy shoppers who love its cheap prices and convenience, the company has attracted criticism for its planning policies and its impact on communities. It also remains to be seen whether Fresh & Easy can replicate Tesco's success in other markets and avoid becoming one of the many British retail ventures to fail in the US.

Another clear challenge is succession. One secret of Sir Terry's success has been the strong and dedicated core team he has assembled in Richard Brasher, Phil Clarke, Andy Higginson, Tim Mason, and David Potts, who have almost all been with the business for at least ten years. However, their quality and Sir Terry's longevity must beg the question of whether there will be more high-profile departures like that of John Browett to become CEO of electrical goods retailer

DSG International. Can Tesco manage Sir Terry's succession and the growth of his lieutenants successfully?

Other driving personal leaders

Driving personal leader commercial executors are focused on industry metrics. In the retail sector, commercial executors like Sir Terry have instant recall of the latest week's like-for-like sales. Insurance commercial executors like Mark Tucker, CEO of life and pensions group Prudential, compete fiercely on quarterly new business figures and on the industry's embedded value metrics that measure the value of in-force policies.

Tucker believes in governing by example. "I believe that a CEO has to be 'hands on' in terms of both strategy and business performance," he says. "But at the same time, you have to avoid becoming a one-man band, so you have to ensure that you have got the right people in and are doing things in the right way.

"The ability to retain focus is also an important attribute. There's a lot of noise in business and a lot of 'advice', whether it is from your broker or your investors or from the press. You have to make sure you have the right strategy and get things done in your plan to prove that you are going the right way."

His view is that being a good commercial executor involves having the ability to articulate a compelling vision that maximizes the benefit to shareholders of both short-term business performance and long-term market positioning, and then the leadership qualities to motivate and inspire successful implementation. "As my track record shows, both in Asia and running the group, I'm about growth not consolidation," he says. "The critical requirement is to balance and achieve simultaneous success at short-term results and longer-term strategic change, when the two can often pull in different directions. I cannot say that one is more important than the other. Short-term performance is no use if it is 'dead end' and not building for the group's future in one way or another. And while strategic vision is essential, strategy divorced from a credible implementation path is self-delusion." He believes that the keys to managing successful implementation of business plans are to put forward a consistent and motivational message and to build a first-rate management team.

Industrial commercial executors, such as Steve Holliday at National Grid, are driven by a quest to raise productivity and eliminate waste. Holliday has a relentless focus on continuous improvement, which he manages through business metrics. "A lot of people think that if you do 5 percent better than last year, that's very good," he says. "But if you just improve by 5 percent, you leave a huge amount of opportunity on the table. We've done a lot of work on getting people's mindsets about what they do when they come to work to change. You have got to really inspire people with vision. It can't just be the old rhetoric about all having to go up the hill together."

He believes in a direct interventionist style, coupled with the humility to recognize that he will make mistakes. "I've had plenty of things that have gone wrong due to my direct style and intervention," he says. "I am still learning and I will be learning until the day I retire. You never stop."

Holliday also does not forget the importance of people. "You have to surround yourself with the best people," he says. "Getting the best people on the bus and making sure they're going in the right direction are part of my job. If you have not got the right people in the job, get them in; and if you are not going in the right direction, get them off."

Another classic commercial executor is Phil Cox, CEO of International Power. "Execution is massively important," he says. "We have earned credibility by delivering exactly what we said we were going to deliver." Chip Hornsby, CEO of Wolseley Group, adds, "Our business is 99 percent execution and 1 percent strategy. If you want to get things right, you have to make sure you execute properly. If you keep coming in with new strategies, you just confuse everyone: your customers, suppliers, and employees."

Team Marshals

While the driving personal leader subtype of commercial executors tend to place an emphasis on their own role, team marshals accent the development of their team as the engine for success.

Team marshals put the emphasis firmly on their management teams. They're often self-effacing individuals wary of media exposure or celebrity status. They exhibit a genuine interest in the people around them and the roles that all team members can play in meeting business targets.

Take the enthusiasm for making a team hum that former Alliance Boots chief executive Richard Baker expresses. "When you get the team to perform above the sum of its parts, anything is possible," he says. "Teams perform amazing things. Average people can produce superstar performances when you get the team right. Yeovil Town can beat Manchester United; you can do anything if you try hard enough. And the buzz when you do it is amazing. Anybody can be brilliant. There's nothing you can't do." Baker says that the measure of a leader is the number of his followers. He sets as his target the best level at which he believes an organization can potentially operate to deliver the potential of the organization and the individuals within it. He is typical of team marshals in using sporting metaphors to explain what he tries to do and how he wants everyone to work together.

Paul Pindar of Capita agrees. "I like a really strong connection between the top 250 people running the business," he says. "My role is being one of the team, energizing, enthusing, and always making sure that people have a glass that's half full rather than half empty. If you can set the right cultural framework, that really adds an enormous amount of value. Then you get personally involved in the things that add value, like sales and acquisitions."

Pindar is more value driven than some other team marshals, but his values center on the connection with the team and a determination to ensure its togetherness. "When I joined the company, we were just 33 people turning over £1m," he says. "We used to have ten golden rules like treating customers and colleagues with respect and no internal politics. People know that if they come into this office and try to knife someone in the back because they think it's the thing to do, they're not going to get a very good audience so it does not tend to go on. As we are growing very quickly, we bring in people from outside but, just as a football club can be spoiled by a few stars who come in and wreck the dressing room, we have to be very careful not to bring in people who will wreck the place."

Paul Walsh of Diageo adds: "I have a huge level of curiosity and I like people. People say that I ask the question 'Why?' five times. I like to penetrate what's going on. I have always been very, very competitive and my competitive nature has been team based. I play as a team. That's something that's always been instilled in me in all the team sports I played. I was always in the team but never captain. What interests me is: are we doing enough with our talent? I engage very deeply with our top 100 managers."

Walsh says that a common thread for team marshals is excellence in "orchestration". "You've got all these people managing in the right direction in the same boat," he says. "You've got to make the destination compelling. Whether it's an ambition to be the best company on the planet or something else, you have to orchestrate your forces and modify the profile of skills you have got in accordance with the objective." With that in mind, he concentrates his efforts on the management team, as a way of making sure that execution of business strategy gets done all the way down the chain. "If you get the management right as a CEO, you are not going to be doing the executing," he says. "I am not going to be going around all our distributors making sure we have got everything right, but someone in the organization had better be doing it. The trick of management is in knowing whether you need to work in algorithms or whether you need a calculator or a sharp pencil. There are times when you need to be at 40,000ft and there are times when you need to dive down and get involved. To my mind, the CEO should be called the chief engagement officer. There are so many people you have to pay attention to."

Perhaps surprisingly, team marshals don't mind being upbraided or coached themselves, especially by their underlings. Pindar says he doesn't worry in the least when others in the company tell him he's going in the wrong direction or not pulling his weight. "It's my team," he says. "My PA will tell me if she thinks I am off the pace and should I be doing something that way. I don't think there's any problem whatsoever in people saying that."

This all sounds very cosy – but can team marshals deliver with this "soft" focus on people? Fear not; they're true to their commercial executor type. Baker recognizes that he is "a strong manager with a focus on people", but also that "you cannot just be a great people leader. You need elements of other leadership styles. You need to be a ruthless inspector." And the people management is distinctly hard-edged. "When I joined Asda, the then chief executive Archie Norman told me that the hardest thing to change is people," recalls Baker, "so I was to interview everyone in my new department and fire four of the 30 by the fourth Friday of my tenure and then hire replacements fast. He said, 'You'll correctly spot the worst two people in the team and even if the other two you fire are not the third and fourth worst, they'll be the fifth or sixth worst, because you'll find the weak people if you ask the right questions. You'll scare the next worst 10 and the best in the team will be energized.' He was right and I've kept this focus on quality. By the end of my first six months at Boots, I had fired two direct reports. It gave me space to hire new people and signaled change. By the end of my tenure I'd changed out everyone in the top team."

PITFALLS OF THE COMMERCIAL EXECUTOR MODEL

While commercial executors can operate in any industry, they are not usually effective in professional services; they're best in businesses that need to be taken from average to great, where pragmatism and an honest confrontation of reality are hugely valuable. Corporate executors excel at setting and meeting targets and combating obstacles to ensure that operations and future strategic ambitions become a reality. They are ruthlessly competitive and have a precise eye for comparing and measuring themselves against their peers, so are typically most focused on business metrics as their measure of success. They're not usually primarily motivated by a wider societal mission.

Therein lie the dangers of the model. One is that the relentless battle to lower costs and increase sales may take too much out of key executives and cause burnout. Another is that without careful management, a commercial executor's company can become overly challenging, with executives vying to outshine each other or seeking to massage their metrics. Then commercial executors risk being unable to attract the best talent, which may be more attracted to value or entrepreneurial-driven opportunities elsewhere.

Corporate executors have an obsessive focus on customer needs and delivering to meet them, but relying too heavily on customers telling you what they need is always risky: no one asked for an iPod, remember. Corporate executors therefore run the risk of being outflanked by a disruptive corporate entrepreneur who changes the rules of the game by spotting a niche in the market and a way of serving customers better. Suddenly it doesn't matter how efficiently commercial executors are running their models; in order to compete, they need to learn to play a new game.

8

FINANCIAL VALUE DRIVERS

Financial value drivers, the category of chief executives that's arguably most loved by the City, focus relentlessly on shareholder value. They are highly skilled at identifying value-enhancing corporate transactions or realizing value from portfolio disposals.

Financial value driver chief executives speak the same language as bankers, analysts, and investors. They're obsessed with generating returns for the shareholders who put up capital to start or grow the business. Value generation is their mission and a single-minded focus on shareholder returns is how they aim to deliver it.

Value drivers want to create the leanest and most streamlined business in their industry; they're aiming to be fat free and rigorously transparent. To reach this objective, they believe in extensive delegation and decentralization, matched with crystal-clear accountability and sheer hard work. In return, they offer exceptional financial rewards to their executives, who in turn have to be comfortable with the unremitting scrutiny and unrelenting assessment that come with working for a value-driving chief executive.

Mick Davis, chief executive of Xstrata since 2001, is one of the best current examples. Xstrata did not exist as a British publicly quoted company seven years ago but, under Davis's leadership, it has barnstormed its way into the list of the nation's 10 biggest.[1] Its phenomenal growth is partly due to being in the right place at the right time. The huge demand for minerals and base materials from China in particular is fueling a commodity metals boom that has seen all miners experience exponential rises in stock market valuations. However, a great deal of the credit has to go to Davis, who put Xstrata in that place at that time.

Before Xstrata was formed in October 2001, its operations were subsumed in the Swiss-based metals group Glencore, which saw an opportunity for a London-based minerals group to join a select band of mining companies attracting London investment. Glencore looked for a chief executive who could drive its idea of transplanting some of its ferroalloy and zinc businesses to a London listing and using this vehicle to consolidate the highly fragmented mining sector. It found Davis at the very top of the industry. He had worked in a similar London minerals transplant as chief financial officer of Billiton, a London company formed out of the assets of South Africa's Gencor. He was a key architect of the merger that Billiton then fashioned with Australia's Broken Hill Properties to form BHP Billiton.

Xstrata started with a value of about $500m ascribed to assets injected into it. Davis then raised nearly £1bn through a flotation on the London Stock Exchange, simultaneously acquiring Glencore's Australian and South African coal assets for $2.5bn. The company immediately entered the FTSE100 and proceeded to use its new paper on a series of acquisitions in Australia and Canada.

Today, Xstrata is the world's largest producer of export thermal coal and ferrochrome, one of the top five producers of coking or metallurgical coal, the fourth largest global producer of copper and nickel, and one of the world's largest miners and producers of zinc. It's also the fifth largest diversified metals and mining company, with operations and projects in 18 countries and top-five market positions in each of its major commodities. With the exception of the short-lived phenomenon of the first dot-com boom, it's hard to think of any other British company achieving so much in so short a time.

Davis on driving a business for value
"I wanted a new company that was nimble and sure-footed and would add value for shareholders and that's what we've built. There was space for us. To be a high-quality CEO, you should be able to lead a company irrespective of which industry it is in or the position it is in. People have leadership capacity or they do not. Whether they are finance people or engineers is not relevant. The reality is that things

happen to companies because the person running the company has the flexibility to be able to manage the risks he is dealing with. You have to wake up every day saying, 'Yesterday was not good enough. Today we have to do better.' Growth is important to me, but it's not growth for growth's sake. You have to protect your values and make sure that you understand the core risks of your business. If you don't do that, your whole business can implode. Making sure that a company can cope with its risks is the CEO's job."

Formative roots and career progression

Davis was born into a Jewish family in Port Elizabeth on the Eastern Cape of South Africa and enjoyed when he calls a "normal middle-class" upbringing with his two brothers. His family was not wealthy but Davis was always keen on going into business. After training as a chartered accountant with KPMG, he worked for South African electricity utility Eskom before joining Gencor, where he served as executive chairman of Ingwe Coal Corporation and later as chief financial officer of Billiton.

The roots of his restless ambition were already apparent. Davis left KPMG because he was not made a partner, even though such an appointment would have meant he was the firm's youngest ever partner at that time. He prospered at Eskom, becoming finance director at the age of 29 under the tutelage of the company's boss John Maree, whom he ranks as his biggest business influence. However, Davis left the firm for similar reasons of unfulfilled ambition three years later after failing to get the chief executive's job – a perhaps unreasonable expectation given that he was still only 32. "My career has been one of leaving companies because they would not recognize the potential I recognized in myself," he says. "I always had the view that I was capable of running the company." At Gencor, Davis joined a young and ambitious team fashioned by the then chief executive Brian Gilbertson and non-executive director Derek Keys.

Davis was hired as a "young Turk alongside people like the now BHP Billiton chief executive Marius Kloppers," says his right-hand man Thras Moraitis. "All the hires were smart, eager, strong-willed, and willing to stand their ground. I think the seeds of Mick's mental model were sown there. Gilbertson molded the young Turks by delegating authority to them."

Davis became chief financial officer, working closely with Gilbertson, but then came Billiton's merger with BHP. He was offered the role of chief development officer in the enlarged group and once again felt he was being undervalued. "It was the right deal," he told *The Times*, "but the result was a completely different company to the one I joined. I didn't think my personal assets would grow."

"I'm speculating," says Moraitis, "but I think that to some degree Mick wanted to show that he was the intellectual force behind Brian Gilbertson when he was managing director. I think there's a sense, perhaps, that he felt he was always the unrecognized number two."

Management style

Davis has very deliberately set about building a value driver model at Xstrata, taking advantage of the company's newness to fashion a group in his image. He describes his management style as "short on process, short on bureaucracy, and long on values" and says that Xstrata has a "unique" business model that relies on complete decentralization.

Davis is a heretical miner. In his view, the mining industry operates on the basis of the myth that you need a large center as a risk-control and scale mechanism, and that head office has to be able to second-guess what people in the field operations are doing. He also doesn't believe that scale in shared information technology and purchasing is essential for a diversified mining company. His insight has been to give full profit-and-loss responsibility to the leader of each of Xstrata's business units, who get complete operational autonomy but are held tightly accountable for results and compliance with group safety and technical standards. Business units can collaborate to share back-office functions and garner the synergies that most mining companies would seek to exploit through a large corporate function, but they are not obliged to. Likewise, while the center executes transformational deals, the business units are under no obligation to use corporate assets in acquiring smaller companies, within their own capital expenditure limits, though they may apply to do so. Thus Xstrata's slim central operations, overseen by Davis, only retain control of the money, targets, health and safety, and technical standards. "I give people the space and support to do their jobs well," he told *The Times*. "I tell them when they haven't."[2]

At Xstrata mistakes are tolerated, as long as they are not repeated and have been made in the context of sensible business risks. The center promises the operations "transformational mergers and acquisitions" that will give them opportunities to make economies of scale within the business units. In return, headquarters demands that the business units deliver operational excellence, meet their financial targets, and never cover up mistakes. Businesses will always be held to account for their actions and inactions.

In effect, Davis has built Xstrata on a form of social contract. Power is devolved from the group in exchange for transparency. "We won't fail" is the strapline to both sides of the deal, "but you have to deliver". At the center of the value system, Davis has a reputation as a robust manager who doesn't suffer fools gladly and has very high intellectual expectations. Definitely not a touchy-feely chief executive, he's also not happy at high-profile dinners, preferring to work and to mix with his management team. "He's very comfortable with silence," says one Xstrata executive. "I've been on executive jets with him and he's not said a word for three hours. He can be awkward in groups at times. He really cuts through it and gets to the crux, to the Achilles' heel of an argument. He frustrates bankers because he'll take their presentation, flick through it, find the slide that really matters – even if it's slide 48 – get the point, and get up and leave."

Acquisitions are where Davis has really made his mark. He has proved a skillful negotiator, strong enough to leave deals on the table if the price is not right. When he does do a deal, he also disciplines himself to be fast and delivery oriented in his decision making, giving himself 30 days to decide who's out of the new combined management team. "He's single-minded when in pursuit of an opportunity – he won't look at even a good deal while doing another," says Moraitis.

But Davis is not a ruthless, cold-hearted accountant. His value driver model is built on a compelling vision of building the most valuable mining group in the world and empowering delegation, creating the freedom and opportunities for ambitious entrepreneurs to build something valuable for the company and themselves.

Moraitis believes that Davis is one of the best delegators he's seen. "He gives a task, he's patient and will watch you flounder with the task and will not intervene, but will wait for you to come for help," he says. "Of course, he'll intervene when necessary. He's not a great, charismatic leader – he's a very shy man – but he is an intellectual giant who lets people get on with stuff. He thinks expansively and excites people, taking them places they would not normally go. Mick paints pictures people would not paint for themselves and gets them to believe they are achievable. He's inspirational."

As a consequence, Davis has been able to hire executives of the highest caliber to drive the phenomenal growth that Xstrata has seen in recent years. "We get the best entrepreneurs in the industry who are self-motivated and stand up to be counted," notes Moraitis. "Our people are not here just to run plants; they are here to find value. Mick has a saying: 'If you tread water for long enough you'll eventually sink.' Momentum is ingrained into us. Everyone is comfortable with accountability and having a bright spotlight on them."

Davis on his management style
"The market has a view that I am a tough individual who does not suffer fools gladly, but there is a softer side to me. If people get themselves into difficulty, my instinct is to help them, not cut them off. We're very loyal to our people. We encourage them to take risks and when they make mistakes we will support them, provided they do not make the same mistake again. We support people so they are challenged, not threatened.

"I go into the business and test the talent. It destabilizes the situation. We give complete freedom and total responsibility to individuals. They get big financial rewards if they deliver and we hold them accountable if they do not. If I can see a weak link in a business unit,

I would say 'I am not sure about Joe Bloggs', but I would never say to them 'Fire Joe Bloggs'. The rule in this company is that you don't give instructions to somebody else's subordinate, but there is no problem with asking somebody else's subordinate for information,

"I have close relationships with people in the organization and try not to be hierarchical. I believe in a style of openness. My natural disposition is to discuss everything with everyone.

"I don't feel lonely. The only time I feel I am alone is when a decision has to be taken about whether to pursue a company-transforming acquisition. My job then is to ensure that I absorb the risks. Absorbing the risks is what I am paid for. I am alone in absorbing those risks. I am not alone on a daily basis, but at the end of the day, it is my decision.

"There's no formula. Anyone who tells you there's a formula is lying. The reason why people get into trouble is they like the myth that they generate that they are omniscient; that they did things because they knew things were going to happen."

Life after Xstrata

Davis is matter of fact about Xstrata existing only as long as its shareholders want it to, and he is likely to take a similar view about his own long-term commitment to the company. In some ways his model is similar to that of a private equity firm and he will be similarly unemotional about selling or leaving the company if he feels that the opportunity is good enough.

He draws personal strength from his Jewish faith and is rounded enough not to be taken in by his own success. "I'm very committed to my career," he told *The Times*, "but it's not those kinds of things that make people intuitively happy. It's things like a decent set of friendships and other interests. I think we all do work–life balance unsuccessfully. It is a big challenge. I do have a life outside work, but I don't think I can claim to have achieved a balance. There are times when I get overburdened."

Like most value driver chief executives, one day he may decide there is more value to be driven elsewhere, whether at another business or in his own personal or religious interests. He continues to nurse an interest in charitable donations and in teaching, and he mistrusts celebrity. "Celebrity CEOs are a danger because in this market people like to see failure," he says. "They do not like to see success. If you have celebrity status, people will seek your downfall and ultimately you will fail, not because you did anything wrong but because you ran out of luck. There are so many things that you don't know you don't know that no matter how good you are, you are going to be faced with uncertainties. There's a danger of linking a company too closely with its CEO. The reality is that it is not the case that a company's success is limited to and attributed to one man. That has never been the case. I don't know where I will be in five or ten years' time, but I am determined it will not be here. When you stay too long in a job, you become less and less effective."

"If someone bought us tomorrow Mick would not shed a tear," says Moraitis. "He's not about building a legacy mining company. He is first and foremost about value for the shareholder." This may also present a challenge for Xstrata under Davis's management, however. His cold management style and frankness about his willingness to exit may lead to difficulties in motivating employees to continue the success story.

OTHER FINANCIAL VALUE DRIVERS

The financial value driver model is best suited to situations where the strategy depends more on smart identification of opportunities to release value, flawless execution, and smart finance and financial control than on inspirational visions, transformational technologies, intellectual property, or highly complex government relations.

While value drivers are rigorous in their focus on shareholder value, the best are not sociopathic accountants unable to inspire people. On the contrary, the value driver model, depending on highly decentralized operations, is heavily reliant on exceptional, supremely motivated executives who are willing to be held to account for meeting, or failing to meet, stretching targets.

Mike Turner is one example. "You have to get the team right, make sure you have people telling you what they really think, make sure your objectives are clear, and then delegate," he says. "You need to keep communicating and remember you're a role model and people will watch what you do very carefully. It's about delegating to people and then holding their feet to the fire. Don't feel guilty about making people do things that are difficult. Don't do it for them. You need to have a very clear strategy. When people say they don't understand the strategy, it's often because they don't like it."

Stephen Hester, chief executive of property group British Land, shares the focus on value. "I think conceptual statements of purpose and values can be overdone," he says. "Companies have to create value or do not exist. Someone will dismantle you."

Delegation is also central to effective value drivers; their skill is partly in identifying which decisions and initiatives will make a difference in the required timeframe. Paul Thompson, former chief executive of closed life insurance funds consolidator Resolution, is another financial value driver. "There are about five or six really good decisions you make every year," he says. "It's about selecting those five and releasing some of the 250 other decisions and getting them done quickly. So you delegate them and people feel they are empowered. I get horrified when I hear about CEOs sending out 150 emails a day. That's far too much detail. You have to delegate things to the people you hire."

Turner agrees. "Home markets have to be managed semi-autonomously by a local so I have to trust my six home markets CEOs to run their market," he says. "Often I can't even know about all projects being undertaken for clients. I'm constantly aware that I'm an alien when I'm on Capitol Hill. Trust is key."

In contrast, Hester emphasizes the need for the CEO sometimes to get into the detail. "Intelligence, drive, and communication skills are important," he says. "It's also important for a CEO to move strategically from the big picture stuff to the nitty-gritty detail. That's not because you have to do the nitty-gritty. That's what you leverage other people for. But to manage people effectively you do have to dive deep into the organization."

Financial value driver chief executives are found most often in diversified industrial businesses like BAE Systems, but also in financial services. Both are sectors where complex businesses often require portfolio rationalization or "buy-and-build" strategies where mergers and acquisitions are seen as the engine for growth. Examples of the former include Sir Roy Gardner, when he was chief executive of British Gas owner Centrica, and Eric Daniels at bank Lloyds TSB. In the acquisitions camp is Sir Fred Goodwin, whose "Fred the Shred" nickname, bestowed on him for his cost-cutting as chief executive at Royal Bank of Scotland, underplays the enormous value he has added to a once provincial Scottish bank by executing and integrating large and risky acquisitions such as NatWest bank and regional US banks.

Financial value drivers measure their success in the same way as the City: through earnings per share and the share price.

PITFALLS OF THE FINANCIAL VALUE DRIVER MODEL

One element of value drivers' agreement with their executives is that they will provide exceptional personal returns. In so doing, they encourage a close alignment of wealth creation for shareholders and the personal enrichment of the management team, particularly the chief executive. When value driver chief executives are successful, therefore, they tend to reap rich rewards in the shape of bonuses and long-term incentive schemes, which also act as valuable carrots to tempt talented executives.

However, the rich rewards offered to their teams by value drivers can lead to some key risks. Because this category of chief executives are driven by financial returns, they and the value driver executives they recruit can be difficult to retain once they've been successful and become independently wealthy. Executives who have striven hard for years, motivated by the promise of financial rewards, may become less committed when they are enjoying the fruits of their success. And as they do so, the job of keeping the talented executives underneath them who have helped in their achievements becomes harder too. Although the best value driving businesses develop strong value systems, there can be a lack of glue bonding people together beyond wealth generation, and this can leave gaping holes at the top of hitherto successful organizations.

Another major risk of the model is that driving value, with its three-year mission plans, can be swiftly overtaken by industry shifts or economic downturns just as the payback for earlier cost cutting, restructuring, or exceptional acquisition-related costs is supposed to be reaping big rewards for shareholders.

There is also a risk that when value driver chief executives make a large acquisition or significant restructuring, the high profile that their returns for investors and personal wealth creation have given them can be their undoing. "People get built up more than they deserve," says Hester, "and then they get ripped to pieces more than they deserve."

9

CORPORATE ENTREPRENEURS

Corporate entrepreneurs have something to prove. They disrupt industries because they believe in a better way of doing things, they excel in spotting breakthrough opportunities and making them a reality, and their vision for their companies is their life vision. Sir Martin Sorrell, chief executive of WPP, is one of the best current examples of the rarest of our five leadership models.

Back in 1986, what is now one of the world's very largest advertising and marketing businesses was yet to be born and the corporate vehicle that would grow into that behemoth was still a shopping-trolley manufacturer called Wire Plastic Products. Martin Sorrell, who until then had been building a career at Saatchi & Saatchi, bought the company, appointed himself as chief executive, and began to use it as a vehicle to acquire "below-the-line" advertising-related companies. In 1987, he stunned the advertising and marketing world with the $566m hostile takeover of J. Walter Thompson (at that time 13 times WPP's size). In 1989, Sorrell followed this with another dramatic hostile deal, this time paying $864m for Ogilvy and Mather, twice as big as WPP. Over the next two decades, WPP became the driving force for consolidation in the global advertising and marketing industry. In 2000 alone, it completed 35 acquisitions.[1]

Today, WPP has amassed one of the largest media-buying groups in the world, Group M. And with its giant creative agency networks, JWT and Ogilvy and Mather, the group is one of the four major players in the global advertising and marketing market. WPP's stock price has soared and, although the company has been through difficult times, including a period in 1989 and 1990 during which it was on the verge of collapse after having overleveraged itself, Sorrell's determination and business acumen have led to significant growth. WPP now has billings of over £31bn and revenues of over £6bn.[2] It has more than 100 brands in more than 100 countries, employing over 100,000 people worldwide and providing national, multinational, and global clients with advertising, media investment management, information and consultancy, public relations, public affairs, branding and identity, healthcare, and specialist communications services.

WPP is now valued on the London Stock Exchange at over £7.5bn and it is ten years since Sir Martin led the company into the FTSE100[3] – not a bad growth story for a company that had a market capitalization of only £1.5m back in 1986.[4] Sir Martin is widely respected throughout the advertising and marketing industry, with his words being scrutinized and quoted by many within the sector; his famed remark that the recession at the beginning of the 2000s was "bath shaped" was one of the most repeated quotes. Indeed, many industry observers credit him with the fact that the UK still has an independent, vibrant communications industry.

Sir Martin as a corporate entrepreneur

Sir Martin built the world's largest advertising and marketing group through daring acquisitions, but he is not simply an aggressive financial wheeler-dealer. What makes him a leading example of a British corporate entrepreneur is that he not only built up WPP Group from nothing, he also successfully diversified its offering in terms of product mix and geographies, growing the group to cover four separate product segments and becoming truly global. As well as doing all that, he developed world-class business acumen to guide WPP's acquisitions. His personal review of the company's fortunes and the wider global economic and business outlook in its annual report has become compulsory reading for anyone wanting to understand the way the global economy is moving. He has a detailed knowledge of modern economic history and an encyclopedic recall of facts and figures, allied to an ability to interpret them seamlessly.

Underpinning all these attributes are the classic characteristics of a corporate entrepreneur. Sir Martin is motivated by proving that he has a better way of running an advertising business and wanting to build something that's better than the offerings of rivals. He's proud of what he has created and the legacy he will leave when he finally retires. As an entrepreneur, his motivation is customer-centric; he is always looking for better ways to serve customers and he has a pragmatic vision to profit from the opportunities that he finds are available. This pragmatism extends to his favorite metric, cash. "Cash tells you what is happening to expenditure, what's happening to acquisitions: the whole thing," he says. "It's not an earth-shattering response, but it's very important. I started in 1975 and actually the same pieces of information we had in 1975 are still as relevant today as they were then."

His is a restless, hands-on management style. He will insist on being personally involved with the first three or four layers of management, taking part in recruitment, and wanting to know details of what's going on in all the businesses. WPP's model places a premium on his personal expertise, market knowledge, deal-making brilliance, and the importance of his physical presence at big pitches to clients. Sir Martin is the critical source of energy in the business.

Sir Martin on being a corporate entrepreneur
"If you start something in a room with two people and you have now got 100,000 people, you're much more emotionally involved with it. We started this business with two people in one room. Moving it from there to whatever demanded a set of characteristics, qualities, attributes, strengths, and then to move it again in another five years demanded another set.

WPP is not a matter of life or death: it's more important

"It's different for me because I started this business. It's the closest a man can come to having a baby... It tends to be very different because it's like the famous Liverpool quote: football is not a matter of life or death, it's more important than that. WPP is not a matter of life or death: it's more important.

"When we win business, I'm delighted; when we lose, I'm physically and mentally upset. That's the founder's difficulty. We started 25 years ago and built it brick by brick.

"Entrepreneurialism means taking risks, so our industry is not entrepreneurial. People in it mean independence when they talk about entrepreneurialism. They mean taking risks with the company's money, not betting their houses. So there are not many true entrepreneurs. There are people who are good at starting things and people who are good at running things, but rarely do you find the same characteristics in the same person.

"It's hard to find someone who's entrepreneurial and managerial. I have been called a trumped-up beancounter many times. We started like a beginner, but we wanted to be a big banana. You had to do it by acquisition. Clearly, the most powerful thing to a shareholder is not to grow by acquisition – it's the top line. What's the variable? What drives success? Well, having the best people round your business, getting the strategy right, getting the people right, and then dealing with all the communities."

Formative years

Sir Martin once described himself as a "spoilt only child", qualifying the statement by revealing that he did have a brother who died at birth.[5] He was born into a business background, with his father working as chief executive of an industrial holding company that had a retail electrical division. "From a very early age, when I was 13 or 14, I remember meeting the chairman of my father's company and him asking me what I wanted to do," he recalled.[6] "Somewhat precociously I said, 'You know I want to go into business' and he said, 'Well, if you want to go into business you should go to Harvard Business School'."

The young Sorrell did go to Harvard, after first taking an economics degree at Cambridge. He was a member of what Sorrell recalls the admissions dean called the "most naive class" at the Ivy League business school. Sir Martin always loved business. Even while he was at Cambridge he wrote an article called "Management today". He remembers going with his father when aged about 12 to look at existing stores or potential new sites. "I think it has always been in the blood," he says.

After Harvard he worked for US consultancy Glendinning Associates, Mark McCormack's International Management Group, and James Gulliver Associates. Then he became the first finance director of Saatchi & Saatchi, an advertising business that was two years old when he joined. "In all these jobs, I profited from the focus, intensity, and determination that I'd gained during my time at Harvard," Sir Martin recalls. "Harvard's hothouse atmosphere stayed with me. Fear of failure drove me. The trouble was that we were made to feel that we could run the world."

Sir Martin on his roots
"I've had two mentors – a lawyer friend in New York and my father – but mentor is not the right word. It's someone you can talk to, someone whose view you can rely on to be independent, someone who has no agenda. I used to talk to my dad four or five times a day. I used to talk to him about what was happening in the business.

"He was an extremely close friend, I think probably the closest friend I've ever had. He was somebody that I could talk to in a very open way and get a view. He was a very clever man, probably never fulfilled his potential. I think certainly he could have done much more than he did."

Sir Martin on his management style
"It's all apple pie and motherhood. No one has any magic formula. It's pretty commonsensical. I think you can overintellectualize these things. Keeping it simple is pretty important. Everyone obfuscates and makes it too sophisticated. Having a clear purpose, vision, and strategy, having the right team, and having them aligned is what's important.

"People accuse me of being a micro-manager. I take it as a compliment. I think the detail is incredibly important.

"I am like a referee in that I bring all the parts of the company to work together. I am the only person, or one of very few people, who sees the whole picture. My Pavlovian reaction is to have everybody in the corporation working together. The Pavlovian reaction of anybody running one of the brands, whether it's 100 companies or 12, is to see it from their point of view.

"My natural inclination is to think of the WPP brand. That is where I am different, in that I was born with this thing and therefore I've seen most and I know 80 to 90 percent of what is there in fairly intimate detail. Therefore I know more about what goes on than most and what the capabilities are. We've got some very good creative people and some very creative insights, so making those available in the corners of the empire is very important. So my role is one of a referee and sort of consolidator or cooperator.

"I don't change. You are what you are. If I'm right I'm right and if I'm not I'm not. I'm not a great believer in the mentor-style approach; I think it's too stylized. I think individuals are very important. Individuals drive businesses. This is not voguish. It's counter to modern theory about leadership and teams, but I still think that individuals are key and probably unreasonably so."

Work–life balance

Sir Martin has never made any pretense of the fact that he lives for his business and has no separation of his business and personal lives. As with all pure corporate entrepreneurs, WPP is his life. "The three circles that matters are family, career, and society," he says. "There are very few people that manage to balance it. I certainly haven't been able to. You could probably balance two, but balancing all three is phenomenally difficult.

"Traveling a lot has caused disruption from a personal point of view and has probably made my personal life more difficult. I haven't actually moved home a lot. I've only had two houses, because I've always made my base in the UK. So, that, at least, has not been a problem."

He does feel that being a chief executive is a very lonely business. And his business life may have been successful at the expense of his personal and family life. In the papers for their divorce, Lady Sandra Sorrell stated that his infidelity, globetrotting, and the long hours he spent building up WPP were the reasons behind the marriage's collapse. She said they led to Sir Martin's workaholic lifestyle, in which she felt "marginalized", "dehumanized" and "discarded".[7]

In fact, it is possible that whenever Sir Martin leaves WPP, it will be the nearest corporate experience to a divorce. He admits that his own succession is one of the biggest threats to WPP's sustainability and one of the biggest issues for the board. "I'm obsessive about things not because I think I can do them better," he told CNN, "but because I am interested. And that's the problem. I'll never be able to let go. Someone will have to tap me on the shoulder."

Just as he is one of Britain's clearest examples of the positive attributes of a corporate entrepreneur, therefore, Sir Martin also illustrates the potential risks of the model. First, corporate entrepreneurs may experience problems in finding people to scale up their businesses without losing the vital entrepreneurial spirit. And while corporate entrepreneurs rely on their vision and brilliance to attract great people, this can also be their downside, resulting in people-related problems that may include allowing themselves and others to get burned out by the demands of their roles. Critics of Sir Martin in particular say that he is so authoritarian and fast-moving that staff sometimes cannot keep up. He remains proud of his legacy, however, and is adamant that he would do it all again.

"Some people can start a company and can't run it and some people can run a company but they can't start it," he told CNN. "I'd like to think that I can do both... so the epitaph should read: 'He was partly responsible' or 'was responsible for initiating the growth and development of the finest advertising marketing and services company in our industry'. It's very pretentious, but that's probably what it's about."

Sir Martin on life after WPP
"There is no such thing as stress, it's just that you're not having fun. Lots of opportunities to deal with problems you might describe as stress, but I think that can be fun. The stress occurs when you feel you can't do it. When people say they're stressed it's because what is coming at them or what they're having to deal with is either too

difficult or they feel it's impossible to deal with or they're not doing their job properly. That doesn't mean that I haven't had times when I've thought this is very difficult and how am I going to deal with it.

"I ultimately chose my direction, so I am very fortunate that I decided at the grand old age of 40 to start to do something. We have to be political, in a sense, but I've chosen a direction and I didn't have to kow-tow. I happened to fall into the advertising business and I've been able to carry on doing what I regard as fun. Our industry is you are as good as your last ad, so the barriers to entry are not that great. You know every day whether you are succeeding or not; there's no hiding. You do a good ad, you win a pitch, you lose a piece of business, you win a piece of business, and you know instantaneously. It's like the entertainment business and sports, you get results very, very quickly.

"My succession is probably one the biggest issues for the board to deal with. I would find it very difficult not to have something central to my work life. I am a doer, not a chairman. If I didn't do this, I would try to do something not dissimilar. I would start again."

OTHER EXAMPLES OF CORPORATE ENTREPRENEURS

There are very few corporate entrepreneurs to be found in the UK but more in India and China, where executives have had to be entre-preneurial to take advantage of opportunities as these markets have opened up. Take Liu Jiren of Neusoft. "When I founded the company, there was no market, a shortage of capital, and a shortage of talent," he says. "The challenge was the lack of conditions usually required to found a company. We didn't know how to run a business, so our approach was to challenge and to learn through making mistakes and by trying."

Corporate entrepreneurs are also more common in the US than the UK and Europe, mainly because of the lead in innovation that has long been established by California's Silicon Valley. One obvious example is Michael Dell, while Oracle co-founder Larry Ellison is another. More recently, the internet revolution has highlighted a plethora of corporate entrepreneurs behind such companies as Yahoo!, Google, and Second Life.

Dell fits the model well, saying that he was sustained through the hard early years of founding his computer company by the fact that "we could clearly see our customers' needs". He adds, "Answering those needs better than our competitors was a terrific motivation. Even during the hardest of times we were clear about the opportunity before us and the advantages of the direct model, which was like rocket fuel for our business." A classic entrepreneur, he believes: "When you use input from your customers as your compass, the right answer is almost always clear."

When you use input from your customers as your compass, the right answer is almost always clear

Corporate entrepreneurs are brilliant visionaries and have the energy, drive, and charisma to bring their business ideas to reality. They start companies not always because making money is their number one priority, but because they believe in something and want to change the way a particular business or industry works. However, that same disruptive mindset can also make them deeply mistrustful of the stock market, the City, and the corporate environment.

Some of Britain's best-known entrepreneurs, therefore, have chosen largely to eschew the quoted environment. Sir Richard Branson and Sir Alan Sugar did so because they had mixed experiences at the hands of analysts and fund managers in the periods during which parts of the Virgin Group and the whole of Amstrad were publicly quoted. Sir James Dyson, on the other hand, has chosen never to bring the company behind his revolutionary bagless vacuum cleaner to the stock market, but summed up a classic entrepreneurial attitude when he told us: "You have to focus on the product and make sure it is appealing. It's about technological breakthroughs and having an edge. I have stepped back from being a professional chief executive; my ultimate role is in being the ongoing creative and innovative force."

Opponents of the public company route cite the increasing burden of regulatory compliance, the dangers of restrictive corporate cultures emerging, and the worry that the City will not understand their entrepreneurial mindsets or be long term enough to back their ideas without immediate returns. Thanks to the growth of the venture capital and private equity industries, moreover, they can find capital from sources other than the traditional equity markets, so they do not always need to overcome their aversion to the capital markets. The contrast can be marked, as a brief look at the two players in the new market for consolidators of so-called zombie funds – closed with-profit life insurance funds – demonstrates.

Here, in an industry sector that did not exist five years ago, Clive Cowdery chose to come to the public capital markets almost as soon as he had formed consolidator Resolution with a pioneering vision of transforming the dull world of closed life insurance funds by aggressively acquiring blocks of business from which economies of scale and other efficiencies could be wrought. His main rival, former Pizza Express entrepreneur Hugh Osmond, chose to fund his Pearl Group in the same sector, steering clear of public capital and turning instead to private equity. Both were innovative, entrepreneurial, and extremely successful. Ultimately Pearl bought Resolution in 2008 and took it private.

Arguably, the best-known corporate entrepreneur is Steve Jobs. As chief executive of Apple, he has shaken up no fewer than four separate industries: the computer, animation, music download, and mobile telecom markets. He has also done so in a publicly quoted environment, though the fortunes of Apple have fluctuated wildly during his two stints at the company.

Elsewhere, an example of a corporate entrepreneur outside a publicly quoted environment is James Bilefield. "I see myself at the growth end," he says. "I like things when they are growing from 0 to 100. I am less interested in 100 onwards. The main thing is belief. You have got to really believe and fight your way. You have to have an end place in mind, but to other people you are ridiculous. It may be a mad idea, but if you have absolute belief in that idea and a team with ability behind you, you can make it happen."

It may be a mad idea, but if you have absolute belief in that idea and a team with ability behind you, you can make it happen

Corporate entrepreneurs are not suited to all industries. It is rare for them to be found in financial services, though the recent emergence of Cowdery and Osmond in life insurance is one exception and the Lloyd's of London commercial insurance market, requiring individuals to take big risks, is another. Technological industries, however, are natural breeding grounds of corporate entrepreneurs, as is biotechnology. Chris Evans, founder of Merlin Biosciences, a specialist venture capital and advisory company dedicated to the biotechnology sector, is a good example. He has set up 20 different biotech companies that are now valued at more than £1bn, including four businesses that have floated on the London Stock Exchange. He says he sees himself as a "commercially driven scientist" whose companies generate ideas and solutions for everyday problems. Elsewhere, the media, consumer, and professional services sectors tend to attract corporate entrepreneurs.

THE PITFALLS OF THE CORPORATE ENTREPRENEUR MODEL

Corporate entrepreneurs tend to rely on their vision and the brilliance of the opportunity, rather than their personal leadership, to attract talented people. The failings of corporate entrepreneurs are therefore typically related to their ability to find, organize, and keep the managers, technicians, and staff they need to make their great ideas work.

The risks of the model are that people burn themselves out, there is inadequate succession planning for when the founder of the business retires or moves on to do something else, and there is difficulty attracting the right people to grow and scale the companies. Corporate entrepreneurs can be weak at managing businesses that are not growing exponentially but are in a steady state; they may have chaotic systems or be distrusting of attempts by managers to instill process and order to their organizations. And they may cause investor disquiet by betting the whole company on a disruptive technology or marketing that may be ahead of its time.

One example of this is the move by Charles Dunstone, one of the few corporate entrepreneurs leading FTSE100 companies, to offer "free" broadband services to customers of his Carphone Warehouse mobile phone retailer. In less than six months, the company signed up 525,000 broadband customers. But its shares dived as it revealed that its TalkTalk "free broadband" offer had become a service nightmare, attracting too many customers to a service that was not ready for that number. "It was an idea that went out of control," Dunstone said. "I thought, 'We've got all these people coming into the shops, what else can we sell them?'"[8] Actually Dunstone, whose fortunes have now revived, doesn't accept that he meets the description of the corporate entrepreneur model. "I'm no entrepreneur," he has said. "I haven't started loads of great businesses. I'm a one-trick pony. I was lucky enough to realize that the real market for mobiles was not giant corporations like BP, but plumbers and builders who previously relied on answering machines."[9] In so saying, he modestly ignores the fact that thousands of competitors stumbled on the same idea at the same time, but only he and John Caudwell of rival Phones4u turned their small businesses into enduring corporations.

10

CORPORATE AMBASSADORS

Corporate ambassadors have a global vision that has a broader societal impact. They operate at the geopolitical level and deliver transactions that transform industries.

Corporate ambassadors are a comparatively rare breed, but a British business leader who illustrates the type well is one of the nation's highest-achieving chief executives in recent times. Corporate ambassadorial skills propelled John Browne to the top of BP, where as chief executive from 1995 to 2007, this son of an immigrant Auschwitz survivor turned a mid-ranking European firm into the third-largest oil company in the Western world and Britain's biggest and most globalized company.

Lord Browne's business record speaks for itself. When he became the youngest chief executive in BP's history in 1995, the company's share price stood at 222p. When he resigned in 2007 it was 563p. During that period, BP returned an 8 percent annual average increase in share price – nearly double the average for the FTSE100 index.[1] He achieved such growth by wreaking major transformational change, leading oil industry consolidation with the takeovers of major US oil companies Amoco and Atlantic Richfield, and moving into Russia by taking a 50 percent stake in what became TNK-BP, which was before its troubles in 2008, after Browne's departure, the largest and most profitable investment in Russia by a western oil company.[2] These moves demonstrated the assured handling of top-level government and corporate players that typifies a corporate ambassador.

Browne also reacted to low oil prices in the 1990s by waging a war on costs. Rival industry executives said that he was the toughest cost cutter in the business. The result was that in 12 years he turned BP into the third largest Western oil company by market capitalization.[3] While driving BP's core businesses, he also exhibited the global vision and eye for societal impact required of a true corporate ambassador by launching a massive sustainability push by BP: "Beyond Petroleum". No wonder he was voted Britain's most admired leader for four years in succession from 1999–2002.[4]

Browne on being a corporate ambassador
"For me it was at the heart of the purpose of the firm. It was about whether I could help shape the business and influence the markets that it would operate in, such as Russia or the entire alternative energy sector. It was about why energy is important in terms of giving as many people as possible the light, heat, and mobility they wanted. And it was about new jobs for a diverse set of people in new places.

   "Leaders need to have a view of the world. The very best leaders are able to pick and trust people. That is hard because people are trained to distrust and often appear to act in a way which destroys trust. Leaders must not be small-minded and must be capable of not being cynical. And they must not be people who want to get everything in place first before anything is done. Life is untidy. In all big things I did, I had to extemporize a bit."

Formative years
Browne was born in Hamburg, Germany, to a British Army officer father and a Hungarian Auschwitz survivor mother, the multilingual Paula Wesz, who had worked for the Allies as a translator and met and married Captain Edmund Browne in 1947. Capt Browne worked in civilian life for Anglo-Persian Oil, which later became British Petroleum. The family settled in Cambridge and the eight-year-old Browne began his education at King's School in Ely. He says that his years there taught him the value of diversity and of not having to bow to "the tremendous pressure to conform". His mother, whom Browne would later regularly take along to BP social events, didn't conform either. Browne once recalled that she was "definitely different",

adding, "She dressed in an elegant way and wore make-up, which was somewhat unusual in the fens in the 1960s. She spoke with an accent which she never lost. I'm sure she did this on purpose."[5]

In 1957 Capt Browne moved out to Iran and by 1959 he had persuaded John's mother to send him to boarding school. His mother thought it was a deeply barbaric thing to do and never reconciled herself to it. Friends of Browne remember him constantly questioning formulas in science and maths classes at Ely. He at first considered an academic career and was offered a Cambridge research fellowship to study continental drift and the ocean bed, but his father persuaded him to take a wider view. "He knew me better than I did myself," Browne recalled. "He kept on saying, 'You need to see the world. Do you really want to live in England for the rest of your life?'"[6]

After initial postings, BP sent Browne to Stanford University in 1980. On rejoining the company, he was appointed commercial manager of the upstream business. The 1980s also saw changes in his personal life. He became closer to his mother after the death of his father at the beginning of the decade and moved her into a flat at the top of his house in London's Notting Hill.

Browne on his roots
"My father gave me the ability to be very comfortable in a world full of different people doing very different things. My mother, who was a foreign worker in the UK in the 1950s, which was very unusual at the time, gave me the confidence to be a little different. Living overseas also shaped me. It's only very recently that I've thought of Britain as my home. I've only really lived here since the late 1980s. I owned a house early for financial reasons, but I did not live in it.

"I didn't have a burning ambition in my 20s. I liked getting great things done and liked it when they were different. That was a purpose in itself. I didn't have a world mission in the early days, but I began to see interesting things as group treasurer at BP. Barriers, such as exchange rate controls, were coming down. Things were about to happen."

Career progression

It was appointment as worldwide chief of exploration and production in 1989 that set Browne up for the chief executive's position. At 41, he was responsible for more than half the company's earnings and expenditure. From this role, he set off on two critical paths that he continued to pursue as CEO. First, he took BP beyond Alaska and the North Sea and saw it become successful in the Gulf of Mexico, Azerbaijan, and Angola. Second, he enforced rigorous discipline and set stretching targets for the division.

As chief executive, he became the company's deal maker. From being a relatively small European oil firm that looked like a target for US consolidation, BP became a major global player in the oil industry. Browne first paid $55bn for Amoco and three months later another $27bn for its fellow US oil company Atlantic Richfield. That put the company just behind what was soon to be ExxonMobil and neck and neck with the Royal Dutch/Shell Group.

"Some CEOs will endeavor to outperform the competition," Browne says. "Other CEOs will look at the industry as a whole and decide whether to change the game, for example through consolidation. My idea of what to do only really came in the late 1980s when the Berlin Wall came down and ultra-high-speed computing opened everything up."

But Browne's vision wasn't restricted to mergers and acquisitions. It also included an early understanding of how sustainability and environmental issues would become a pivotal part of business. Back in the late 1990s when green measures were still regarded as somewhat peripheral, he gave a speech at Stanford University in California, committing BP to reducing greenhouse gases. He changed the company's slogan to Beyond Petroleum and used it as the clarion call for a series of alternative and renewable energy initiatives. "For those of us who have long been advocates of a greener economy, the change of British Petroleum to Beyond Petroleum was a single moment that marked the mainstream business world's adoption of sustainable development," wrote the *Sydney Morning Herald*.

It wasn't just the corporate logo that turned green. Browne was convinced that the company had to lower its impact on the environment and began positioning the group to succeed in the post-hydrocarbon world. Seven years later, BP is the world's largest producer of solar panels. It has also invested heavily in alternative and renewable energy projects and has reduced its greenhouse gas emissions while raising its energy output every year for the past decade.

Management style

Browne's management style is characterized by attention to problem solving, recruiting and managing the best talent of his generation to work for him, and wielding the power that he possessed as chief executive with a comparatively light touch.

His friend Peter Hennessy argued that Browne ran BP "like a research scientist" and Browne himself admitted as much. "I have great satisfaction in solving problems," he once said. "I have great satisfaction in exciting, different and new things. And that's why, at the beginning, I tried to find exciting things to do, challenging problems, things which were a bit more difficult to solve. If driving for that sort of thing is ambition, then that's a definition of ambition."[7]

One of Browne's most impressive characteristics as a leader, and one that was evident when we interviewed him, is his tremendous clarity of thought. He is able crisply and persuasively to frame complex geopolitical and business issues at will.

His success at recruiting and managing talent, moreover, is evidenced by the fact that his succession was always an internal issue, despite the troubles that BP encountered after the Texas refinery explosion toward the end of his tenure as chief executive. It was also probably not a coincidence that his successor, Tony Hayward, came from the same exploration and production path that Browne had himself taken at BP. Browne maintains the intense interest in developing the next generation of talent that he exhibited at BP; he continues to be active in addressing people early in their careers. His clarity of thought is matched by an impressive ability to inspire people at these events.

Browne's views on how power should be wielded epitomize the views of corporate ambassadors, who do not tend to develop huge egos. "Power is something that has to be used very, very carefully," he says. "It's much better to think you have none, rather than to think you have a lot. That is the way, I hope, you can make more sensible decisions. I have the sense that power – the ability to get things done, to make changes – is limited. And perhaps it's most effectively used from a position of humility rather than strength."

Power is most effectively used from a position of humility rather than strength

Browne on his management style
"I found that effective business leadership required a tight focus on the plot. Set a clear strategy and organize your resources behind it. Strong values and careful delegation are essential, but above all, keep clear where you're driving for.

"Make sure you have enough time to get out there and develop people and markets. You need a great chief operating officer because the job is changing a lot. It's a little team approach. It can be two or three people but not four.

"There are too many things for one person now because the nature of competition has changed. Competition is not in your backyard: it's everywhere. You need a radar, but there's always too much information so you need people with experience to help you pick places to go.

"No company can survive without reinventing itself. Go and expose yourself to new ideas. Search, listen to people, and train yourself to be interested in things. Then you assemble a pattern of the world. Sometimes you get a good idea, but they don't arrive every day."

Browne's downfall and the risks of the corporate ambassador model
Lord Browne's reputation suffered a blow in May 2007 when he resigned after misleading a court during an action aimed at preventing a newspaper revealing personal details given to them by a former boyfriend. However, since Browne has left there has been comment on suggestions that he became too distant from the daily workings of BP and that he allowed some business processes to weaken.

There were rumblings about Browne's "huge power" from early in the new century. For example, one former director told the press anonymously in 2002 that "the longer he is there, the more a feeling of a court develops".[8] More damagingly, Tony Hayward, then BP's five-year veteran chief executive of exploration and production, wrote on the company's internal website in December 2006 that "the top of the organisation doesn't listen hard enough to what the bottom of the organisation is saying" – a posting that rapidly made the newspapers and was widely viewed as a criticism of Browne's management style.[9] Browne had long been a media figure, nicknamed "the sun king", and this cultured, successful, renaissance man was increasingly portrayed in the press as appearing and acting rather like a monarch.

The accusation of a weakness in process control came to the fore with the results of an investigation into the series of tragic explosions at BP's Texas City refinery, which killed 15 people and injured 180 others in 2005.[10] Led by former US Secretary of State James A. Baker, a panel found "material deficiencies" in BP's safety procedures at its American oil refineries. The report found that prior to the Texas City tragedy, BP had emphasized personal safety over process safety. Indeed, at that time BP was proud of its achievements in personal safety, which it believed probably saved hundreds of lives. Although the report stressed that it did not find any deliberate or conscious efforts on BP's part to short-circuit safety, the panel said that BP mistakenly interpreted improving personal injury rates as an indication of acceptable process safety performance at its US refineries. It found instances of "a lack of operating discipline, toleration of serious deviations from safe operating practices, and apparent complacency toward serious safety risks" at each US refinery, albeit adding, "we are under no illusion that deficiencies in process safety culture, management, or corporate oversight are limited to BP". In addition, BP suffered fallout, in summer 2006, from a spill caused by poor maintenance of a key oil pipeline in the Alaskan exploration and production division. Critics put these two high-profile incidents together and alleged a systematic failure by Browne and his top management to monitor process controls adequately.

These criticisms highlight the key risk in the ambassadorial model, but need nuancing and pegging back. Corporate ambassadors are by their nature outward looking, so great ambassadors build a team around them to keep tight control over the internal operations of their business. Browne made a conscious effort to do this by appointing a very strong deputy chief executive in Rodney Chase in 1998 and building a set of highly trusted personal advisers around him. This model worked phenomenally well for five years. However, Chase retired in 2003 after 38 years at BP.[11] It is from this point that concerns about BP seem to mount. "I could not get approval to keep Rodney beyond 60, he left and left a big hole," admits Browne. "It was a tremendous partnership, which allowed us to achieve a huge amount."

Browne had been trying to bring on a fresh generation of talent, a move that was undoubtedly one cause of concerns by some that he was sidelining some of the old guard. In response to Chase's departure, Browne moved some of these younger executives up and added additional processes at the center. In one sense this worked; Tony Hayward, after all, flourished under Browne. However, the transition was not competely successful and the problems discussed above developed. While the Texas explosion was a tragedy, Browne's misfortune lay not in a deep failing as a leader, but in not transitioning his management team.

Browne on his support network
"Being single doesn't mean you don't have a family life. It's actually just a little bit more difficult. I always think of my closest friends as my surrogate family. When my mother died – she was the last member of my family – that became even more important to me.

"There's a deep loyalty that you might find in a family in the people I am closest to. They do actually behave as members of my family. They're just not related by blood or by marriage."

Life after BP
Browne has continued with his vision in his life after BP, mixing business with a focus on the environment and giving back to society. His

work in London with New York-based private equity group Riverstone Holdings will see him advise on buyouts and growth capital investments in the midstream, upstream, power, oilfield services, and renewable sectors of the energy industry, while he began his term as president of the British Association for the Advancement of Science with a plea for the creation of an international climate agency to coordinate action against global warming.[12] He said that the responsibilities of such a body would include setting a long-term goal for stabilizing carbon dioxide in the atmosphere; setting carbon emission targets and allowances; monitoring and verification; and providing incentives for developing countries to invest in clean energy.[13] In line with these concerns, Browne joined the advisory board of Sustainable Forestry Management, a business that owns large tracts of forests and trades in carbon credits.

Like most ambassadors, it does not look as if Browne will ever actually retire. His global corporate ambassadorial skills will continue to be trained on the same issues as they focused on during his tenure as chief executive.

Indeed, from our interviews it is clear that Browne is still the most highly regarded CEO of his generation. Most CEOs see him as typical of a twenty-first-century leader and were disappointed about how he was forced to leave. Most feel that the press focused on titillation and recent problems rather than examining properly what he built and the transformation he wrought at BP. To us Browne remains the CEO's CEO.

Browne's advice to aspiring CEOs
"New CEOS in successful businesses should generally seek to evolve the business and build on what is there, rather than starting from scratch.

"Nobody leaves early enough. Try to remember that as you go through your tenure. I forgot it. I think a lot of people forget it. But remembering when to bow off the stage is more important than remembering when to go on the stage. The reality is that, despite the press speculation, I thought very carefully about leaving in late 2005 and it might have been a good thing to do."

OTHER CORPORATE AMBASSADORS

Corporate ambassadors almost exclusively lead long-established businesses with global footprints. They're most frequently found in resource businesses, such as oil and minerals, or global banking groups. Much like their diplomatic brethren, corporate ambassadors have a calm and measured management style. They're most effective in situations where interaction with regulators, governments, and other authorities is critical. They thrive on solving high-profile problems and they possess the vision to see how their companies have to change to maintain and enhance their roles in the future.

John Varley at Barclays is an example of a corporate ambassador who realizes the importance of how he is seen to lead. "I am clear that a chief executive who is wild and unpredictable is a menace," he says. "A CEO must be balanced. You cannot have an organization which is twisting in the wind of the chief executive's mood swings. People have to be able to predict me; I cannot be moody. Moodiness is something I am very suspicious of."

Corporate ambassadors lead by example. Sir John Bond, the Vodafone chairman who also fits the bill, famously refused to fly in first class on short-haul flights when he was chief executive and then chairman of banking group HSBC. He was renowned at the bank for his smooth, affable style. He always took time to talk to even the lowliest staffer on his tours around operations, checking the temperature of the organization and boosting morale. Even trade unions found it hard to dent his measured ambassadorial style. At one stormy annual meeting, unions arranged for the immigrant worker who cleaned the offices in Sir John's office at the bank to ask a question about the difference between his pay and that of the chairman.

"You probably don't know who I am, but I get up at 5 a.m. to clean your windows," the cleaner told Sir John.

"Of course I know who you are," came the friendly retort. "I've often seen you and wanted to have a chat. Next time you do the windows, why don't you stop by for a cup of tea?"

Stylistically, corporate ambassadors tend to be traditional in their bearing, fastidious about their appearance, and fiercely protective of their reputations. Varley is known for his braces and formal dress sense, while BP public relations advisers always took great care to ensure that the diminutive Browne was pictured from below, for example on a staircase, to boost his stature.

The distance that some corporate ambassadors tend to cultivate is also one of the risks of the model, however. It is an easy target for the media and can be damaging for businesses with a strong consumer presence. "With his high-cut trousers, stiff-collared shirt, blue braces and monogrammed cufflinks, he looks at times like a man who might not even know who David Beckham is," commented *Sunday Times* interviewer Andrew Davidson in a profile of Varley.[14] Corporate ambassadors risk becoming so distant from their business's operations that they are not able to dive deep into detail if a crisis blows up. In addition, the media profile that their high-visibility leadership attracts means that their personal reputations can become so inextricably linked to that of their employer that they can inflict collateral damage on their company if they fall from grace.

Nevertheless, corporate ambassadors do possess the leadership talent necessary to cope with the transforming changes of globalization, sustainability, technology, alternative capital, and the war for talent. They not only possess great vision for the future of their industries, but are also personally engaging and able to generate support from a range of stakeholders, allowing them to follow an ambitious path. As chairman of shipping group P&O, Sir John Parker foresaw how the rapid development of container shipping would drive world trade and globalization.

Similarly at Lonmin, Brad Mills defied predictions that a minerals company that mined only one commodity could not survive in the fiercely competitive industry. He saw that demand from China and India would be so great that a global monoline supplier could still thrive. "Great chief executives have an ability to see change coming and prepare their people and organizations for change," he says.

But global ambassadors also run their companies along strict moral codes. Mills has plaques on the wall that visitors can see as soon as they arrive, declaring the company's commitment to working in its communities and trying to tackle the environmental problems inherent in an extraction business. Sir John Parker adds, "Whether you are a big company or a small company, whether you're in one country or in 30, the same principles apply. You create one company in terms of values and ethics and you have to make sure that the standards by which you deliver customer service, safety management, and everything else are exactly the same wherever you go in the company."

GLOBAL MISSIONARIES

lobal missionaries are on a personal mission to make a signifi-cant difference and a corporate mission to make their company great. They are typically customer champions and lead by inspiring people and energizing them to tap into their full potential.

Global missionaries possess strong beliefs and values that drive them to bring transformational change to the companies they lead. They're passionate in their belief that changing and revitalizing people is the key to refreshing businesses that have lost their way and need renewal. And they have the personal and leadership skills to inspire their workforces to attack the change agenda with similar zeal.

A good example is the way in which Ben Verwaayen used the model to transform telecoms company BT. When Verwaayen was recruited as chief executive in 2001, the company was in a mess. Its leadership was discredited after taking the company into an ulti-mately unsuccessful US joint venture and loading the group up with £30bn of debts, so heavy a burden that it was forced to organize a record rights issue and divest itself of Cellnet, the mobile phone com-pany now called O2, which was its fastest-growing business.[1] Five years on, the company's share price showed 35 percent growth between February 2002 and November 2007, outstripping the 26 per-cent growth in the FTSE100 index during that period. On the way, it posted more than 20 consecutive quarters of growth in earnings per share.[2]

More holistic measures of the deep-seated cultural change that he brought to the company would resonate even more greatly with Verwaayen. What he calls the "disease of consensus" was a hangover from the company's days as a nationalized industry and meant that meetings were carefully scripted in advance so that there would be no open conflict or disagreements. Verwaayen sought to make employee engagement a flagstone of the new BT, rejoicing when staff questioned his logic or management style and openly encouraging them to be innovative and entrepreneurial and to adopt a relentless focus on the customer.

Verwaayen embraced the sustainability agenda after discerning that it was highly prized by BT's customers and also had the advantage of making employees believe in the company and work harder to play their part in its success. Such cultural change has underpinned business success that can also be measured in financial terms. After virtually missing out on the first internet boom, BT has now put itself at the center of the converging media worlds of broadband internet, television, and fixed and mobile telephony, which it has re-entered. It has also re-engineered itself as a services company and is using this model to globalize the business in a way that the disastrous Concert joint venture with MCI WorldCom failed to do in the late 1990s and early part of the 2000s.

Verwaayen as a global missionary
Verwaayen sees his mission at BT as much more than simply getting the financials right and putting the company on the track that its investors want. To do that, he believes, requires the company also to stand out from its competitors as having a meaningful purpose. Like other global missionaries, Verwaayen has a need for significance. His mission is to make an extraordinary difference to BT's customers and the world at large. It needs to be accomplished in accordance with his core values of being accessible, approachable, and treating people with respect. And it does not have an end point.

He has put the customer at the center of the company and changed the corporate culture so that it revolves around customers. That has acted to protect the core business, Verwaayen has built an innovative mindset that empowers employees to think about what services the group can provide in the future. His leadership incorporates conventional management, such as making hard decisions about hiring, firing, eradicating bureaucracy, and eliminating waste. However, it is also unconventional in many ways, due to his willingness to be challenged and to allow his employees to be disruptive and innovative.

At the heart of his missionary model is a passion for people. He is genuinely committed to talent development, believing that running an organization is the greatest contribution that one can make in the development of young people, giving them chances to try different things. And he's equally committed to employees and staff, priding himself on personally answering every single email he receives – in our experience often within the hour. But Verwaayen is hard-nosed too: his insight is that superior long-term returns require fired-up employees satisfied with the meaning in their work rather than demotivated people pursuing bald financial targets.

Verwaayen is highly authentic, with his passion for Arsenal football club and his strong conviction that he needs a healthy work–life balance and time away from the business with the friends and family he grew up with.

As with all missionaries, not everyone wants to be converted and some observers question how effective Verwaayen really was at handling detail at BT, noting that the company's bureaucracy is still awesome and its customer service poor. Like many other global missionaries, however, he is low-ego. "For sure I know that I am not the most suitable candidate to run BT," he says, "because by definition given the fact that there are six billion people on earth somebody else is out there that for whatever reason is more suitable than I am. I'm the lucky guy sitting here because of time and circumstance and it's OK. That's the concept you should bear in mind. You're not the objectively best person."

Verwaayen on being a global missionary
"Leadership for me is to set the agenda, set the tone, and choose the right people. It's about hearts and minds. If it's just highbrow and the rest of the organization waves the middle finger to you, nothing will happen. If you don't portray your respect for the past, whatever you

think personally about it, you have just condemned everybody's efforts in the past. You have to continue to make radical change in the people, to create new ideas, and get diversity. It's *It's about the culture to disagree and to* about experience, it's about viewpoints, it's about *make disagreement into a positive* the culture to disagree and to make disagreement into a positive. That's the most important ingredient of success. A strategy is a result of the people sitting around the table. It's not an abstract.

"I think I'm now more leader than manager, but when I started here I was more manager than leader. I took an enormous amount of decisions, immediately, bang, bang, bang, bang. But if I look over the last month I have a hard time finding any decision that I took. I ensured that other people took the right decisions. If you take the decision, you are responsible for the legitimacy of the decision and you are also responsible for the execution of the decision. It's your decision, so it's your problem.

"What you want is a culture in which people take the right decision as close to the problem as possible, in a collective perspective in which they know it's the right decision. So they have to ask less and they know, from the culture and the values and the targets that you have set, what the right decisions are. Because they own it, it's their decision. It's a much easier sell. So that behavior means that you grow over time from the manager to much more a leader. A leader role is much more long term. It's much more instrumental for change.

"It isn't black and white. It's not that we have a ring of dummies around the table and here comes the enlightened person and says, 'I went to the mountain; here are the Ten Commandments.' No, that's not what works. You start to talk about issues and the philosophy is the customer. The first word that I introduce is customer, customer service, customer capability. What is it that we have? What are our pluses and minuses? What's irritating the customers, what's delighting your customers, where can we expand our customer base?

"You get a dialogue. Then you find people who are believers, people who are doubters, people who are progressing, and those who are slightly stifled.

"Those who are stifled you try to ignore quickly. Then you try to have a dialogue with the other people, bring one or two new brains in, and bring them into the dialogue. Sometimes it's a consultant and sometimes it's a new hire. Then it gels, but it's a gelling that happens collectively."

Formative years

Verwaayen was born the fifth of six children to Dutch parents who ran a family chemicals firm in a small village in The Netherlands. He says he discovered early in his life that he wanted to be a "change agent". He organized the first student parliament at his school and set up a union to argue for better conditions during his time as a conscript in the army. He graduated with a degree in law and international relations from Utrecht University in 1975. He originally wanted to be a journalist or politician and took a first job at a small insurance company, just because it gave him time to sit on a state committee to reform the army. However, after that company was bombed, he discovered it was a subsidiary of US conglomerate ITT, a target of left-wing anger because of its alleged role in the overthrow of Salvador Allende's government in Chile.

Upset by this hiding of ownership, Verwaayen headed off to Brussels to protest at ITT's European head office. In response, the group promoted him to be their PR chief for The Netherlands.[3] He is still deeply involved in Dutch politics as a member of the People's Party for Freedom and Democracy.[4] He sat on its executive committee for ten years and wrote its program for the 2006 Dutch elections. "I don't play golf or do receptions but I love public policy," he told the *Sunday Times.*[5]

Verwaayen on the importance of his roots

"I eat at McDonald's and I eat at Gordon Ramsay. Both are excellent in their own right. For the time that I'm here, I am 100 percent BT's person and I'm loyal to the last second, but it's not who I am. It's my company as long as I'm here, but it's not my company. If tomorrow somebody says to me 'Ben, please leave', am I devastated? I will kick myself because I should have left before somebody asks, and believe me that's what I will do. But the 'who' in me is not affected at all, because the 'who' is what I am with my family, what my grandson thinks about me, what my friend that I've known since high school thinks about me.

"People think that this is a job that consumes your personality. Wrong. That's why you get people panicking and doing strange things. I once worked for a company where people would change their friends when they changed their jobs. That's not me at all. My real life is about family fun and sharing with friends. That's what drives me. It's not ego. I get hundreds of emails from customers every day and I answer them all the same day, but this is activity; it's not me. I'm Ben."

Career progression

After ITT, Verwaayen became a director at PTT Telecom, the Dutch publicly owned telecoms group that was a forerunner of today's KPN. After nine years he moved to New York to join the board of Lucent Technologies, the telecoms technology spinout from AT&T that had become the US's biggest ever initial public offering and was a stock market darling.

By the time he arrived at BT in 2002, however, the dot-com boom had turned into a crash and Lucent had fallen from its lofty perch. Verwaayen was a surprise choice, arriving to a chorus of "Ben who?" from investors who were seeking a more established name to turn around the company after its high-profile failures. Observers pointed out that he was arriving from a failing business, but he quickly set about silencing his doubters. Thomson Reuters chief executive Tom Glocer believes that Verwaayen's global missionary model could have been tailor-made for the company. "He's unpretentious, smart, full of energy, and leads by example," he says. "He's exactly what a stodgy, hidebound institution like BT needed."

Verwaayen's success at BT was based on three main business missions. BT's slowness to embrace the internet was tackled with a determination to grow the company's broadband business, competing aggressively with established providers and winning 10m customer accounts.[6] Verwaayen also turned BT into a services company by championing BT Global Services, the division that supplies data and voice services to multinational companies and large organizations around the world. BT now partners with retailers to advise them on how technology such as radio frequency identification can transform their relationships with customers, telling managers when customers are in the stores, and providing opportunities for special promotions that are targeted at a particular customer group. It works with global oil companies to construct communication frameworks on remote oil rigs that enable some drilling problems to be solved over video link, saving the cost and delay of sending out engineers to distant parts of the world. And it's busy with transport firms, advising rail companies on smartcard technology that would allow passengers to buy tickets over their mobile phones. Finally, Verwaayen struck a groundbreaking deal with British telecoms regulator Ofcom, hiving off BT's local network access in the UK into BT Open Reach. This allowed rivals into this market, but had the benefit of freeing BT to compete with fewer restrictions.

Underpinning all these developments, however, was Verwaayen's emphasis on empowering BT's huge workforce. Despite lots of cuts, the company still employs more than 100,000 people.[7]

Verwaayen on his management style
"You fly like an eagle very high, but you also need to dive very deep into the ocean. You need the ability to inspect the detail. I am a deep diver. If you fly over, you get fed what people want you to hear. The biggest disease at companies is that it is more important to please your boss than to please yourself. It is very hard to get rid of because it is in people's DNA. People want to please their boss so if he wants nonsense, they will serve it hot or cold or however he wants it. Entrepreneurial people get lost in the mindset of an organization.

"I think a CEO needs to be unreasonable. If you start off being compassionate with everyone, nothing ever happens. I need to be unreasonable with targets, but I also need to be passionate about people. I also believe very strongly that you always have to see the other side. You have to look at the little guy.

"I believe in constructive conflict. The first meeting I went to had 17 people around the table and the discussion was scripted, because the social regime was that there was not allowed to be conflict. Everything was socialized. There was no issue that anybody knew about where the outcome was not already decided. One guy made a presentation and half of what he said was a bunch of nonsense. I told him so, but he said, 'Do you think I agree with this?' I was stunned and asked him why he was presenting something he did not agree with. He had to say something he knew was wrong because it was what everyone wanted to hear.

"Once I talked to 800 of our people and said I wanted them to be change agents. I offered to remove the biggest hurdle they had. There was dead silence in the room. Then a guy at the back stood up and said, 'Actually the biggest hurdle is you.'

"I asked why. He said, 'In most organizations people want to do what the boss wants, so everything is done how he wants it. But how is a guy in his 50s going to know what's in the head of a 25 year old?' He was absolutely right. We have to leave behind this kind of hierarchical control behavior or our success will be limited by the ability of the CEO.

"We had a 'John' who could never go on holiday because he was indispensable. The first thing I did was fire John, because he was on top of his mount and pushed everyone else down. You have to have a very strong values agenda and you have to have the guts to pursue them. I said to everyone, 'It's over, it's done. We're going to do things totally differently.'

"The first time someone pounded the table, I stopped the meeting and said, 'Can we please celebrate this moment. This is passion. This is fantastic.' We need to have people who are confident enough to be wrong and to be called wrong and to change their opinion when they see they are wrong."

Verwaayen on the risks of global missionaries

"I was a CEO when I was 36. I was running the largest Dutch company, so I could have been a celebrity if I'd wanted to. I don't think it is an opportunity. It is a choice.

"Everybody in a role like this needs to have a certain ego. If you don't have a certain ego you will not put in the effort. But the question is, can you control your ego? That has to do with personality, it has to do with your environment. Do you like criticism, do you like people to say no, can you kick yourself? Can you look in the mirror and laugh? A lot of those attributes are forgotten after a while.

"It is a very egocentric definition to leave your legacy because you want to be on the podium, in the books with everybody talking about you. Actually, they will talk about you with respect, fondness, and care if you touch the people's hearts and minds. A company is very cruel in that sense. The company doesn't exist; it's always people. I don't think in legacy terms at all. I do my utmost for the company I work for, 24 hours a day, 7 days a week, but not in terms of a legacy.

"My legacy will be what the people that I worked with in the past think about me, and how I have shared relationships with them, and we still have a good time. I don't think in abstract terms about legacy at all. I think that's chasing the impossible."

Life after BT

Verwaayen stepped down as BT chief executive in May 2008 and left the company a month later, having said consistently that he would leave well before anyone asked him to. He is likely to have no shortage of options for future roles. He clearly has the capacity to lead a business even larger than BT. Equally, he is still active on the Dutch political scene, has written a political manifesto in The Netherlands, and is vocal in Brussels on public debates.

Although he says he's not interested in philanthropy in the classical sense, because he sees it as having a lot to do with ego, Verwaayen is heavily involved in a range of other fora, having a high profile at Davos and chairing the Confederation of British Industry's Climate

Change Task Force, so he could build a very interesting portfolio of on-mission roles as a global citizen.

Certainly, he's unlikely to fall from the public eye. "Personally, I think that you have to participate in the public debate," he says. "I think public policies are too important to leave to a selective part of society."

OTHER GLOBAL MISSIONARIES

Global missionaries are most commonly found in established businesses that have struggled and need to be reinvigorated; they're not overawed by the prospect of doing this with large numbers of people. They can bring their value-rich approach to bear on any industry.

Dame Marjorie Scardino is a good example, having transformed Pearson from a sprawling conglomerate into a focused, world-leading publisher. And Tom Glocer has an evangelical zeal about making sure that the company's customers are well looked after. "I spend as much time as I can with our customers," he says. "No matter what I am doing, even if I am in a board meeting, if a customer calls I will try to break out and take it. We're a service company with 17,000 people and doing this is vital for two reasons. Most customers I speak to like that are happy that they have called, but far more important is the example you give to your employees. It is about answering the phone and not letting it go on to voicemail and not letting an opportunity go to waste."

Although global missionaries exist worldwide, there's a heavy concentration of them in emerging markets. These CEOs are on a mission to establish their countries as world players by growing world-class global companies and, by so doing, to raise the standard of living in their country. Take Ruben Vardanian, CEO of Troika Dialog, Russia's largest investment bank. "I decided early on that I would devote my life to working to build Russia's capital markets," he says. "I have tried to help take Russia to the next level, economically. I spend 30 percent of my time on building the infrastructure of new Russia and the new standards and principles of the country. I see myself as a pioneer for Russia." Equally, Narayana Murthy, previously a strong leftist, return to India from France having spent time with high-profile French left-wing thinkers like Jean-Paul Sartre. He says he was "convinced that the only way to solve the problem of poverty was entrepreneurship".

Predictably, global missionaries measure their own success by the success or failure of their mission, so what resonates with them most are their achievements according to holistic management measures, rather than purely financial metrics. This might be redirecting a traditional company to focus on sustainability issues and the environment as a way of appealing to customers and motivating employees. Or it could be a greater company-wide vision of engaging with customers in a more tailored and personal fashion, with the aim of not simply bringing in more business but achieving a total transformation of a company's brand image and culture.

Culture and values are particularly important to global missionaries, whether they be living inside the company or on prominent display in its advertisements. But most importantly of all, the global missionary is on a mission for hearts and minds. He or she seeks believers and, in that quest, welcomes open discussion and even disruptive opposition as a necessary process through which to convert followers.

James Murdoch has an evangelical zeal about the environment that has driven the change agenda at BSkyB. "It's about having a positive attitude to change," he says. "Change is undervalued in organizations and continuity is overvalued. We need to have people in this organization who are very comfortable grappling with things they don't understand because there's no shortage of those things in this business, even for the most senior people." Murdoch is a paid-up guardian of BSkyB's values. "Values must stay consistent," he says. "We don't have a plaque in the corner of the lobby, but we do have some words that everyone knows: we're tuned in, we're irrepressible, we have fun, and we are inviting."

Some global missionaries may be driven by an actual religious zeal. Philip Green is unusual both for his openness about his Christian faith and in that he has run companies in three different industries, holding key roles at information group Reuters and container shipping business P&O Nedlloyd before taking over at United Utilities. He is very clear about the underpinnings of leadership. "Leadership is about hearts and minds; it's about marshaling the troops," he says. "It's about what people need. Yes, you can do some of that with management, but people don't understand the distinction. Leadership is beyond rationality. It's about maturity and inspiring people. I don't put our values on the wall. If people see them on the wall, they're just on the wall. It's about getting them immersed in the company's culture."

I regret the times I just let things happen more than I regret the times I took action over something

Equally, Murdoch stresses that global missionaries are hard-nosed businesspeople who are grounded in the detail and achieve stellar financial results. "A lot of CEOs are very hands-off and I try not to micro-manage," he says. "But I regret the times I just let things happen more than I regret the times I took action over something. When you see something bad going on, you have to stop it."

Global missionaries have a tendency to be all-encompassing. They try not to manage everything directly themselves, but they do ensure that they receive the maximum amount of information about what's going on in the company and with the mission. "I tend to go down into the organization a long way," admits Green, who is nicknamed "CEO Direct" within United Utilities because of this management approach. "It's my style to find out what's going on. There are certain things a chief executive should take interest in and have a personal commitment to. Talent development is one of them. I am known as a feedback junkie. Everyone can email me directly and you can also do it anonymously. Everyone gets a reply."

It's this fervor that makes global missionaries stand out from the crowd as chief executives. Sometimes their missions can make them appear so single-minded and focused that they become controversial figures, evoking opposition in the workforce.

John Neill of Unipart, for example, has the zeal of a convert because that's exactly what he is. He vowed not to repeat the mistakes of his father and developed a set of extremely strong values to which he keeps very close. Neill admires his father, who started life as an office boy and as a young man played the stock market on margin by gearing up and made a lot of money, but when the market crashed he lost everything. He then worked incredibly hard to pay back his debts and continued to work hard all his life, becoming a successful businessman, but he never played the market on margin again. "I've seen risky no-brainers to make fast money, but I've never taken them because of dad's experience," explains Neill. "My primary objective is to have control of my life for me and my family, but after that it is to help others grow. Material things you get bored with; people you don't."

When Neill arrived at Unipart, it was a nationalized company and he was shocked by how poor the management was. "It was management by anecdote," he says. "Top management did not know their business. Our traditional markets were dropping and so it was clear to me that we needed to build a brand. We needed to control our destiny by owning the consumer, rather than being controlled by politicians. We needed to control our destiny for our staff." His solution was not only to draw up a commercial plan for the company that saw it diversify from its motor parts roots into sectors that were broader and more sustainable, it was about creating a different kind of organization. "We created a long-term, shared-destiny relationship with our stakeholders," he says. "We try to inspire employees to come to work to eliminate waste by training them in a formidable world-class body of knowledge on continuous improvement. Everyone is challenged to live up to the corporate goal of delivering 'outstanding personal customer service' and living by the company philosophy 'to understand the real and perceived needs of our customers better than anyone else and serve them better than anyone else'."

It was this vision that led Neill not only to spin Unipart out of British Leyland so that it became owned by staff and investors, but to transform its culture and ethos and provide a "university" where staff could get the training and skills they needed to excel in the new business environment in which the company was going to compete. "The chief executive must create a vision but also a picture," Neill comments. "Over time, this picture becomes more and more clear. Binding the company together requires mental constructs and a consistency of leadership. That means people believe in the vision; they can see it and they have it constantly reinforced as it gets ever clearer. It leads to a cadre of signed-up missionaries. Then people are not relying on the CEO, so it's about leadership and communication." Indeed, Neill's belief in communication is so strong that it led him to set up a separate division of the company that not only delivers Unipart's own communications and marketing needs, through video, film, and television, but also offers these as services to external customers.

Like many models, however, the strengths of global missionaries can also become their weaknesses. If it is not carefully controlled by a company's board, the strength of character of a global missionary chief executive can develop into almost a cult of personality, leading to a situation where a dynamic leader and his or her personal whims become too important to the organization. People may identify too strongly with such leaders and be unable to function properly without them, so that decision making suffers lower down the chain, succession planning is inadequate, and a vacuum is left when they depart. The global missionary may be in effect the glue that holds the company together.

LEADING AT THE TOP TODAY

You've now seen the main categories that most of the top CEOs we interviewed fall into, when each type of leadership typically comes into its own, and how some outstanding examples of these CEO types actually do the job of leading today. At the highest level, the types compare as in the table overleaf.

There are clear similarities but also stark differences. For example, corporate entrepreneurs' drive and focus echo those of value-driving CEOs, but their personal attachment to the business they started could not be further from the cold-blooded detachment of the shareholder value-focused value driver. Equally, commercial executors share a metric-driven style with value drivers, but these leaders focus on different priorities. Similarly, although corporate ambassadors resemble global missionaries in valuing a societal purpose very highly, the typical personal leadership approaches of each type differ markedly.

As with any categorization, much information about the individual can be lost in the act of characterization, and we would not suggest that the leaders profiled are either fault-free or only capable in the ways we've described when illustrating the leadership type. Equally, the leaders profiled may in the future develop their style, for example from a corporate executor focus to a missionary focus, if circumstances demand. On the other hand, we think that these categories highlight striking similarities across the CEO population, and allow illuminating conclusions to be drawn about the leaders we have today and which of them may be better placed for success in the future.

One interesting illustration of how this categorization can be applied is to examine which leadership types are typically favored by private equity and public equity owners respectively; a hot topic at the moment. Although examples of each type are currently found in both settings, at present most private equity firms tend to prefer commercial executors and value drivers for their focus on driving

	COMMERCIAL EXECUTOR	FINANCIAL VALUE DRIVER	CORPORATE ENTREPRENEUR	CORPORATE AMBASSADOR	GLOBAL MISSIONARY
CASE STUDY	Sir Terry Leahy	Mick Davis	Sir Martin Sorrell	Lord Browne	Ben Verwaayen
FOCUS	Results	Shareholder value	Personal mission	Society	Corporate potential
MEASURE OF SUCCESS	Business metrics	EPS	Cash	Market capitalization	Holistic management
DEFINITION	• Driving focus on achieving best results in industry • Relentless focus and attention to detail to ensure operational and strategic ambitions become reality	• Relentless focus on shareholder value • Understand value metrics of industry and often highly skilled in identifying value-enhancing corporate transactions or realizing value from portfolio disposals	• Have something to prove • Disrupt industries because believe in better way of doing things • Excel in spotting breakthrough opportunities and making them reality • Their vision for companies is their life vision	• Have a global vision with broader societal impact • Operate at geopolitical level and deliver transactions that transform industries	• On personal mission to make significant difference, as well as corporate mission to make company great • Typically customer champions, lead by inspiring people and energizing them to tap into their potential
SITUATIONS BEST AT SOLVING	Businesses that need to be taken from average to great	Complex businesses requiring portfolio rationalization, or buy-and-build strategies where transaction-based growth needed	Young businesses and those where industry-changing opportunity exists	Where interaction with regulators, governments, and other authorities is critical. Thrive on high-profile problems. Almost certainly established businesses	Established businesses that have lost their way and need to be renewed. Dealing with large workforces a particular strength
TYPE OF INDUSTRY MOST OFTEN SEEN IN	Can operate in any industry but not usually effective in professional services	Diversified industrial businesses, financial services	Technology, biotech, consumer, professional services	Global resource businesses, global banks, industrials	Broad range
RISKS OF MODEL	• Taking on too much and burning out • Organization risks being political • Risk if corporate entrepreneur changes industry game • Not attracting very best talent	• Managing economic downturns • Being blinkered, not seeing industry shifts • Lack of people glue beyond wealth generation • Loss of successful executives when become independently wealthy	• People burn-out • Succession • Getting right people to scale business • Weak at managing steady-state businesses • Chaotic processes • Shareholder heartache as may "bet the company"	• Getting distant from business's operations • Not being able to dive deep into detail if crisis blows up	• Succession • Personality of CEO may be too important to company, people may identify too strongly with him or her

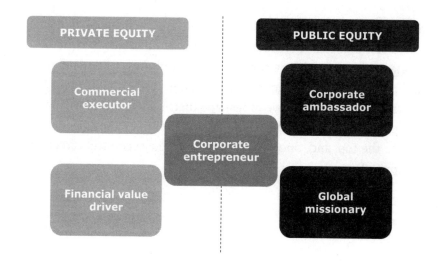

financial and operational results. Equally, most public companies tend to prefer corporate ambassadors and global missionaries. Corporate entrepreneurs sit a little uneasily with both sets of owners. Because private equity firms are increasingly taking note of their wider societal impact and public company leadership is fast taking lessons from private equity, the distinction laid out in our illustration may erode over the coming decade, although it remains in active play today.

There is another application of the categorization: self-analysis. We hope that these chapters will have assisted you in identifying your own leadership type. Most people are clear by the middle of their career what their dominant leadership style is. However, beware: a substantial minority find that they have only a weakly dominant primary type alongside an important secondary type. For example, you might find that you've spent a long time thriving on the freedom to act in entrepreneurial businesses, but that in reality you are a global missionary who needs a corporate platform and a mission to be properly fulfilled and have the full impact of which you are capable. The trick to using these insights to plan your career is to consider where you are now and where you want to be in the future, and in so doing to balance what situations you thrive in, where your leadership type is best suited to being used, your personal strengths and weaknesses, and whether each concrete opportunity that presents itself matches your values and personal mission.

Having examined how some of the world's best CEOs lead today and perhaps what you can learn from them, read on to discover how CEOs expect they will have to reshape their leadership styles and the companies they lead in the coming years, the advice they give for getting to the top, and, once there, how to have a successful career and a happy life.

PART III

LEADING INTO THE FUTURE

In Part I we showed you the five critical shaping themes for the next decade and top CEOs' tips on how to respond to them. In Part II we explored the way in which some of the world's best CEOs run their businesses today.

In this final part of the book, we set out:

❏ CEOs' secrets on how to organize and lead tomorrow's businesses.

❏ CEOs' guidance to ambitious young people on how to get the apprenticeship you need to set you up for a fulfilling career, to succeed, and to get to the top.

❏ Tips from leading CEOs on how to stop the role dominating your existence and forcing your personal life to one side.

12

DITCHING COMMAND
AND CONTROL

"Command and control is dead. Management in the classical sense is dead. That will be scary, very scary, to boards."

Ben Verwaayen, former chief executive, BT

"To me, leadership is primarily about raising the aspirations of people, making people say that they will walk on water."

Narayana Murthy, chairman and chief mentor, Infosys

CEOs will face two fundamental challenges in the coming decade. There will be a shift from domestically focused international businesses to truly global businesses, as well as the necessity to earn, and retain, a license to operate in all countries around the world. World-beating companies will also have the consumer and the needs of their talent at the heart of their businesses. They will have to respond swiftly and innovatively to shifts in their environment, exploit the power of the web, form close partnerships, develop best-in-world solutions to local problems, and take a broader view of success than simple financial profits, so becoming welcome neighbors in communities around the world.

This chapter sets out how CEOs will have to change in order to ensure that their companies are successful, sustainable twenty-first-century businesses.

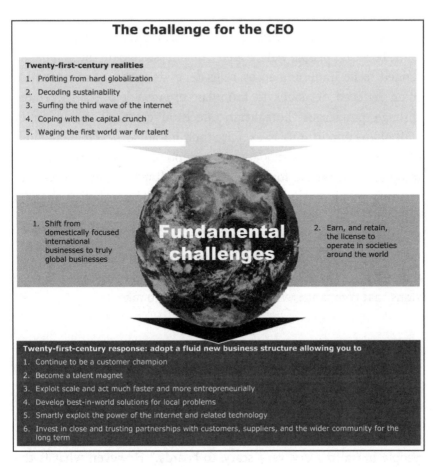

The challenge for the CEO

Twenty-first-century realities
1. Profiting from hard globalization
2. Decoding sustainability
3. Surfing the third wave of the internet
4. Coping with the capital crunch
5. Waging the first world war for talent

1. Shift from domestically focused international businesses to truly global businesses

Fundamental challenges

2. Earn, and retain, the license to operate in societies around the world

Twenty-first-century response: adopt a fluid new business structure allowing you to
1. Continue to be a customer champion
2. Become a talent magnet
3. Exploit scale and act much faster and more entrepreneurially
4. Develop best-in-world solutions for local problems
5. Smartly exploit the power of the internet and related technology
6. Invest in close and trusting partnerships with customers, suppliers, and the wider community for the long term

COMMAND AND CONTROL IS DEAD

Leading CEOs believe that the 200-year-old Western manufacturing-derived model of efficiency driving businesses will be inadequate in coming years and will need to be rethought. They also recognize that the Western command-and-control style of management is out of date in most situations. Command and control is characterized by issues being funneled to the top and then decisions being passed back down from on high – but they're often the wrong decisions taken by managers who are removed from customers and the day-to-day reality. This approach will continue to be useful from time to time, mostly in turnaround situations requiring tight control, but it will not be adequate in most mainstream businesses.

Mervyn Davies remembers when "memos came from the autocratic boss and people were scared". Businesses where this happened tended to be underpinned by rules-dependent management, which often reduced decisions to formulaic approval processes operated through ponderous, bureaucratic decision gates, denuding junior staff of any opportunity to exercise their initiative. Severe hierarchies of this sort find accommodation of exceptions or innovation hard or impossible and make for incremental and linear career progression. Treating people in this way leads to trapped human potential and a consequent lack of fulfillment for workers.

Above all, such businesses are not appropriate settings in which to take long-term decisions that require multi-constituency decisions that are as yet hard to quantify in financial terms – the kind of decisions that companies will increasingly have to take.

The alternative: Unleash the talent within

"I think command and control is dead," states Ben Verwaayen. "Location and time is dead. Management in the classical sense is dead. It has to be on different notions. That will be appealing to many people but also scary, very scary, to boards." However, what is the replacement?

The central problem with command and control is its failure to engage people by offering them meaningful work and freedom to innovate. John Weston, former CEO of BAE Systems, says, "Throwing tablets of stone from the top just does not work. But getting people fired up about what they can achieve and giving them the freedom to be masters of their own destiny is a better way – and they appreciate it."

Great businesses will provide employees with space to think and a global meritocracy to grow within. A good example is Google, which claims to be committed to making itself a natural home for a diverse group of the most talented people in its industry. The company states, "We believe we have created a work environment that attracts exceptional people. We know that people value meaning in their work; they want to be involved with things that are important and that are going to make a difference... Talented people are attracted to Google because we empower them to change the world."[1]

If providing fulfillment to employees is the central challenge, we need briefly to consider what people want out of their work. As Todd Stitzer states, "People want meaning in their work experience; they don't want merely to be a wage earner. They're searching for several levels of meaning – for themselves, their families, and society."

Tony Robbins is the world's best-known personal development coach and has worked with several US Presidents, including Bill Clinton, and a number of leading CEOs.[2] Through his research, he has concluded that humans have six core needs. The more needs that are met more fully, the more fulfilling the work experience will be for the employee. While command and control gives people a high degree of a very narrow form of certainty in their lives, it cannot satisfy any of the other needs adequately. Furthermore, the critical shift in the talent that businesses will rely on in coming years is the rise to prominence of Generations X and Y; these generations have significantly

HUMAN NEEDS (Robbins)	THRESHOLD CRITERION FOR FULFILLMENT THROUGH WORK	PARTICULAR NEEDS OF GEN X/GEN Y IN CONTRAST TO BABY BOOMERS
Certainty	Feel secure that I will continue to have a job and be paid for a living	Lower need for job security than baby boomers, higher propensity to move
Variety	Require a variety of responsibilities to avoid monotony	Higher need for job moves or internal progression and for variety while in role
Significance	Feel that I have the opportunity to make a difference professionally both as an individual and through the company's actions	Not willing to be micro-managed, deep desire to make a personal difference to company and industry
Connection	Sense a personal connection with peers, management, and leaders	Expect to connect deeply both at work and at home and so less likely to accept work–life imbalance
Growth	See opportunities to learn and develop capabilities	Expect to grow faster and demand focused personal development
Contribution	Confident that through work I am able to contribute to society beyond simple commercial success	Higher expectations that company will be responsible and make a significant contribution to society as a matter of course

different parameters for needs fulfillment than the baby boomers who are typically managing them. The previous table summarizes the core needs and the differences.

As Generation Y expert Bruce Morton underlined to us, "Gen Y demand more from their employers than their predecessors. Though it may have an effect, more money is not the answer to making your Gen Y employees more passionate. Above all it is the leader's passion that will make the difference, and that passion needs to be embedded in a cause that the people can buy into – something they can be known for."

Gen Y demand more from their employers than their predecessors

Command and control is not only too slow and cumbersome for the next decade, but is also likely to be rejected by the younger generations.

THE CELL METAPHOR

Command-and-control businesses use military metaphors and rely on vertical and rigid structures. From our research, we believe that a better metaphor for a global business is a human cell. Cells have elastic edges that can dynamically expand and contract and are porous; a central nucleus that regulates semi-independent processes; and a fluid body that allows the free circulation of critical nutrients and energy. And cells are alive! Visualizing the corporation as a cell allows leaders to make the most of three critical insights.

Soften the corporate boundaries

The CEOs we interviewed believe that most tangible and intangible assets will increasingly be shared through partnerships, joint ventures, and the further fragmentation of the supply chain in the coming decade. To keep up with the fast-changing environment, businesses will need new rules of engagement allowing quicker, more flexible, and deeper collaboration with external parties. They will have to assimilate information quickly, form technical and business

The cell model

partnerships speedily in response to market change – and dissolve them as rapidly – foster proprietary innovation as extensively as possible, and be open to working with communities and governments more closely than ever before. Liu Jiren states, "To be a leading global player, competing with firms with a 100-year history, we need to create a new business model. We need to know how to make innovation happen through open collaboration." Julia Middleton, CEO of Common Purpose, believes that we "need leaders who understand the value of networks which extend far beyond the traditional confines – and, more importantly, know how to lead them".[3]

Change the role of the CEO

To unleash the inventiveness of their employees, CEOs cannot be generals directing every action of their team members. Rather, they must be facilitators for the talent and energy of their teams, removing critical roadblocks to brilliant execution.

Cris Conde urges, "Redefine the role of the CEO. If different employees can share information with each other, they do not need to rely on bosses to do that. Therefore, one of the major roles of old-world bosses (being an information conduit) disappears. The imperial

CEO has to disappear – the CEO now has to ensure that everyone can play their part to the full. The CEO is like a conductor – he creates and orchestrates a system. It is very arrogant to think

The CEO is like a conductor – he creates and orchestrates a system

you can make better decisions than the thousands of people below you. This may be true if you have more information. But in the last five years I have maybe made one decision (to take the company private) that no one else could make. The role of the boss is to make the handful of decisions that cannot be made by anyone else and to maintain the collaboration systems. I really think that the rise of these collaborative systems is redefining organizational structures and the role of the CEO; they are the last nail in the coffin of the imperial CEO."

Nikesh Arora adds, "The real engine of Google's success is innovation. Consequently, we look to our managers to encourage innovation and guide it to scale, so that it can make a global impact. Google's success has been built squarely on the shoulders of our amazing employees. Google has done well because we've provided a great work environment where people can literally change the world. As Google grows, we're still committed to this culture that fosters rapid innovation."

It's not just technology businesses who believe this. Thras Moraitis is on the same wavelength. "It's impossible for people at the center to have more information than guys on the ground," he says.

To unleash your teams, you have to face up to another truth: that the bureaucracy of command-and-control businesses avoids, rather than rewards, risk taking. Lenovo has recognized this. Says Bill Amelio, "We try to eliminate organizational obstacles that might hinder idea development, such as functional silos and hierarchical decision making. How well we foster such a mindset internally dictates our success globally. It directly impacts our flexibility in adapting quickly to changing market conditions and fast-changing customer tastes. Our approach of organizing around hubs in diverse regions to specialize in major functions, rather than having a single headquarters for all significant decisions, is an innovative departure from the traditional single hub-and-spoke management approach of most other "global" companies.

"With no designated headquarters office, our multicultural management team is free to convene wherever and whenever it makes the most sense. Similarly, world-sourced business functions are located solely on the basis of concentrations of specific talent, skills, proximity to key markets, infrastructure, language proficiency, IT capabilities, costs, and facilities."

Todd Stitzer adds: "You have to be able to iterate on the ground all the time. The goal is to create a framework and then find people who can run within the framework."

Give the center a fundamentally different role: The nucleus

The final insight on organizational design from our research requires greater discussion than the first two. The cell approach depends on the center orchestrating rather than rigidly controlling the global business by focusing on a few critical areas, while providing soft leadership that releases the latent energy in the operating units and results in better performance across the entire organization. Let's look at what this model means in terms of both business and personal leadership.

Business leadership requirements

The CEO remains guardian of purpose and strategy
Day-to-day pressures mean that some big, developed companies are distracted from their underlying purpose by fire-fighting and short-term priorities. This problem needs to be addressed, but many professional managers find it hard to make the changes necessary to bring soulless companies back to life.

The CEO must make clear the company's purpose ("What is our company here to do?") and its strategy ("How do we beat the competition?"). A company's purpose has to inspire it to outperform, capturing the imagination of all stakeholders and instilling a sense of pride in employees that they are part of the company. And clearly, the strategy needs to be dovetailed to this, because if a company does not have an effective strategy, it will not succeed in its purpose.

Ian Coull says, "This is probably the message that I talk to my people about most often, because if we are going to have a business that we are going to persuade shareholders to invest in, they have to know and understand what the company is about and how it's going to behave. If we don't have the right purpose and values, we're going to lose some of the potential appeal to these investors."

Archie Norman has observed a distinct shift in people's aspirations and a concomitant increase in the importance of purpose and strategy in recent years. "In my view," he says, "what's really changed is at most Western developed companies, the way you attract people and employ people, and the way you obtain performance from them, has become so much more demanding because people have so many options. They're much more transactional. Good people can go and get a job somewhere else tomorrow. Therefore, enlisting from them

Good people can go and get a job somewhere else tomorrow

some loyalty that goes beyond the salary you are paying has become a much more challenging task. That's why creating something they feel they can be loyal to – a sense of belief, purpose, a project we're all on – has become so much more important for people, and it requires a very different style of leadership."

The CEO must also make sure that the organization lives out its goals. Too many company mission statements are not compelling and too many business strategies do not properly set out how the company intends to outcompete its rivals and succeed across sectoral, industrial, and national boundaries. Philip Green states, "In my experience, we get the best from people when they derive a sense of meaning from their work activity: few are driven solely by the promise of material reward. At P&O, our vision was concise, short enough to be remembered by all in the company, specific so progress and achievement could be measured, and ambitious. Visions are of little value if they are not stretching and carry with them the possibility of failure."

The CEO must therefore ensure that every employee understands what the company is there to do and how it will win against the competition through communicating purpose and values clearly, consistently, and with great impact.

The CEO lives and celebrates the company's universal values
Values answer the question "What do we stand for?". They stem from a company's history, its market proposition, the values of its leader and employees, and the external environment in which it operates. In global businesses values need to be universal, setting the framework for how the company should act at every level, wherever its people are and whatever the context.

Universal values do not trample over or ignore local cultures in global organizations. In contrast, they act as a golden thread that can hold the company together, while recognizing the importance of local traditions. Says Narayana Murthy, "You need to have universal values that are celebrated in every culture and are modeled on every culture, while still leveraging local norms. You need to be very open-minded to adapt to and leverage other cultures."

> You need to have universal values that are celebrated in every culture and are modeled on every culture, while still leveraging local norms

Bill Amelio also sees common global values as vital to bind a company together. "It's these organizational values that hold the key to motivation and keeping such a diverse company moving in the same direction," he says. "At Lenovo, the heart of our newly melded culture quickly became tied to innovation and technology. Despite our predecessor companies having vastly different origins – one created in the East and the other in the West – both had distinct similarities in their development as both led the evolution of computing and IT in their respective parts of the world."

The trick to formulating values, however, lies in making them granular enough that they can guide action. As Whitbread CEO Alan Parker states, "Too many companies' values are just words, rather than actual beliefs of the organization." A recent study concluded that six universal moral values could be identified in companies' codes of ethics and associated literature: trustworthiness, respect, responsibility, fairness, caring, and citizenship.[4] Although some bad businesses struggle even with these, who would not want their business to observe them? Great businesses go beyond these level one values and create level two values that, with some basic principles of human interaction taken for granted, are more specific to what the business is trying to achieve and, as such, provide stronger guidance to the business's employees in their daily lives. Where level one values secure a sound footing for business, level two values describe the qualities that tomorrow's business requires to win. For example, Standard Chartered has "courage" as a really meaningful, strong value.

If you cannot create level two values, your company will struggle to maintain itself. Infosys is a good example of a company with level two values, which are expressed succinctly in an acronym – C-LIFE, standing for Customer delight, Leadership by example, Integrity and transparency, Fairness, and pursuit of Excellence. Samir Brikho at AMEC observes that "values need to go beyond the superficial and standard – you need level one, two, three, four values. For example, saying you believe in people is one thing, but really a modern company must ask 'What more can we do to develop our people?'. That's when people are really a value."

Values must also be actionable: people need to see how they fit into their daily activities. To this end, the CEO of General Healthcare Group, Adrian Fawcett, has gone so far as to draw a "pictorial values map which reminds us where we came from and how we serve our customer base today, our aspirations for the customer and company and the journey for tomorrow". To be actionable, values must be rooted in the business as it is now, rather than the board's vision of how it will be. Archie Norman says, "Values have to come from the people you're employing, not from the boardroom. You may be chang-

Values have to come from the people you're employing, not from the boardroom

ing and reshaping the company so they don't want the old values, they want the new ones, but it's still got to be their language to ring true. They've got to say, 'Yes, that's what we believe in'. Sometimes the values that are expressed are boardroom pontification."

Values must be embedded deep into the business's culture so that they guide action. This takes a long time and concerted effort at a senior level. BT chairman Sir Michael Rake says, "We've put our values at the heart of our business. We've engaged over 3,000 people from around the world, from different countries, levels of seniority, gen-der, and so forth, which allowed us to build a set of global values which now underpin how we conduct day-to-day business and how we treat each other and our clients. It's taken seven years to embed them. They help our recruitment enormously and also our retention."

Values take a tremendous effort to distill and it requires still more energy to embed them and make the business breathe them daily. However, they're both extremely powerful profit drivers and key to sustainable success once established.

The CEO gives wide freedom to act and ensures innovation is rewarded
The key advantage of the cell model of governance lies in the way it allows the smart devolution of power, with the objective to trust and empower staff so that the right decisions are made as close to the front line as possible. The energy will increasingly flow up from knowledge workers close to or on the front line, rather than being forced down from on high.

Ben Verwaayen wants "a culture in which people take the right decision as close to the problem as possible in a collective perspective that you have developed in which they know it's the right decision. So, first of all, they have to ask less," he adds. "Second, they know in the culture and in the values and in the targets that you have set, what the right decisions are, and therefore, because they own it, it's their decision, it's a much easier sell."

Shiv Nadar, chairman and chief strategy officer of India's HCL Technologies, focuses on making sure the entrepreneurs in his busi-ness are unbound. "You can see entrepreneurs: it's screaming on their foreheads," he says. "So we actively look for entrepreneurs. Real stars join HCL every day and it's on their foreheads. If it's not, they are not stars. We give them the tools and empower them to drive the business from the bottom." Nadar recognizes that "once you grow to a certain size, you need processes to manage the business", but emphasizes that "you also need to ensure that the entrepreneurship emanates from the bottom of the business".

The same applies online. Mitch Garber, former CEO of PartyGaming, believes, "In twenty-first-century companies, it is important to hire great people and to give them flexibility and have confidence in their decision making. As CEO, you can't take decisions in India, Israel, or America, but you can create a business framework whereby the big decisions come up to the top and you can make the right call."

To release the talents you have in the business does not require a mere change in tone. As a CEO, you must fundamentally reassess how you see your role. You must learn, as Sir Bill Castell puts it, "to suppress your ego so that you can then be a champion and help others learn, like you do your children". He adds, "CEOs are going to have to get used to being at the bottom of the hierarchy, supporting the 460 managers above them."

CEOs are going to have to get used to being at the bottom of the hierarchy, supporting the managers above them

You must also ensure that your incentive system encourages employees to experiment and be innovative. Google is a good example here. Its aim is to provide "an environment where talented, hard-working people are rewarded for their contributions to Google and for making the world a better place". And it has flexible rewards to make this happen. For example, its "founders' award" is designed to give "extraordinary rewards for extraordinary team accomplishments". While there's no single yardstick for measuring achievement, a general rule of thumb is that the team accomplished something that created tremendous value for the company. The awards pay out in the form of Google stock units that vest over time. Team members receive awards based on their level of involvement and contribution, and the largest awards can reach several million dollars. In 2005 Google awarded about $45m in restricted stock to 11 different projects, citing the recipients for creating "tremendous value" for the company. Cynics question whether Google sees a profitable return from the awards. However, these initiatives have been at least a key factor in attracting and motivating the top talent to the business and there can be no doubt that Google developers turn out a large number of innovative products.[5]

The ability to give individuals the space and incentives to act innovatively while channeling that energy productively will distinguish leading CEOs from the rest of the field over the next ten years.

The CEO is primarily responsible for talent
As we saw in Chapter 6, talent-magnet companies will build talent development partnerships between the chief executive, human resources department, and the search industry. The CEO will have to be the talent champion and ensure that talent stays at the top of the business's agenda and that talent development is driven down into all line managers' performance metrics.

Top CEOs will make sure that their key executives are drawn from the top 1 percent of global talent and that attracting the top talent is as high a priority as serving customers. These CEOs will be committed to investing money and at least 25 percent of their time to talent development. Not satisfied with a process-based approach to HR, these CEOs will push their HR teams to become true internal talent champions and to find a global search partner who knows the top 1 percent of global talent.

The CEO monitors the company radar and future-proofs the business
Chief executives don't read enough, states Val Gooding. "They need a political, social, and economic view on the world." Tomorrow's leaders need to have a great feel for what's happening in and around their companies and then have flexible resources with which to reshape their core businesses and to develop novel businesses to capture value from shifts in the environment. Too many twentieth-century companies were caught out by swift changes in technology or the entry into their core markets of new foreign competitors. The quickening pace of globalization makes these dangers all the more prevalent.

A FTSE100 CEO told us, "Countries and companies have wonderful assets but also carry baggage. You need a radar to understand what's coming up across the different regions in your business. For example, Europe's outlook, with social costs rising and labor inflexibility, is very different to what's happening in Asia." Meanwhile, Sir

Bill Castell has some practical advice. "CEOs must get out there and test their vision," he says. "CEOs should use universities to help with their radar. For example, I had Massachusetts Institute of Technology help me to understand the future of world energy." Finally, as Sir Roy Gardner emphasizes, "It is important that the center does not delegate away the radar: it needs to keep an eye on the future of the customer."

It is important that the center does not delegate away the radar: it needs to keep an eye on the future of the customer

Inside their organizations, CEOs need to discern what's going well and badly in regard to customers, competitors, and talent. Archie Norman says, "You've got to understand what's happening on the front line, and you've got to understand in some cases more about that than the line manager. The good leader today in business is complex and fast moving, and there are ways of informing the inner circle. You have a grapevine. So, you walk the stores or you walk the customers, you have people who pick up the phone and tell you things. You have an internet blog with suggestions; you have lots of different ways which tell you what's really happening. The line never tells the truth, never, even in great organizations. Good news travels fast, bad news travels slowly, and so you've got to know."

These insights are no use if they are not actionable. The radar has to drive CEOs' efforts to prevent themselves being wrong-footed by shifts in the future. Brent Hoberman comments, "The best corporates will have a team focused on future-proofing their own business, spending time bettering and breaking their own processes. These groups should not worry about existing investment cases: their mission is to create the next generation and to avoid the company betting its future on what it does today."

Such teams will be available to CEOs to work on growth initiatives, scope major strategic moves and mergers and acquisitions, and continually re-examine how to use corporate assets to create disruptive new businesses. CEOs should therefore consciously build teams to create wide-ranging insights about the world and to incubate significant new ventures.

The CEO polices business performance and ensures global minimum acceptable standards are met
Freedom to act does not mean that the business units and employees are unregulated and totally unconstrained by the center – far from it. Great businesses regulate themselves along two axes. First, to drive value there is rigorous transparency on performance: these businesses compile financial and non-financial data that is comparable and timely. And they monitor the security of their corporate assets – financial, tangible, or intangible.

Xstrata provides a good example. The center sets very demanding targets and executives are rewarded lavishly for meeting them but, equally, failure to meet targets is investigated very carefully and consistent failure is not tolerated. That's performance policing: the question of whether people are reaching high enough.

However, to guarantee the integrity of your business you also need to ensure that all operations meet quality and sustainability standards. Therefore, great businesses set and monitor minimum acceptable standards – they ensure that people are standing on the right foundations. Bernd Scheifele says, "The challenge is in reaching technical standards globally, principally in production and sustainability. Whereas sales and marketing are managed locally because cement is a local market business, we use global best practices for production and sustainability."

Sir John Parker wraps performance policing and minimum acceptable standards together neatly. "At National Grid, the model is very simple," he says. "We have to have leading governance practices, visibility on accountability, and transparency, because governance at the end of the day is about discipline. You need to decentralize management decision taking to the lowest possible level, but with well-defined responsibility and accountability all the way down the line. You need strong audit control with a solid line from the board to every audit controller, sound administration, strong compliance, and very strong legal teams ensuring you are conducting your business correctly. Whether you are a big company or a small company and whether you're in one country or 30, the same principles apply."

Ron Havner says that reconciling the freedom to innovate and the
bottom-up energy of businesses with rigorous performance policing
and minimum acceptable standards will be one of
the trickiest balances that tomorrow's CEOs will
face. "The trick with the cell model is to ensure
decentralization to the regions and front line," he
says, "but to also retain central policing of risks and
financial management to ensure that accountabili-
ties are followed and no one bets the company."

The trick with the cell model is to ensure decentralization to the front line, but to also retain central policing of risks and financial management

People leadership requirements

The CEO inspires
Ketan Patel, founder of investment firm Greater Pacific Capital,
states, "Big adventures require visionaries, charismatic leaders, and
controversial thinkers. Such qualities are rare. So instead, many leaders focus on those things that do not require vision (we call them
pragmatism), do not require personality (we call them reliable)."[6]
    "Hold on," you may be thinking, "I thought the era of the inspira-
tional, big-ego CEO was dead?" Absolutely right. However, the current
generation of professional managers are not going to be able to provide the personal leadership that companies will require either. Fresh
role models for global companies are needed. Great CEOs find inspiration for themselves and their team in their passion for the company, what everyone can do together, and their personal purpose.
Inspirational leaders don't have to jump up and down frantically and
be on the front cover of *Time* magazine. Great examples are often
found in the emerging champion companies.
    In the new world of work, chief executives need to be able to lift
their people to go beyond themselves. Comments Narayana Murthy,
"To me, leadership is primarily about raising the aspirations of people, making people say that they will walk on water. A plausible
impossibility is better than a convincing possibility."
    Sir Bill Castell recognizes that this is intimately linked to human
needs. "People want a CEO who inspires them and a job that they

don't think is wasting their time: a job that makes a difference."
Samir Brikho contrasts leadership with managing. "You give a manager targets and he is determined to meet them,
you coach him to meet them, and he meets them,"   When you think you can only jump 2m,
he says. "A leader inspires. He articulates a com-   a leader can get you to jump 2.5m
pelling vision, has certain values and lives accord-
ing to them and, when you think you can only jump 2m, he can get
you to jump 2.5m."

For Archie Norman, the leader can no longer be a deadpan numbers
person. "The chief executive who was primarily the cold analyst gaz-
ing at the numbers around the boardroom table: that model is going to
be more difficult to make work," he says. Richard Baker points out that
the inspirational leader has to be focused on team success and derive
satisfaction from moving others. "When you get the team to perform
above the sum of their parts, anything is possible," he says. "Teams
perform amazing things. Average people can produce super-star performance." Chairman and former CEO of the Financial Times Sir David
Bell agrees: "When you assume that people don't have ambition, can't
do more than they are already doing, and really therefore they don't
matter very much – you're almost always wrong."

Inspiring leaders bring to life for every employee or partner what
they, their team, and the company can do. Inspiration is about raising
the aspirations of the group for the group.

The CEO elicits trust and belief
People need to be inspired by a compelling vision to make them want
to go somewhere. However, the leader also has to get them to step out
on the journey and then sustain them along the way. Getting them to
cross the starting line requires that they believe that you, the leader,
and they, the team, can get there together. They need to believe in
you as an authentic person with the ability to help them overcome
the roadblocks on the way; they need to trust that you are leading
them toward a meaningful and decent future. In other words, where
inspiration establishes a high bar as a worthwhile and achievable
goal, trust and belief keep your team going through the hard times. In

Narayana Murthy's words, "Achieving dreams means making sacrifices in the short term to achieve in the long term. It means that one
of the most important attributes of a leader is trust. Trust means people will give their lives for you because people see
Achieving dreams means making   that 'if it is good for him it is good for me'."
sacrifices in the short term to achieve in   Trust and belief are built through the decisions
the long term   you make and the way you are seen to be with peo-
ple. You have to ask whether people think you are
a decent person trying to do the right thing. John Neill emphasizes the
personal element. "The people in the front line of the company need
to know you. They need to know that you care about them and all the
company's stakeholders. They need to know that you know their business and care about their process problems and personal problems at
work. You need to get onto the values level of all of the people at every
level in the business and while building respect for the past, clearly
signpost the future." So too does Sir John Parker. "Good leaders walk
the talk," he says. "They're consistent in their behavior. They live out
the words. I can think of no higher risk to a leader's credibility than
not living out the words."

Murthy is blunter still. "Walking the talk is the most powerful
instrument of adherence to a value system that our people adhere to,"
he says. "If you eat your own dog food, trust is automatically built."

Leadership does not have to involve the consumption of pet food.
However, people's trust in you as a person is essential to their belief
in their ability, with you, to reach the desired goal, so you must work
to build trust in you as a person. If you manage to sustain trust and
belief in you among your teams, you stand a good chance of getting
the team across the finish line.

The CEO brings clarity
Errors made at the top are magnified as their implications spread
through the business and the original instruction is reinterpreted. As
the lead delegator in the business, chief executives have to give the
business clarity on strategy, objectives, tasks, values, and all other critical issues. It's very much easier if you are a natural communicator,

though you can learn to improve your skills in this area. Being a great communicator means understanding what you're trying to say and how it's likely to be understood by the different audiences you're addressing. Sir John Parker calls communication "the sister of leadership". "Can you describe your vision of the future in two sentences?" he asks. "Without being able to communicate effectively, a CEO can't instruct people."

Communication is the sister of leadership. Without being able to communicate effectively, a CEO can't instruct people

Experts say that communicating is actually one of the most complicated things human beings do. Certainly, miscommunication, misunderstanding, and the subsequent confusion and lack of clarity are at the heart of many business difficulties. Although chief executives normally receive training in presentation skills, they are rarely trained in the art of communication, part of which involves being an effective *receiver* of information.

"The real art of communication is in understanding what message is received by the listener rather than what is transmitted by the speaker," says Alan Watkins. "Many CEOs make the mistake of believing that just because they said something or sent out a signal, they communicated. Rarely do leaders check what was received by the listener, but this simple discipline of checking what was received, when applied appropriately, can transform the quality of communication. The quality of communication can be significantly enhanced by understanding the type of person you are speaking to and how they see the world. The message has to be adjusted to fit the audience, not out of some manipulative Machiavellian intent, but simply because the message will fail to land or become distorted if such adjustment is not made."

Gifted communicators make this kind of adjustment naturally. Nevertheless, this flexibility is a skill worth developing, because it helps you ensure that listeners understand what you intend so that you can reduce the risk of them misunderstanding your guidance.

CEOs are a role model in their dedication, consistency, and personal balance
Malon Wilkus, CEO of private equity group American Capital, insists that leaders "must have a passion, integrity, and personally work hard

to make the business even better. If everyone can see and understand what you are about, then they in turn will be fired up to go the extra yard to do the same."

People will judge your dedication by your visibility to them. That means that you have to travel and meet with those in your distributed operations around the world. GE taught Sir Bill Castell that "the CEO needs to get around the world and see people face to face once a year. After that, he can do things by telephone." Indeed, when Philip Green became chief executive of P&O Nedlloyd, he set himself a target of seeing and being seen by 80 percent of the company's employees in his first 12 months. He achieved that goal and made sure he did it again when he moved on to become chief executive at United Utilities.

The CEO is always on display. John Weston believes that "on an average day, a senior manager has about 100 opportunities to provide leadership to the team. The problem is that they only take one and the team see the other 99."

For Sir John Parker, "the key to demonstrating personal dedication is consistency. Your people see you doing this day in day out and they start to trust and believe in you. Consistency is key to integrity, which for me is the most important value for a CEO."

However, your actions will inform those of others, so you have to be smart in your balancing of travel and technology. Todd Stitzer sends his top 100 employees a monthly voicemail, communicates with his top 1,000 every two months, and sends a newsletter to the next 10,000 every quarter. Smart use of technology can protect your time and energy while still preserving your work–life balance. Remember that your working style and work–life balance will set the tone for the whole business, so by not looking after yourself and staying fresh you are indirectly reducing your business's energy, a point we'll come back to in Chapter 13.

The CEO judges and moderates organizational pace and energy
CEOs must make a judgment call on how much pace and change their company needs, and can handle, at this point in time. They then

need to decide how well the business is achieving the necessary pace, increasing it if necessary or slowing the organization down before it overheats.

Sometimes the energy has to come from CEOs themselves. "You need a high level of energy and the ability to bring together teams with different backgrounds and skills, take risks with them, and get the organization results oriented," says Mervyn Davies. "It's relentless, but all the successful chief executives that I know love the job and thrive on it."

Equally, it's very unhealthy for the CEO to be the business's sole dynamo. John Neill says that Unipart has developed a vast number of carefully thought-out mechanisms by which management creates and spreads energy throughout the business. Every six weeks it has a glitzy "Mark in Action" awards event, where it celebrates significant achievements and recognizes the people who have made them. "Those who've been recognized then wear a hologram on their badge so it's clear that they've been celebrated," he says. "I have not missed a Mark in Action meeting in 20 years. So you do not have to bring all the energy. You get it from the groups you assemble and it's part of your job to transport that energy around the organization. You don't have to have the great idea, but you need to spot it and propagate it. All these events serve to identify *You don't have to have the great idea, but* and hold up exemplars within the organization *you need to spot it and propagate it* and their stories get around the business. But they also help me to judge the pace the organization is moving at and where to speed it up and where to slow it down."

Sir Terry Leahy has more cautionary words. "Energy and pace matter," he argues, "but you can be too energetic or frenetic. The bigger the organization, the bigger the ripple effect, and too much noise at the center can lead to chaos at the edge. Quiet leadership can be best. You still need lots of energy to be quiet. You have to cover the ground. Also remember that energy and freedom may conflict."

Finally, the level of pace and energy required will depend on the company you run. "You have to understand the pace and pulse of different organizations," says Philip Green, comparing life at the three companies he's led. "At DHL, you can't try to execute an order until you've received it. At Reuters, most of the revenues are through subscription and the concept of an order doesn't really exist. At United, we are a utility and there is no order book at all – it's a monopoly. The pace and pulse is very different."

As we warned you at the start of the book, being a CEO carries a health warning because of the amount of personal effort required in the role. However, the best CEOs channel the energy of the organization rather than trying to overcome sticking points and inertia single-handedly.

The CEO is flexible in the face of reality
The necessary flipside of clarity and the hard business output of performance policing is flexibility. Great CEOs have the unshakeable conviction that there's always a way. However, they must also be grounded in reality; there's no point leaving employees deflated by expecting them to do what really is impossible. Martina King underlines this, saying, "You have to paint an exciting future, but you must also face reality. You cannot be credible about the future unless you face reality." The CEO must recognize when brick walls are being confronted and the team needs to regroup and attack from another angle.

Flexibility is a key soft leadership element and a key distinguisher from twentieth-century approaches, because it is fundamental to the increased devolution of power and decentralization of authority that lies at the core of tomorrow's leadership. As Mick Davis showed in Chapter 8, the CEO has to distinguish "good" failure and "bad" failure – the failure of anticipated returns to be reaped following the pursuit of an intelligent, carefully thought-through business risk is no failure at all. Deciding when to push and when to regroup is a classic leadership skill, but one on which a premium will continued to be placed.

The CEO develops and promotes the firm's personality
Personality is the character of a business; it is described whenever your employees are asked over dinner what it's like to work for your

company. If it's a good personality for the employee, it will resonate with them and they will express it with pride and enthusiasm. On the other hand, in underperforming businesses personality can be flat or toxic. The CEO must then tune into the underlying energy of the business, such as it is, and create a new personality that feels authentic but energizing to the high-quality employees already in the firm and compelling to talents outside it. The CEO has a very direct influence on the personality of a business because he or she will typically be seen as personifying it.

Many chief executives say that being a CEO is like being on television all the time. They are aware that whether they are in corporate headquarters or out in the field visiting operations, they are being continually observed. Even the most casual remark can change someone's day or get tongues wagging. "If you're a CEO, everyone in your company watches you all the time," says Leigh Clifford. "If you do something that's inconsistent with the values you espouse, it goes around the organization and everyone knows."

But there's a flipside to the high profile: every situation is an opportunity to evangelize the business's values and a chance to lead by personal example. John Neill once had to practice what he preaches when he was lecturing at Unipart's staff "university" and Jenny, the coffee lady, was struggling to serve 100 people in their 15-minute break. "She got overwhelmed and her broad smile faded as she became highly stressed realizing she couldn't achieve the task," he recalls. "So I started serving coffee with her, but we still struggled. So when Jenny went home that day and her family asked what kind of day did you have, the answer was obvious and clearly she wasn't looking forward to the next course." Neill encouraged Jenny to learn the relevant components of the Unipart Way, the core of its business model, and apply them to her area of responsibility. The result was exactly the sort of continuous improvement exercise he was teaching about. "Now using the Unipart Way," he reports, "Jenny manages the system and uses her new-found skills to continuously improve the process. Today everyone gets served in less than 2 minutes and Jenny takes pride in chopping seconds off the process. Her family would get a very different answer now when asked, 'What kind of day did you have?'" Neill tells the story as part of the Philosophies and Principles course that he continues to teach at Unipart U.

And of course, businesses, like people, should not be entirely serious all the time. As the late Sir John Harvey-Jones, former chairman of ICI, once modestly explained his role: "Basically, I try to jolly things along."

Conclusion: The nature of the cell

The cell metaphor is designed to bring to life how the center of an organization should respond to the new business realities and the new world of work. Tom Peters, author of the bestselling *In Search of Excellence*, captures much of the essence of the cell when he says, "Passionate servant leaders, determined to create a legacy of earth-shaking transformation in their domain... must necessarily create organizations which are... no less than cathedrals in which the full and awesome power of the imagination and spirit and native entrepreneurial flair of diverse individuals is unleashed... in passionate pursuit of jointly perceived soaring purpose and personal and community and client service excellence."[7] Peters' language is a bit over the top for us and for most CEOs, but its direction is definitely right.

THE FELLOWSHIP

So are we moving toward a breed of superhuman CEOs who can lead a complicated cell business while at the same time having a fulfilling life outside work? Probably not.

Step back for a second and try to imagine a new global powerhouse. Imagine a "dream team" of Lord Browne filling a global ambassadorial role, Sir Terry Leahy driving operational execution, Sir Martin Sorrell developing entrepreneurial new ventures and markets, Mick Davis pulling together massive value-adding deals, and Ben Verwaayen focusing on inspiring the troops. What a team that would be!

Clearly, in practice this would probably be a disaster, as each of these CEOs works in his own way and all are used to being the boss. Equally, however, it's clear from our interviews that top global companies, while on the surface operating as a conventional management group, are really run by a close-knit team of key executives with extraordinary and complementary skills. We believe that the outstanding companies of the next decade will be led by a tightly bonded fellowship of remarkable leaders operating as one.

Arguably the most well-documented fellowship is the so-called dream team that drove mobile phone manufacturer Nokia's phenomenal growth through the 1990s. Jorma Ollila worked in super-close partnership with Matti Alahuhta, Pekka Ala-Pietilä, Sari Baldauf, and his replacement as president and COO, Olli-Pekka Kallasvuo. A fellowship has also driven Infosys, as Deepak Satwalekar, lead independent director there, explained to us: "At the heart of Infosys is a fellowship which was formed over 20 years ago, based on a mission, strong values, and a firm commitment to doing the right thing and integrity." Indeed, a similarly close top team has led National Australia Bank through a fêted revitalization. Ahmed Fahour states, "CEO John Stewart runs the business more like a private equity business than a traditional corporate. John's really a managing partner and his reports are partners. This approach trickles a long way down the organization – for example, I run my business with 'partners' too.

"This is important because (1) in truth John doesn't have the same information we have about our businesses, so it's better that most decisions are taken where the most information is; and (2) because, frankly, we'd all leave if he micro-managed us! The partnership is based on mutual respect, clear principles and behavioral rules, and careful mentoring, which starts with John's expert mentoring of his business heads. At the end of the day, if you don't understand what you should do in the fellowship, you're not good enough to be in it." At Resolution, Paul Thompson also thought of his top team as "partners, not people run by command and control".

The truth is that fellowships feel radically different from a conventional leadership team in the closeness of their binding, the total openness between their members, the level of conflict and disagreement the members can tolerate with each other, and the high level of interchangeability of the fellowship members. Archie Norman fondly recalls his time at Asda, which spawned a generation of FTSE100 CEOs, including Richard Baker, Andy Hornby, Justin King, and Allan Leighton. "A real team is a rarity," he admits. "All chief executives tell you they've got a great team but when you say who is the great team, 80 percent of them tell you it's these 20 people or these 12 people. I know what they're trying to say, but that's not a team. You very, very rarely find a team of 12 people, in fact pretty much never. That's not a real team.

"A real team is typically three or four people, because the real team in fast-moving companies is one where, when things are going wrong, they share things with each other completely openly. When they have a rotten day, they come in and say, 'I've made a right mess of that, can you help me out, just tell me where you think I should pick it up.'

"Or someone comes in and says, 'I've got this idea, do you think we should do it?' and somebody else will say, 'No, I think that's rubbish actually.' You can have that sort of joint, heavy lifting. There are high levels of inter-changeability – if I can't make that meeting, OK, I'll go and pick it up for you. No sweat, no problem. That is a huge advantage to have, but it's unusual.

We all respect each other for what we are doing, but we are able to have an open argument about things, like a family row

"The right culture to create is one where there is total transparency. There are no secrets. Everybody knows what everybody else is doing. We all respect each other for what we are doing, but we are able to have an open argument about things, like a family row. I like businesses where people feel able to shout at each other, in a professional way obviously. They are emotional about it and have a go. We may be incredibly aggressive and abrasive, but afterwards we're all friends. We respect each other and we feel better."

Lenovo has a such a fellowship. Kenneth DiPietro remarks wryly, "We have some awesome arguments; we make it a rule to discuss the undiscussables." Importantly, at Lenovo Bill Amelio and chairman

Yang Yuanqing have succeeded in building a vibrant fellowship drawing on people from a wide range of cultures.

Sir John Parker expands on this idea. "In the executive cell, there will be ideally three to four people who collectively drive at pace and with integrity, releasing energy across the whole organization," he says. Ron Havner thinks that the key thing about his fellowship is that it "promotes more sharing of ideas and issues between fellowship members than in a conventional company management team". Indeed, the most significant danger with a fellowship model is that, in Mervyn Davies' words, "You have to be careful the top team does not become a cult. In a world of fast change, you continually need new blood and fresh ideas in teams."

A fellowship is a much more effective way to lead a cell business than a more conventional CEO plus strong line manager model for several reasons. First, a cell's leaders need to propagate messages through a dispersed and non-hierarchical organization. Having a group of perfectly aligned executives close to the CEO and core mission allows for a fast-acting viral information flow. Second, fellowship members, by being close to the center, are more empowered to take major decisions, visibly dispersing power right at the top. Finally, entry into the fellowship generates tremendous loyalty and so aids in the retention of top talent.

Being a CEO in a fellowship

Taking the lead remains the role of the CEO. Mitch Garber says, "The true test of a CEO is not when things are going well, but when things are not going well and you have to go off course and ski off piste. It needs real self-belief to change course and make tough unpopular decisions, but ultimately this is the difference between the success and failure of a leader."

Certainly, businesses should not be governed by majority vote. In that way lies vacillation. However, many CEOs observed how infrequently they take unilateral decisions or override their top teams. Although some situations, such as turnarounds, require strong leadership more than others, most CEOs recognize the value of working in a team.

Rather than robbing the CEO of the initiative or exchanging him or her for a consensus-seeking council, a fellowship model strengthens the CEO significantly. What could have been impossible becomes possible. A CEO in a fellowship is stronger with regard to internal opposition or inertia, as there is a core team of really close advocates within the business. The fellowship can give the CEO valuable support in hard times and the trust they share with him or her can make it easier to face reality in tough spots.

A trusted fellowship can work particularly well during transformation phases. At Tesco, for example, Tim Mason is setting up the Fresh and Easy venture in the US while the rest of the fellowship focuses on the core business.

John Waples, business editor of the *Sunday Times*, warns that one danger with fellowships is that they are often forged in periods of super-growth but then their spirit and speed are lost as the business grows and solidifies. However, having a really close team provides the CEO with the chance to be supported through the lows by people with unshakeable conviction in the mission, and to celebrate the highs of success with people with as deep a commitment to the outcome as the leader.

Building a fellowship

Martin Halusa says, "Every portfolio company needs a different kind of investment style at a different time in their lifecycle. When we invest there are always areas that have been neglected under the previous ownership, and it is our job to identify these blind spots and make sure we have the appropriate resource and capital structure to address them. One of our key skills at Apax Partners is to identify what kind of guy a portfolio company needs at the time we invest."

Leadership is situational – you should choose a CEO whose leadership type best matches the challenges the business will face in the future. For example, a global missionary is likely to be best placed to revitalize a large global company that has lost its way. However, the cell model works with any situation and with any CEO type and always requires that the CEO be supported by a close-knit fellowship.

The closeness of fellowship members requires a much closer alignment of personal values than most leadership teams manage. The fellowship members have to be very clear on what moves them individually and as a team. They must invest heavily in probing and really understanding the other members' values, so that they can all align their beliefs on how to conduct business and be fully frank and open with each other as disagreements arise. Fellowship members must also respect and value each other's skills so that there can be mutual respect and equality of contribution. Finally, there must be a sense of collective responsibility, so that all fellowship members back the decision of the CEO whatever the previous argument and its intensity.

Several CEOs told us that their fellowships do not map to the company's senior management team; some of that team may well be excluded and some more junior executives may be part of the fellowship. The most important questions in selecting members are:

❏ What specific skills do you need?
❏ Who in the fellowship is outstanding in each skill area?
❏ Do all of the fellowship have a deep commitment to the cause and the right values and beliefs?
❏ Is there a natural chemistry between the fellowship members?

The non-executive board in a fellowship

Clearly, the board in the future will increasingly have to be prepared to work effectively with executives operating in more tightly knit fellowships. Consequently, as Paul Manduca, former chief executive of Deutsche Asset Management, states, "The non-executive boards of tomorrow will have to be highly supportive of these talent teams but still not be afraid of testing strategy and key operational risks. In addition, the boards of fellowship-led companies are more likely to be successful, but they must ensure that the company continues to adapt to changes. It will be their role to check that the fellowship still has the right members to address each phase in the company's development."

In an ideal world, the non-executives would be a close-knit team too that would work closely with the executive fellowship and maintain a constructive dialogue about the business. Such a dialogue can allow boards to continue their strong testing and challenge of executive decisions, but also develop a careful, guiding rapport with the leadership team that allows them to reduce the need for heavy direct interventions in the business.

CONCLUSION

Tomorrow's CEOs will abandon the outmoded command-and-control model that is too inflexible for the modern business environment. Instead they will assemble a fellowship to work with the CEO to make sure that the business unleashes the collective power of its people.

Fellowships will be close-knit and contain people with complementary skills who truly pull together. Fellowship members will work together at the heart of the business and their deep relationships will lay the foundations for constructive conflict and stronger performance driving throughout the company. Such organizations will be super-charged and respond to market changes in a much more entrepreneurial way.

SECRETS OF CEOs: DITCHING COMMAND AND CONTROL

❑ Most businesses will face two fundamental challenges in the coming decade:
  • Shifting from running domestically focused international businesses to truly global businesses
  • Earning, and retaining, a license to operate in societies around the world
❑ To meet these challenges, successful companies will:
  • Continue to be a customer champion.
  • Become a talent magnet.
  • Exploit scale and act much faster and more entrepreneurially.
  • Develop best-in-world solutions for local problems.
  • Smartly exploit the power of the internet and related technology.
  • Invest in close and trusting partnerships with customers, suppliers, and the wider community for the long term.
❑ CEOs will operate more cell-like businesses, not command-and-control structures.
❑ CEOs will master both business and people leadership and be able to operate and energize globally dispersed businesses.
❑ CEOs will run their businesses in a close-knit fellowship of top executives as opposed to through a traditional management team approach.

13

PREPARING TO LEAD

"If you want to be a CEO, then you must focus on being a great leader."
Richard Baker, former chief executive, Alliance Boots

"I want to learn the ways of the Force and become a Jedi."
Luke Skywalker to Obi-Wan Kenobi, Star Wars

For those of you at the start of your career in the new world of work, the first and most important thing to do if you believe you want to be a CEO is to unpick your motives and understand why. Wanting the title and money, power and status is understandable and not unusual. However, as an audacious life goal, setting your sights on that title alone is probably a recipe for disappointment. Remember that, where the Top Gun fighter pilot school aims for the top 1 percent of pilots, the CEO of a large international business is in the top 0.001 percent of the company, so it's a tough position to go for. If, on the other hand, your aspiration to be a CEO is really an expression of wanting to realize your potential and make a significant difference in business and beyond, then you must recognize that you are not talking about a title – you're talking about a career mission. And critical to its successful fulfillment will be becoming a leader skilled in both business and personal leadership.

To become a complete leader for tomorrow requires an apprenticeship. Learning leadership is like a quest – there's no defined path to success.

In this chapter we provide advice from visionary CEOs on how to start your quest, share views on the career foundations you need to build, and then, for those of you preparing to become CEO soon, we

Journey to become tomorrow's global CEO

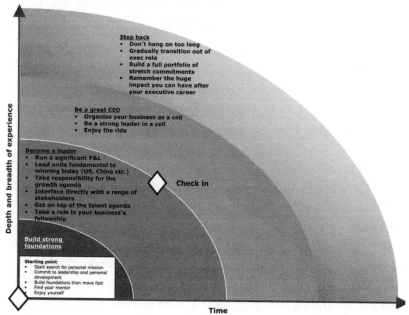

lay out the way to pull up mid-career and check on your progress and reassess your aspirations. We've discussed how to lead a twenty-first-century company in Chapter 12, but at the end of this chapter we also share thoughts on how to step back from the CEO role and look beyond building an orthodox "plural" career.

Where most conventional career advice is linear, most CEOs we talked to thought that traditional career planning is outdated and that it is better to think of your career as divided into broad phases of leadership development. However, we are well aware of how life tends to upset carefully laid plans, so this chapter is designed to help you roll with the ups and downs.

WHAT DO YOU WANT FROM YOUR CAREER?

Very few people know what they want to do from the outset. Keith Butler-Wheelhouse was in that camp. He recalls, "I always wanted to be a general manager. I was 19 when Henry Ford II came to the Ford plant I worked at. He asked what we wanted to do in life. I said I wanted to run Ford. I got a lot of ribbing for that from the others, who had been less ambitious in their aim, but Ford respected the question and asked me why. I said I wanted to learn to integrate the facets of the business together. And I spent the following 20 years at Ford training myself in all elements of the business. That education has stood me in great stead."

However, the majority of our CEOs only got a sense of their career mission in their late 20s or 30s. Paul Thompson would hope that you do not want to be CEO of the business you are in at 25. "You should be more of a rebel than that," he says. "Wanting to be the boss shows too much empathy for the establishment." Meanwhile, Eric Daniels says, "I guess I was a late developer. My career's really been a series of lucky accidents. I've done all kinds of jobs. I worked in a grocery store at 15, on a construction site at 18, then a petrol station, a library, and a shop, and I had two stints at a paint factory. When you're working in a paint factory, you cannot imagine what a dirty, dangerous job it is. Work on enough of those jobs and you'll want to make the world better. My 17-year-old son doesn't know the answer to that at the moment. This doesn't bother me."

Over time, your career mission will emerge and become clearer. At Tiger Airways, Tony Davis advises that instead of a fixed plan, "you need a thread to your life". His own career is connected to an early passion for flying: like many boys, including a young Paul Walsh, he wanted to be a pilot in the RAF.

Remember that insight into your career mission need not come just from business experience. Narayana Murthy tells of a formative experience hitchhiking home to Mysore in southern India that decided him on entering business. He reached the city of Nis in what is now Serbia and Montenegro at night and slept on the platform of the train station for two nights running, as he had no local currency. He eventually caught a train into Bulgaria and tried to engage two fellow travelers in conversation. Having struggled with the boy, who spoke neither English nor French, Murthy spoke instead to the girl. Somehow angered, the boy called the police. "They threw me into an

8ft by 8ft cell," recalls Murthy. "I had no food or water for another 72 hours and the floors in Bulgaria are very cold in winter. Eventually, after 108 hours without food, they put me in the guard's compartment on a freight train to Istanbul and would only return my passport when I got there. That long, hungry journey gave me time for introspection and I decided to conduct an experiment in entrepreneurship in India."

By the end of your 20s you will know the sort of direction you want to head in. Many of the CEOs we interviewed realized in their late 20s that they were driven by a desire for freedom out of a frustration with poorly managed command-and-control enterprises. For Nick Basing, a serial venturer who has grown several businesses and is former CEO of Paramount Restaurants, a key motivator has always been "feeling restless about missed opportunities. I always got frustrated that lots of opportunities were being missed by the organizations I was in," he says. Paul Thompson adds, "Above all, I hated being told by anyone what to do, even if they were right. For me, being CEO is all about freedom; people who find making big decisions lonely are not cut out to be CEO." Richard Baker was driven through his retail career by "two main driving forces: (1) to not be bossed around and to have the freedom to act; (2) to be economically independent and to be able to walk away from work if I wanted to". He says he "realized early on that the only way not to be bossed around was to be the boss".

The only critical element at the beginning of your career is to be determined to do great things. The truth is that most people are afraid to be bold and to commit to achieving their career mission. So although you don't know how things will turn out, dare to be great. Thras Moraitis has only one regret. "I started and sold several very good businesses as a young man, but for the same effort I could have done great things," he muses. "Aim for great things."

Tan Pheng Hock values passion in young leaders. "Coming from humble beginnings has taught me never to take anything for granted and to treasure every bit I have," he says. "Never be afraid to dream, and to work hard towards that dream. There are no short cuts in life, and no promises. But if you're passionate enough about what you believe in, you can succeed." Of course, as Philip Green says, "the best foundation will be to work with a twenty-first-century global leader – but there aren't many of those around."

If you are committed to undertaking a leadership apprenticeship, five points are fundamental in starting out:

- ❑ Commit to finding your ultimate career mission and to doing something great.
- ❑ Commit yourself to excellent leadership and personal development from the outset.
- ❑ Lay solid foundations, but then move faster and take bigger risks and ignore conventional advice founded in the old world of work.
- ❑ Find your mentor: work for a great leader.
- ❑ Don't neglect family and friends and enjoying your 20s.

BUILDING THE RIGHT FOUNDATIONS

To become a CEO for tomorrow you will need a very broad range of experiences. Lord Browne states, "The first few years of a career have to be about investing to understand. Be an apprentice, get your hands dirty, and take risks. It's generally better to do it early. It's a really bad idea to have a rigid life plan. You know nothing early on; you only really get to see what business is all about once you're past 40. Before then, it's about getting loads of experience." Damian Reece, head of business at the Daily and Sunday Telegraph, observes that "the younger generation of CEOs are less conservative, probably because they have been schooled in an internet decade and are naturally, therefore, more ambitious, confident, commercial, aggressive, and 'can do'. Build a career: ignore conventional advice, take more risk at an earlier age, and aim to be a great leader."

Eric Daniels adds, "If you set your heart on being a chief executive, your chances of being disappointed are very high so that aspiration is likely a waste of your life. The question is: 'What do you like?' Try a lot of things and figure out what you like during your early life and career.

"Apprenticeships take many forms, but never forget that the objective is to become a leader. You need to discover whether you have got leadership qualities or not and you can only discover that through experience, because leadership is a very personal quality. It can't be taught and you don't know until you've tried to lead."

CEO apprenticeship requires you to have a medium-term goal but not to overplan. Tony Davis thinks that youngsters try to plan their careers too much. "You cannot lay out an objective and a route to it when you're young," he says. "You should be more flexible and take more risks. Broaden your perspectives and experience; change country and industry: that depth of experience marks you out to employers."

But don't read this as counsel for an easy life, as skilling up is a very serious business. "You need to know where you are," says Daniels. "The 20s are the new teens. They're all about discovery about yourself, but they're also about building skills because, if you don't, you're unlikely to be happy down the track."

The 20s are the new teens. They're all about discovery about yourself, but they're also about building skills

Life is not a game of chess in which every move can be planned out. The first phase of your career is about the serious business of exploration: exploration of yourself, business, and the wider world. Potential CEOs need to accumulate a broad range of business and personal experiences, build a platform of hard business skills, and learn about themselves early on.

Your parents' advice when choosing a career was almost certainly to get a great education, get a profession, and work for an already well-established and well-known company. That advice is rooted in the old world of work. It remains good advice in the twenty-first century – but only at the very start of your career. The new world of work is where those entering the workforce today will have 13 jobs by the age of 38, as we saw in Chapter 6. More than ever, a great education will be the bedrock of your career. Even today, 59 percent of Fortune 100 CEOs and 45 percent of FTSE100 CEOs have advanced degrees;

indeed, only 4 percent of FTSE100 CEOs do not have a degree at all (in 1996 that figure was 37 percent).[1]

Getting experience at a good company at the start gives you a platform to allow you to take more risks and to move quickly later. Not only that, but in the future employers will expect you to move faster and get broader experience than people did in the past. Equally, those same employers will be open to you having done "unconventional" things. Historically in Europe, for example, a failed early-stage business was a CV stain. Increasingly, however, CEOs today see work in new ventures as the experience accelerator it really is.

As importantly, doing "adventurous" things is fun and, in fact, you will underperform against your potential maximum if you get too comfortable. James Bilefield remarks, "Every time I've moved company, people have thought me mad. I've left successful positions with great prospects for riskier options because I get frustrated if things aren't moving fast. The key thing is to keep life fun and not to get bored. I've been lucky to be able to do that. Get out there and take risks."

Lord Browne agrees. "It's dangerous when a person or a company says that things are so good that they don't want to do anything or change anything; that's the time to check out and do it again," he says. If you're still hesitating, remember a point on which Browne was emphatic: "The risk downside is lower than you think at any point in your life." In most decisions, you are probably overestimating the personal career risk involved. Thras Moraitis also speaks from experience on this point. "Find a trend, get a foothold, raise capital, and take an expansive view; there's no issue if you blow out early," he says. "I had 13 ventures before Xstrata."

Remember that the financial sums you put at risk early on in your career are tiny compared to your likely earnings later, as Tony Davis learnt. "When I was leaving British Airways at 29 to go to the Middle East, I was really concerned about my pension," he says. "That's now a tiny sum of money for me."

Make your first job a fast stable

Your first job has to be in what Archie Norman calls "a fast stable". He believes that the great leadership brands, companies like Mars and Tesco and many professional services firms, give employees "fast experience. It will be tough at times, but will take you through the hoop. You want leaders to have come through a variety of different situations and been challenged, who have known failure, who have felt the fire."

> You want leaders to have come through a variety of different situations and been challenged, who have known failure, who have felt the fire

At the very outset of your career, your main priority has to be to learn the basic technical skills of business as quickly as possible and to find some of your personal limits. And joining a fast stable will probably keep your mum off your back and put money in your pocket.

Get broad experience as fast as possible

A fast stable will also set you up to broaden and collect business and personal leadership experiences and take on calculated risk even more quickly.

Having decided aged 19 that he wanted to run Ford, Keith Butler-Wheelhouse trained himself in all aspects of the business: "manufacturing, product development and engineering, finance and treasury, sales and marketing". He credits a measure of his success as a CEO to having a broad grounding in business.

Similarly, Paul Thompson says, "I was a young man in a hurry. I would not have had the patience to plot a career through a big organization. I wanted to get to the City and do deals and get that excitement and rub shoulders with CEO clients. I got a look at boardroom issues, what it's like to get into tight spots, and saw the sharp commercial end of delivering or not getting promoted or paid. But at 25, I was thinking about getting some grounding. I went to an accounting firm, because I thought, 'Let's get a bit of professional training.' I knew I would not stay five minutes after qualification." Stanley

Cheung, managing director of Walt Disney China, has placed "a huge commitment to learn and a desire to lead" at the core of his career.

At both the fast stable and broadening stages, some experiences carry a premium. Arguably, with the high value on flexibility and growth that will be seen in the next 10 years, strategy consulting and global operations consulting firms will be an even stronger background than accounting. Like investment banks, consultancies can give you exposure to CEOs and some of their most important problems as well as broad cross-industry experience very quickly. Professional services firms also put you under pressure to perform from the get-go. You'll find your personal limits pretty quickly.

Mitch Garber agrees. "The professions are a great grounding: accounting firms, consultancies, investment banks, and search firms all give you business experience in deals, finance, and people, but also complex problem solving, presentation at board level, and also performing under pressure." It's the route Brent Hoberman took. "In my mind, I always knew I wanted to set up my own business," he says. "But I went into consulting first for a couple of years to give me an experience base. It also gave me the ability to simplify complex problems and build business models. If starting again, I would join a start-up or early-stage consultancy with a focus on business transformation to maximize the experience. In the future, it will also be key for a CEO to have a period in an entrepreneurial high-growth business; it helps you not be afraid to change if things are not working and also to take more commercial risk. There are also operational benefits such as the ability to bring urgency and get things done by doing things in parallel rather than in series."

Equally, this is not to say that the great industrial brands like GE and Procter & Gamble will not continue to be training academies for world-beating CEOs. However, the trick will be to judge at what point in your career a move into one of the behemoths makes sense and what to jump out of them for.

As you move around, try to get experience of two to three industries, three to four functions within them, and of working under different capital structures, such as for private equity owners or a family office.

Ahmed Fahour provides a great example of a twenty-first-century career. An Arabic-speaking Lebanese, he was brought up in Australia and joined Boston Consulting Group there. Having made partner with BCG, he co-founded a private equity firm, iFormation, backed by Goldman Sachs and General Atlantic Partners. A few years later, he was headhunted to run corporate development for Citigroup before being made CEO of Global Alternative Investments in his 30s. After four years, and wanting to raise his family in Australia, Fahour returned there and joined National Australia Bank – where his father was once a cleaner – to help John Stewart with its turnaround. It is clear that the start in BCG's fast stable and a mix of private equity and large corporate experiences have rounded Ahmed out and helped in his fast progression.

Wherever you're working, stay close to the customer, where the money is made, and solve today's problems or build a growth engine for the future.

Go where the growth and future opportunities are going to be
From early on in your career, try to put yourself in some kind of historical context. As Tony Robbins reminds us, "Most people predict tomorrow looking at yesterday, but the great leaders recognize the cyclical nature of the world." You should also recognize the cycles that markets and the economy go through and position yourself to take advantage.

Take Richard Baker. "In my mind, it is clear you have to be in the right industry," he says. "I started as an engineer in the UK motor industry, but figured out that was not going to be a winning industry in the long term. Moving from industry to retail was a huge leap of faith for me, but I knew that there was a shift in power going on in the UK economy. So moving from Asda to Boots was a conscious move into healthcare. Today, the obvious move is into the emerging markets. Rising tides lift all boats; only go into a winning company or a winning sector – you can be as good as you like in a poor environment and it won't do you any good."

Rising tides lift all boats: only go into a winning company or a winning sector

Growth industries mean disruption and innovation. As Michael Dell is keen to emphasize, this means that "learning to thrive in an era of constant change is a competitive advantage that every business leader has to embrace. Success comes down to listening – listen to the customer you want to serve and fully understand their needs. Then, and only then, can you offer products and services that are truly differentiated and valued by your customers."

Work globally
Philip Green advises, "You'll need to have a feel for the world in terms of the history and cultures of western countries, but also emerging markets and undiscovered countries to be an effective global CEO in the future." Frank Brown, dean of Paris-based business school INSEAD, believes that future business executives should make a deliberate effort to become global by spending periods in foreign cultures. "It's about not going from the US or the UK to Australia for a six-month pub crawl," he says, "but going to Tokyo, Beijing, or São Paulo, really experiencing a different culture and trying to get by in a different language. It's about understanding that things there are much, much different. It's critically important that people get that experience early on so they are open to it later on."

Muhtar Kent, president and CEO, The Coca-Cola Company, "needs people who can move seamlessly across borders and cultures and who feel as comfortable working in Mumbai as they do in Atlanta; people who can speak the language of sophisticated modern trade. We're looking for people who are flexible enough to understand the pressures and local cultural nuances associated with being a sole proprietor of a small street-corner bodega or kiosk." Make your career global as early as possible.

Damian Reece agrees. "For UK leaders, one problem is that the FTSE is a bit like the premier league," he says. "It has attracted some of the top management talent from around the world and there is a danger that local talent get crowded out. Also, if you are pursuing a global career, better to be 'schooled' in international experiences earlier rather than later."

Ideally, work for a great leader
As we have seen from Part II, only a limited number of CEOs and senior executives today are true leaders for tomorow. However, such leaders do exist – leaders who are brilliant at bringing on young talent. In the UK, two good examples are the late Sir John Harvey-Jones and Archie Norman. If you have the opportunity to work for a similar leader today, ideally as part of their fellowship as they transform an industry, then this experience is the best learning you can get. If you do get the chance, hang on tight!

Develop tomorow's leadership habits

Alongside taking the concrete actions above, you'll be speeded through your apprenticeship if you develop the following habits.

Adopt the mindset of a CEO
Whatever your responsibilities and lack of seniority, you should always seek to adopt the mindset of a CEO. You can think of this at two levels. From the bottom up, assume the mindset of a CEO in your core work activities: deliver first, but take a broader view on how to help the wider business be more successful. From the top down, learn to assess the business from the point of view of the CEO: how is it faring against the elements of the cell described in Chapter 12? Are there gaps that you can develop new projects to fill? For example, if you think carbon footprints are important, is the business carbon neutral? If not, why not set up a task force to make it so?

Develop winning habits, but know how to lose
Many of the CEOs we interviewed had experienced serious failure or very difficult situations at work or in their life at some stage, and almost all of them believed that these were some of their most valuable experiences. In developing your career, never forget that, as Lord Browne puts it, "Everything adds to you: a book read, a business, traveling to somewhere that you fail. Experiences build character and you grow your intelligence, skill, and judgment." Another

FTSE 100 CEO added, "It is better to fail early and badly and bank the learning rather than fail big and publicly later on when the stakes are high."

Indeed, Ron Havner and Archie Norman actively look for people who have faced really tough times when hiring senior executives. Havner says, "When I'm hiring I test whether the candidate has faced adversity and failure at work, like going into liquidation, or tough times at home, like a death in the family. Dealing with these troubles and bouncing back breeds inner belief and deep confidence."

Norman adds, "By the time it comes to 35, if it's all gone swimmingly and it's all pulled through and they have been mentored by the chief executive and been on programs, that's fine, but it's a bit of case unproven." When he hires people he wants to know: "What has been the moment that you have stared into the cavern? What did you have to do where you had to confront really difficult people, people you just didn't get along with or you didn't like? You had to work with them and they didn't perform, but how did you do that?" Failure can make you a much better leader.

What has been the moment that you have stared into the cavern?

Be a student of personal development
Try to pick up a coach and a mentor pretty early on. Hone your strengths and work on your weaknesses where you can. For example, is poor energy management what really holds you back? Vitally, integrate what you learn about yourself into your everyday life.

Have a life
Early in your career, you are balancing money with gaining top-drawer experience quickly. But you have to unpack the question of experience and measure it against the elements of tomorrow's leadership that we've discussed in this book: business leadership, personal leadership, and your own needs.

Take investment banking: this provides a fantastic grounding in finance (a critical technical skill), it gives you a good network, and it certainly means that you work in a fast stable. However, it is likely to give you an inadequate grounding in the softer side of personal leadership. Banking can also be grueling. For example, one CEO told us about his son's experience in investment banking. The son only took two days' holiday in two years and once fell asleep during a client board meeting. Shaken by how exhausted he had become, he decided to resign, even though he was highly regarded by the bank. When he revealed his decision, the incredulous boss offered him double and then four times his salary to stay. He still quit. The truth was that although he was becoming wealthy, he hadn't had time to find a partner or buy a house or have any life beyond work.

Many CEOs are like Mitch Garber and make a point of hiring people with life experience outside work. "It's important to have not just strategic and business leadership experiences but a broad enough experience of life," he says. "For me life experience has included my marriage, bringing up my kids, setting up a shop at 14, being a lawyer, being a professional skier, and my interests in food and travel. It is diverse experiences which allow me to talk to and relate to employees at all levels."

There's a lot more to life than work and money. If you can't manage your work–life balance in your 20s, you won't stand a chance later in life as personal and professional obligations become more significant.

Learn to celebrate your successes

The top executives we meet in our day jobs are typically single-minded in the pursuit of their objectives and are often quick to identify the next objective as soon as they have achieved a goal. Clearly, this ability to prioritize and deliver is a strength to develop early in one's career. Equally, however, Tony Robbins stresses that great leaders also take the time to celebrate their successes, because "if you do not celebrate your successes, then your quality of life will be poor. Don't be superstitious – if you celebrate, you will actually achieve more in life."

Show total commitment but ruthlessly change role if you're not being stretched
Sir Bill Gammell, CEO of Cairn Energy, has a philosophy called "go or grow". "If any part of the business is less than 10 percent of the value, it has got to go unless I can see it growing," he says. "I am always looking to see if I can double our value every three years." A similar mentality will serve you well in developing your career.

A number of CEOs said that it was vital to absorb everything you can from every role before moving on; do not only excel in your job, but observe how the business you're in works and what's going on around you. You must balance your ambition and goals with 1,000 percent commitment to the role in hand and an absolute determination to achieve the goals you set yourself. Variety of experience is no excuse for throwing in the towel. Alexey Mordashov, chief executive of Russian steel company Severstal, says, "Always you'll come up against reality. Then you need to come around again. However, weak people too easily say, 'You can do nothing about this.'" Move on without regret only when you've sucked the experience dry.

Above all, be true to yourself
The biggest risk is to lose sight of your career mission so that you don't fulfill your potential or – worse – you are not true to yourself at work. This can be a lasting disappointment at the end of your life.

Bill Amelio tries always to stay true to his roots. "Having spent the first 21 years of my life in Pittsburgh, I like to think I now have a 'True Grit' spirit. With our blue-collar, no-nonsense style, Pittsburghers are tough-minded people who talk straight and are driven. I am proud of my formative years, and I would encourage CEOs in training to leverage the values and ethics of their individual upbringings to ground themselves. While their professional development may never end, it's their respective early years that will never change. These roots must always be valued and respected.

"Many memories still flood my mind when I visit my dad's shoe-repair shop in Pittsburgh. At 'the shop', as we affectionately call it, he taught me the importance of customer service, quality, and a strong work ethic. Additionally, I watched and learnt as he dealt with a wide variety of customers and customer problems. It's these roots that form the core of the person I am today and, like any effective leader, I'll always try to be true to this core."

Ben Verwaayen highlights the importance of the self-knowledge he sees in his senior teams at BT. "If you look to our top teams, I like to think you'll find much more authentic, different individuals whose personal choices they articulate, that they can put words around, and know why they do things, and therefore they are better in the role that they play," he says. "Authenticity is only possible with confidence because the temptation to be a conformist is enormous." You may feel that your beliefs and values are fully formed on leaving school or university, but you will find that they mature and are reshaped as you experience the world.

In short, be yourself. When push comes to shove, you have to make all your big decisions with your heart; you can't lead if you're acting.

If you follow the advice from our CEOs, you'll be well equipped for the next phase of your career, becoming a leader for tomorrow.

BECOME A LEADER FOR TOMORROW

Having laid the basic foundations, you will naturally start to take on bigger and bigger business responsibilities and greater leadership challenges. As you do so, bear in mind the key experiences that CEOs told us are needed to prepare you to be the CEO of a global company. Heed the advice from Gigi Levy, CEO of online casino 888: "In mid-career, the trick is to look for quantum leaps in experience, not just in middle to top management but also in technical domains, different industries in small to big business, and in public or private equity settings."

There's no doubt that successfully taking responsibility for driving performance and operations in a number of significant profit-and-loss accounts is critical experience for becoming CEO of a major business. Direct accountability for business units fundamental to winning today and in the future, such as a major country like the US or China or a key region like Asia, will be invaluable experience for later. Likewise, successfully taking responsibility for key elements of the company's growth agenda, ideally a mix of acquisitions, partnerships, new ventures, and key game-changing or future-proofing projects, will give you an understanding of how to drive super-growth in the future. As the world becomes more multipolar and business comes to interact with wider constituencies than pre-viously, make sure you've had the opportunity to interface directly with a range of stakeholders such as shareholders, regulatory bod-ies and politicians, lobbyists, and pressure groups. You also need to be on top of the talent agenda. Clearly, you have to not only take responsibility but also excel and ensure that your success is sustain-able when you move on.

Ideally, in getting these experiences you will find yourself increas-ingly involved in your business's CEO fellowship and build a role in that fellowship that plays directly to your unique strengths and what you enjoy.

Interestingly, as they collected ever more valuable experiences through this period of blossoming in their career, most CEOs found that their world view shifted and became much broader. This prompted many to reflect more deeply than they had previously on their motivations:

❑ Can I be the CEO?
❑ Do I *really* want to be the CEO?
❑ Should I be here or somewhere else?

The iterative process of action and reflection helped them develop a better sense of what situations and companies they would thrive in if they were to become a CEO.

Reality check

Eric Daniels advises, "By your 30s, you need to be managing some considerable part of a firm with people and a profit-and-loss account.

This is when you distinguish yourself or don't; it's when you go up or sideways." Many CEOs agreed that the critical part of their career came between about 35 and 45. Lord Browne says that he found his understanding of the world and his career underwent a massive acceleration from about 40. Likewise, Richard Baker has for a long time believed that "if you're not in the big job by 40 you are gone; a few people make it there before 40 but very few make it there after 40 – there's then a younger generation coming through. I applied for the Boots job in part because I was 40 and thought I had to act."

Indeed, research by Heidrick & Struggles has shown that the average age of FTSE100 CEOs is dropping, so it may be that in the coming years the critical point will be earlier than 40.[2] The inescapable conclusion is that by your mid-30s you need to be actively focused on whether or not you are going to step up to the CEO job and what you need to do to get there. You have to take a mid-career reality check.

You should weigh up the strength of your current position and prospects against leaping into a new role and the risk of that not working out. Assuming that you are on track within your current business, internally you will have a track record of achievements and successes, you will have career momentum in terms of promotions and increased responsibility, you will be senior and ideally in the CEO's fellowship, and you will have some sense of the likelihood of future progression and whether you are on path to becoming CEO. You will also have some degree of lock-in, either financial or emotional, in terms of invested effort and loyalty to people and the company mission. You have to balance these known quantities against new opportunities and their relative attractiveness in terms of scale of responsibilities, degree of promotion compared to your current role, company reputation and the prestige of the new role, your ability to make a huge success of the new venture, the level of remuneration, and the opportunity cost of closing out as yet unavailable moves. These are tricky decisions – not to mention the personal assessment of what is right for your family.

However, if your ambition is to be a great global leader, it is more complicated still. You have to ask whether your current business, and those you are trading it off against, constitute your final target, your Mount Everest, or whether you are actually looking at a Mount Kilimanjaro that will help you further build your capabilities ready for the final assault on Everest. The assets differ but include:

❑ Relevant business and personal leadership skills and experiences that you've been building up over time.
❑ Your responsibilities.
❑ Your reputation in the market.
❑ Your personal network and access to key industry forums and influential opinion formers.

Many CEOs emphasized two further points. First, you should always move if you stop believing in the value and culture of the business you're in, even it's prospering and you're doing well. Second, in most cases, if you're unsure whether to stay it's usually better to move.

You'll probably feel like you're standing on a Snakes and Ladders board looking for the long ladders of momentum and personal asset accumulation, and squinting to see whether the opportunity you jump on is going to turn out to have been a treacherous snake that will set you back. But in a sense, that's the essence of being a CEO. Taking a new leadership role is always a leap of faith. As Paul Thompson says, "The challenge of the CEO is stretching out. If you don't, no one else is going to."

In reality, you should never feel 100 percent confident that you know you can do the next job. If you do, you're not stretching yourself and learning. The risk is always lower than you think at any point in your life.

STEPPING DOWN FROM THE BIG JOB DOESN'T MEAN RETIREMENT!

Retiring as CEO need no longer signal the end of your career. Many retired CEOs we talked to felt like Brent Hoberman: "After you have succeeded in growing a successful business early in your career, then I have found that you move towards trying to find a balance between family/kids time, potentially wanting to invest, and also wanting to share experience and mentor others in a chairman role." Such former CEOs are finding that there are many ways to take a leadership role.

In the past decade, most CEOs have tended to move into a plural career of non-executive positions as a way of continuing in business and sharing the benefit of their experience and wisdom. They have then in time replaced their non-executive roles with lead director or chairman roles, once they have become experienced non-executives. However, off the record many ex-CEOs, while enjoying having more free time, find non-executive roles unrewarding from a business point of view (not least because most consider non-executive boards to be too heavily focused on corporate governance and not sufficiently value adding or commercial).

In the next decade, CEOs expect stepping back from an executive career to be a more gradual process. Some will move into chairperson roles at their own businesses while remaining hands-on in their approach. You see this already in particular among entrepreneurs: Sir Stelios Haji-Ioannou of easyGroup and Sir Richard Branson at Virgin Group are active chairmen. There are, of course, questions of ensuring good corporate governance by balancing strong chairpeople with strong senior independent directors. Equally clearly, there must be closely defined responsibilities between the new CEO and the heavily involved chairperson to allow a new partnership to develop. Other CEOs will combine chairmanships with pursuing their personal passions in not-for-profit activities or business activist forums such as the World Economic Forum.

If a business has been a roaring success, huge care has to be taken that the loss of a star CEO from the fellowship does not wound the company. As several CEOs and chairmen emphasized to us, imagination has to be used to make sure that momentum is passed to the next generation and continuity of leadership is assured.

The best twenty-first-century leaders will learn from the small group of twentieth-century CEOs who saw themselves as CEOs second and leaders first. They viewed their role as giving back by bringing on the next generation of CEOs; that mission did not finish with the end of their CEO job. Sir John Harvey-Jones was a great example. He had an impact on a large number of organizations after his executive career and mentored a number of today's top leaders.

Never lose sight of the starting point

So even toward the end of your career, don't forget that you set out on an apprenticeship to become a global leader and achieve your mission. You wanted an adventure on the rollercoaster and you wanted to learn how to change the world. Hopefully you will have. However, as Lord Browne states, "You are always learning. At the age of 55, for example, you could start to learn from people at the start of their lives who have a different mindset and watch the changing values and the changing incentives." Every day of your life is about training.

You need to be able to look back at what you've done and feel both that you've achieved something and that you've had some magic moments through your work. So stay fresh and make room for all those non-work-related ambitions you harbor. Learn to take advantage of the calmer spells in your career so that you're not constantly being hard on yourself, as well as determinedly seizing the key opportunities to grow. You do need to ride the waves of career momentum when they come, but equally you must welcome the lulls as periods to reflect and refresh. Take these opportunities to step back and commit time to family and friends and your wider interests.

As Apple CEO Steve Jobs says, "We don't get a chance to do that many things, and every one should be really excellent. Because this is our life. Life is brief, and then you die, you know? ... We've all chosen to do this with our lives. So it'd better be damn good."[3]

SECRETS OF CEOs: PREPARING TO LEAD

Starting out
❏ Commit to finding your ultimate career mission and to doing something great.
❏ Commit yourself to excellent leadership and personal development from the outset.
❏ Lay solid foundations, but then move faster and take bigger risks, and ignore conventional advice founded in the old world of work.
❏ Work for a great leader.
❏ Don't neglect family and friends and enjoying your 20s.

Building the right foundations
❏ A strong sense of your ultimate career mission.
❏ A broad collection of business and leadership experiences – multifunctional, multigeographic, multibusiness, multi-industry – linked by a strong and consistent career thread.
❏ A pattern of success and winning habits – but recognize that this will be tempered with the odd failure or two.
❏ A sense of your technical and leadership strengths and weaknesses and also your personal limits, developed from your experience and personal development.
❏ Ideally, you will be in the fellowship of a great leader, but also enjoying life with your family and close friends.

Stepping back
❏ It's better to step back too early than too late.
❏ Ensure the business does not lose momentum by gradually transitioning out.
❏ Consider taking an active chairing role to allow a phased transition.
❏ Build a full portfolio of stretch commitments.
❏ Remember the huge impact you can have after your executive career is over.

14
HEEDING THE CEO
HEALTH WARNING

"Leaders need a deep sense of self and how they feel about the world... The very best leaders first start with a sense of being."

Lord Browne

"I can't remember the first two boys growing up when I was with my first wife."

FTSE100 CEO

The fantasy comedy *Click* carries an important warning for every global CEO. Adam Sandler plays a loving family man with the modest aspiration of becoming a partner in the firm of architects he works for so that he can spend more time with his picture-perfect wife and children, and their dog. One night, he gets frustrated with his television remote control and decides to get a universal control for all his gadgetry. In the event, he accidentally comes home from the shops with a control for reality that allows him to fast forward through his own life and see how it turns out.

The experience is not pleasant. Sure enough, he gets promoted, but the film charts the future life his workaholism is leading to. His marriage breaks down and his wife remarries, his weight balloons then shrinks under unpleasant liposuction, his children act in ways he does not approve of at all, he is diagnosed with cancer, is distracted by work in what turns out to be his last conversation with his father, and, eventually, dies of a heart attack.

As Sandler lies dying, he despairs of the choices he's made through his life. Then, with a flash, he wakes to find he's been whisked back from death to the evening he started playing with the universal remote control, and has the opportunity to prevent the future unwinding in the way he's seen. Elated, he leaps into action, rushing to show his affection for his father and his family.

None of us has a time-accelerating remote control so we cannot be certain how our own life will turn out. However, there is no doubt that CEOs run all the risks parodied in *Click*. For example, one FTSE100 CEO confided to us, "I have been married twice and have four kids and one grandchild. I can't remember the first two boys growing up when I was with my first wife. We separated when they were 8 and 9. I can't remember them when they were young." Another equally senior CEO admitted ruefully, "I didn't see my son grow up; we're only now building a relationship in his late teens."

In fact, not only do the demands of the role often rob CEOs of life's pleasures, they even strip the role of some of the allure that had them chasing the promotion in the first place. As Archie Norman relates, "If you ask chief executives, there is a peculiar phenomenon that very few of them say, 'I have a terrific time, I love doing this.' They're all thinking, 'Oh, another couple of years and then, you know, maybe I'll take a few chairmanships.'"

It is clear that the CEO role can get on top of you, damage your body, mind, and spirit, and ruin your personal relationships. But why wait for your death bed to wish you'd done the right thing? Surely you want to have a satisfying family and personal life? CEOs and their closest advisers tell us that there are three things you need to do to achieve just that:

❑ Drive your agenda, don't let the business drive you.
❑ Build an active support network.
❑ Ensure you are always at your best.

DRIVING YOUR AGENDA

The happiest CEOs we've met are those who have managed either to build strong boundaries between their work and home lives, so that home refreshes them for work and work does not impinge on home; or those who have fully integrated their work and their personal lives and do not see a massive tension between the two.

Steven Crawshaw, former chief executive of bank Bradford & Bingley, falls into the first camp. "I'm firmly of the view that it's possible to have a work–life balance but you need to draw some very clear line," he says. "I have a *cordon sanitaire* between work and home. I don't need my wife to make my business decisions." In the latter camp, Ian Coull's wife has given up a high-powered career to travel around with him while he is CEO of Segro. Paul Thompson is of a similar persuasion, thinking that "fixing firm boundaries is too structured and naive. Life has to be much more interlinked, but you have to be very disciplined about how you manage yourself." While both approaches seem to work, both require tremendous personal discipline.

We know this is hard. There are times when business takes over everything. We've all been there: "We have to close this round of funding next week or we close the business", "I have to do this investor roadshow in Shanghai over our wedding anniversary", and so on. Even when there is no abnormal event, the fact is that when you're looking after a whole company – perhaps hundreds of thousands of people – there's always something that might go wrong or a project that could be improved. Modern technology, far from being a useful tool, can seem to create a treadmill of urgent priorities with no end in sight. Tony Davis knows the feeling only too well: "The train seems to be going faster and faster and every now and then you need to apply the brakes so that it does not become a runaway train."

> The train seems to be going faster and faster and every now and then you need to apply the brakes so that it does not become a runaway train

But hold on, you're the CEO. You control the agenda. Paul Walker says that you can run a wildly successful company and be in control of all other aspects of your life: "It is possible to organize life in such a way that you can balance private life and business. If you work hard and have the right people around you, you can make it work. If you delegate, put in controls, you can have a good home life."

Make time work for you as well as the business

Sir John Parker is insistent that you are paid to be smart, not tired, so keeping mentally fresh and alert is part of your job. For him, managing your personal life is part of being a complete CEO. "It is totally possible to have a balance and in fact it's essential," he says. "It's totally easy to become stale when you don't have time to sit with family and friends. Treadmills do not make for good leaders and managers: stressed people do not get the best results. What's work–life balance about? It's about managing your time. My father used to say to me that if you cannot manage your time you cannot manage anything. You need to ask yourself: 'What am I doing two weeks from today?'"

Create protected time every week

Harriet Green warns against losing the initiative on a daily basis. She argues that one should not "be too responsive. I've taken to walking to the train from home. It takes 35 minutes, but gives me time when I'm not on the Blackberry and I can think, really think. You must not let the technology control you." Philip Moore has a weekly routine: "At the weekend, I walk my dog for about an hour and I think a lot about my work. The dog is irrelevant really, but the walk is quite helpful." Richard Baker says that at Alliance Boots he always managed every week so that he had a thinking day to reflect on events and gain perspective.

Know what can refresh you daily

Keith Butler-Wheelhouse refreshed himself while CEO through routines based on exercise and domesticity. "I go to the gym and play tennis frequently," he says. "I'm also a fixer. One of the kids kicked in the swimming pool light over the weekend. I pulled the part out, stripped it down, found the faulty part, and my driver's purchasing it now. I'll spend 20 minutes installing the replacement tonight. It matters to me that I can still do ordinary things – that's important."

Set simple rules that impose structure on your life

Cris Conde thinks that the answer to balance is having bright-line rules: "Twenty years ago, I set two very simple rules for myself: I do not take or make calls in the evening and I take my vacation. These rules clear time to think and be with my family and they are all I need. I advise everyone to come up with rules that work for them and apply them carefully."

Be as serious about time "off" as time "on"

At times of peak stress, most of us assure ourselves that we will take time off to destress completely. However, for most people the dips in activity are rarely as deep as the peaks. How many of us are guilty of being chained to the Blackberry by the holiday pool? Therefore, a critical piece of advice from CEOs is to make sure you do take time to let your internal spring uncoil completely.

For Richard Baker, "The most important thing is my family and friends; I take every holiday day I'm entitled to." Brad Mills is even more extreme and has developed a technique of complete isolation. "As for me, I go for two weeks each year of hardcore fishing," he explains. "I leave my wife and kids and don't take anyone with me. You need to recharge your spirituality and you cannot do that easily in an urban environment or working situation. When you are sitting in a stream, and your cellphone doesn't work, and there's absolutely no way that anyone can contact you, your mind roams around for the first few days. Then you get on with it. Fishing is meditation for me."

Know your source

Philip Green marries the physical, the spiritual, and business in how he seeks satisfaction, which boils down to "the 5Fs – Faith, Family, Fitness, Fun, and the Firm where I work. My Christian faith is at the core of who I am and the first three are the bedrock for my own performance and allow me to be at my best in my role." He is one of a small but increasing group of CEOs who are explicit about how their faith underpins their leadership. There are also a growing number of CEOs who draw on spiritual values in leading their businesses – especially in the emerging markets.

BUILDING AN ACTIVE SUPPORT NETWORK

Leadership is lonely. More than half the CEOs we surveyed say so. And most of the rest admit that they would be lonely if they hadn't taken deliberate action to build the support networks they need. Many CEOs draw on a tailored support network in their professional and personal lives.

CEOs do also need to be able to get a perspective on themselves, their colleagues, and the performance of the fellowship as a whole. They draw on three principal elements: their chairperson, external coaches, and their family and friends. Finding the right blend of support – chairman, coaches, mentors, family, and friends – depends on your preferences and needs, but top CEOs were insistent that building and maintaining the right support network is essential and takes careful thought and the investment of quality time.

The chair as sounding board

Unfortunately, in many cases a key role of the chairperson is to sack the CEO if he or she is not performing. Worse, in many cases that's also the chairperson's default position when bad news hits – they are often very concerned to protect their own reputation and personal brand. This is equally often a significant mistake. However, good chairpeople see themselves as absorbing some of the flack for the CEO.

Certainly, that's the view of BAA chairman Sir Nigel Rudd. "As chair, I see my role as a lightning conductor to take some of the heat when it gets a bit stormy," he says. Paul Adams says that he is fortunate to be able to use his chairman as a sounding board. "If I wanted to chew something over I would go and talk to the chairman because that's his job," he explains. "If his job is not to help the CEO then you've got the wrong CEO, in my view. I tend to go and see him when I'm ruminating on something. He says 'Oh yes' and he listens while I talk. By the time I have finished talking I have come up with the answer. I say 'Thank you very much' and the chairman says 'I haven't done anything'. That's the job of a good chairman." There's no doubt that chairpeople like that can really empower their CEOs.

A coach for gaining perspective

Richard Baker says, "It is extraordinary to think you can be excellent at something without a coach. The notion that Roger Federer would not have several coaches is ridiculous. One of the best things that happened to me was to get a coach. I think it's been massively helpful. When the waves were breaking over me, I got a coach. Within 10 minutes, he'd correctly identified the one thing I needed to do. As a CEO, the idea you can do it on your own is extraordinarily arrogant. I think the coaching industry is a whole industry that has yet to be born; it needs to be developed."

About 40 percent of FTSE100 CEOs have used coaches and an even higher proportion advise their top team to use one.[1] Executive coaches are just like sports coaches: they help you with your technique. As Alan Watkins observes, they typically fall into one of two camps: "The first type, which includes the majority of coaches working with CEOs, operate tactically. They help the CEO consider the tasks he is engaged in and his behavior on key issues. Then there is the second type, a much smaller group of coaches who work more fundamentally and are focused on helping the CEO become a better leader. Their conversations are focused on equipping the leader to lead, inspire, and cope much more effectively with whatever tasks he is facing. The first type of coach focuses on 'doing', the second on 'being'. In reality, the first type is a management coach, the second is a leadership coach." Both are useful depending on the situation you find yourself in.

At Standard Chartered, Mervyn Davies used a management coach. He recalls, "I got someone who catalogued how I spent my time and went through my diaries and measured my progress on a 360-degree basis. It was brutal, but I am a great believer in courageous conversation. I don't think I agreed with him; I was allowed to argue." Equally, one FTSE100 CEO says of his adviser, "If I called her a coach she would be furious. She's one of the smartest people I've ever met. We talk about leadership. She always comes up with three or four questions and I come away with an action list."

Paul Thompson also values the independent view, counseling, and energy recharge that his coach provides him with, but he is clear that he does not discuss every issue he faces. "It's a lonely job. There's no way you can please all the people all the time and there's no way you can be everyone's friend," he explains. "You have this difficulty of being able to relate to people and like people and still use people well. Everyone wants to be liked, but you have to be able to put all your energy into other people and then you need to get your personal energy from somewhere else. It's quite challenging. My coach has given me the personal energy and maturity to deal with things. It gives me more inner strength and helps me to cope with having to give lots to other people and often getting nothing back, because that's what it's about. But I do not need to talk to someone about all the issues. You need to be able to make decisions yourself."

Many CEOs also have mentors. They tell us that they benefit from having someone experienced outside the business who has their success as the sole objective, and so can provide both robust counsel and a sympathetic ear. Ideally, a mentor has been through the type of role you are currently in, so can really relate to the pressures and advise you from real personal experience. Ruby McGregor-Smith, CEO of support services business MITIE, says, "As you get more senior in your career, you need someone outside your business who can give you cold clarity of thought. Close colleagues and friends and family cannot give this. And you especially need help at times of change in your career (e.g., having a family). This is something I wish I'd had."

Indeed, one former CEO of a major financial company took this approach to its logical extreme. "In my later days as sales director, I knew the CEO was going to move on at some stage and I wanted to work out whether I really wanted to be a CEO," he says. "I worked out the pluses and minuses and got my head around it. At the time I thought I had only a 20 percent chance of getting the job, so I went to see a coach and asked him what I needed to do to get that up to a 50 percent chance within a year. Some of the coaches I went to see could not understand this at all, but I found one who really helped me with it.

"Six weeks afterwards, I was appointed as CEO. The board was braver than I thought it would be and the coach was fantastic. It was a question of getting the right discipline. The coach I saw was an ex-CEO who had been through some really bad times as well as some good times. He helped me get it clear in my head and I now encourage my people to go through a similar exercise."

Above all, coaches and mentors are not there to take ultimate responsibility – that's the role of the CEO. So in choosing a coach, it is important to be clear why; it may be that you need a mirror held up to you, or counseling support on a particular technical aspect of your role or leadership. You also need to be very disciplined and discerning about the coach you choose for the task identified. Finally, CEOs agree that you must not over-rely on one coach and, above all, not become dependent.

Family and friends to keep you grounded

There has to be more to your life than your job. Having a happy family is good in itself. However, if you need a cold business reason to justify creating room for a family life, the truth is that spending time with family can get you back to the business refreshed and refocused.

It's very simple for Terry Duddy, CEO of Home Retail Group, owner of UK household names Argos and Homebase. "My support network is my wife, because she's in charge of all the things that are really, really important," he says. "I don't lie in bed worrying about what's going to happen tomorrow. My business is on my mind all day, but the next business day does not arrive until 5 a.m. the next day."

Recognizing the potential conflict between work and home, some CEOs have found ways to integrate their families completely into their professional lives so that the apparent tension dissolves. Gareth Davis says, "I talk a lot to my wife about the business but we only see each other at weekends. Weekends are quite precious and we talk a lot about work. She loves to talk about it."

You need to show your colleagues that you have more to your life than your work otherwise you look like a deal-junkie or a megalomaniac. Remember that they are probably not going to gain so heavily in personal terms from whatever deal or growth you are currently working on.

You must nurture your family relationships for another reason; if your long-term happiness becomes entirely bound up in your job, you'll find it very hard to recover at the end of your career.

CEOs told us that there are three tricks that most miss. The first is that the intensity of the effort made during a big push has to be matched by the intensity of the effort after that push; effective recuperation is vital. But, as Alan Watkins states, recuperation is not just a case of putting your feet up: "The antidote to exhaustion is not rest but doing something that makes your heart sing."

> The antidote to exhaustion is not rest but doing something that makes your heart sing

The second, and more important trick is that top CEOs don't compromise on significant personal moments such as births, deaths, critical childhood successes, which are non-negotiable – the business has to wait. Your family will judge you on these and your performance will be the foundation of your long-term relationship with family and friends.

Finally, one very successful CEO told us, "However tense it gets, you have to demonstrate to others that it is not your life. It might be the little things – like a text to the kids at the height of the deal. My wife is hugely sympathetic during the tough events, the all-nighters on a deal, and so forth. She understands that I can't run the kids to school at those times. But I need to demonstrate that I keep some time for them still – something to keep the family together and protect me. For example, it might be a call to them while they're on the school run."

Ultimately, as another former FTSE100 CEO observed, "At the end of the day, you have to play like the job's as important as life and death but recognize that it is not life and death, because when it goes wrong (as it sometimes will) you need the safety valve. You also need other things in your life because if you don't, you will not be detached in your thinking, and you have to be detached." Mitch Garber agrees that perspective is vital in good decisions, as well as essential to keeping a balance: "When you are faced with big and difficult life experiences, you must take a deep breath and realize that business experiences are seldom the end of the world. This also allows you to step back and make better decisions."

BEING AT YOUR BEST

Most CEOs have confidence in their business abilities and belief in their own leadership or they would not take on the job. However, most of our interviewees told us that they find it difficult to be at their best day in and day out, while at the same time concluding that the role will become increasingly global and correspondingly harder in the next 10 years. Given this, as we have said we expect that a majority of CEOs will use one or more coaches within a few years.

In addition, in recent years there have been a number of break-throughs in our understanding of the human system and its perform-ance, which have significant implications for our ability to improve the performance of global business leaders. These advances have mostly been made in the fields of psychology, neuroscience, peak per-formance, neuro-linguistic programming, and by trainers drawn from a range of disciplines working with elite sportspeople. Many of the latest advances have already started to be used to accelerate sporting performance, but have yet to be applied widely within the corporate world.

From our interviews, it was clear that there are a number of differ-ent challenges with which CEOs are grappling and which stop most from being at their best. These issues typically concern energy man-agement, achieving mental clarity, and maintaining emotional stabil-ity. However, some CEOs even find themselves questioning their sense of self. The diagram below breaks these challenges down into the four fundamental aspects of peak performance and gives an indi-cation of the most relevant fields of human development that can help CEOs to maximize their performance.

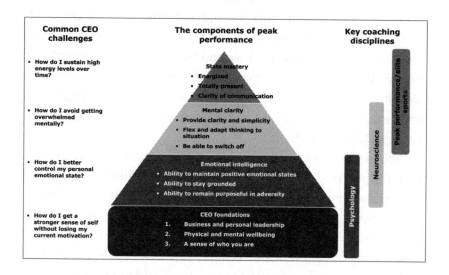

CEO foundations: Do you know who you are?

The truth is that, in Lord Browne's words, "Leaders need to understand themselves and the world around them. This takes time, success, and failures to develop. You need to become more free of your own prejudices so as to listen to others, to reflect, to pick and choose people. With that understanding, you can trust and then you can really achieve." As Mike Roney says, "You have to have strong emotional security. You have to believe in yourself and be able to continue to drive the business without instant feedback." Another senior CEO states, "The most important thing CEOs are paid for is judgment. You have to be centered to do that. It is vital to do personal development so you can be centered in all situations and be more consistent."

To lead effectively, you need to know what you believe in and what you are here to achieve. States Tony Robbins, "When you find a top performer in any field, including CEOs, part of what makes every one of them great is that they are clear on who they are – their true nature. If a person does not have a personal sense of meaning in their life, they will not succeed. No matter how cerebral they are, unless they have a clear mission and outcome, they cannot fulfill themselves." This foundation of self-knowledge is essential to maintaining the drive and focus to win professionally and personally through the ups and downs of a career and life. Unfortunately, as executive coach Peter Hogarth acknowledges, "Few chief executives have done an analysis of what drives them and what success looks like to them."

Ido van der Heijden, a corporate psychologist with 30 years' experience of working with top executives, agrees. "Chief executives face a dilemma: when you climb to that level, you do so at a cost," he says. "To get there, you need to be psychologically well defended, be very ambitious, and may have a pretty big ego. In being top dog, you risk losing some of your human freedom. This lack of freedom can limit and stifle personal development and can lead to uninspired leadership. The challenge is to continually define your sense of meaning and purpose, which is very hard if you are disconnected from the deeper aspects of yourself."

One of the most effective ways of deepening your sense of self is to frame and reframe key life experiences with an expert, drawing on the latest developments in psychology. Doing this helps you recognize crucibles in your personal and professional life when you go through them and actively learn from the experience, and it enables you to formalize your motives and objectives at any point in your life.

This is easier said than done. Van der Heijden observes that frequently people have become very senior because of a powerful psychological circumstance, such as poverty in childhood or a sense of duty to parents who sacrificed a lot to get them their start in life. "Often people are not aware of what drives them. They need someone to encourage them to turn over untouched stones and examine what's underneath them," he says. "I find that often people come to look for this self-examination between 35 and 45. This is the stage in their lives when typically wives and children start to complain that they are not providing the intimacy desired.

"These executives need to rebalance their lives. They come to me fearing they will lose their drive, but in fact they learn that their identity can be far broader than their position of power. We all have programs running in the background and unless one is aware of them one cannot control their effects. To understand them requires an exercise of digging through history, the good bits as well as the more painful experiences. The very qualities that helped you to get to the top may also be the ones that can cause a divorce. To integrate your history gives you more freedom in being able to express yourself in different ways. It can give you the emotional courage needed to lead and inspire."

Unfortunately, many chief executives seem resistant to embracing such an approach. Van der Heijden says, "Although a lot of senior executives and teams approach me to work with them, it's rare that a chief executive is willing to submit to the same treatment. My clients may work with me just before the big promotion, then have me work with their team, but, once promoted, sitting CEOs very rarely submit. It's a real challenge for CEOs to realize that emotional courage, self-awareness, and the willingness to examine yourself are qualities that can make the difference between effective and inspired leadership."

Do you have high emotional intelligence?

Generally, CEOs assume that there is a certain base level of IQ among all corporate leaders. Most therefore value EQ over IQ as a way of discriminating between great leaders. However, CEOs – albeit with a few notable exceptions – do not have a deep understanding of emotional intelligence and have not invested in developing their own EQ beyond their experience of dealing with the business situations they have encountered.

The human body can experience a vast array of emotions. Daniel Goleman, author of *Destructive Emotions* written in conjunction with the Dalai Lama, documents an estimate by Tibetan Buddhists that they can attain 34,000 distinct emotional states. To put that in context, research undertaken by Cardiac Coherence on CEOs indicates rather worryingly that an average CEO will manage fewer than 15 of these states in a typical 24-hour period.[2] It seems clear that there is much for CEOs to learn about emotions!

Research into this phenomenon and others by neuroscientists like Antonio Damasio[3] has shown that every decision is shaped by your emotions. The measurable and dramatic effect of emotions on decisions and performance means that great CEOs must develop more sophisticated emotional intelligence. They need to understand how their emotions affect their decision making, and their ability to influence and lead others is greatly improved if they can spot emotions in others, both individually and collectively.

The good news is that over the last ten years scientists have started to subject emotions to proper study and a few sophisticated coaches are now able to help leaders increase their awareness, manage their stress and anxiety better, and empathize with others so they can manage their own emotions more effectively.

Tony Robbins' research suggests that human emotional states are driven by positive values, which we move toward, and negative values, which we move away from. In his advanced coaching programs he gives participants the tools to elicit their own values, helps people to understand their subconscious rules, and – having understood them – to reprogram them to create the mental toolkit they need to move ahead as they desire. Bob Quintana, a former senior Robbins trainer and CEO coach, says, "Many top CEOs are driven by the desire for significance and the need to make a difference, but have very demanding rules which don't allow them easily to feel successful or fulfilled. One CEO I work with had subconscious rules that he would only feel successful if he had changed an industry and done something no one had thought possible with a team that's widely recognized in the business world. Not surprisingly, he didn't feel successful, despite having achieved things which most others would judge remarkable."

Developments such as these across science and peak performance coaching will in the coming years be increasingly helpful to CEOs seeking to boost their emotional intelligence.

Do you have sufficient mental clarity?

Many CEOs complain of being mentally overwhelmed for significant periods during their time in the role due to the relentless demands of switching focus continually throughout a day. One moment you're finishing a strategy session, the next minute taking a call requiring a decision on the basis of detailed data, then you're dealing with an unhappy customer straight after. In addition, you are at risk of being thrown a curve ball – the one question from an analyst you weren't expecting, for example. In these situations, it's all too common for the brain to almost shut down; if it does, you're sunk. Taking the analyst as an example, the biological source of the "mind going blank", as it does under pressure sometimes, is well understood and is called "cortical inhibition". The curve ball puts you into a chaotic mindset and effectively reduces mental clarity and creativity, as well as lessening the ability to solve problems and make effective decisions. As ever, your body and your mind are intimately linked.

In short, great CEOs need to have mental clarity on demand. Here again, recent developments have much to offer and there is strong scientific evidence to show that we can train ourselves to generate a coherent signal to the brain and therefore enhance clarity, creativity, and speed of thinking. For example, we're all told to take some deep breaths before a speech to calm and energize ourselves. The latest research shows that in fact there are 12 elements of breathing that can change your physiology, and that each of the 12 elements can be controlled and turned to use in calming and focusing you. Alan Watkins comments, "Many negative emotional states are associated with disordered breathing patterns. There is good evidence to show that rhythmic breathing may explain the health benefits of meditation and rosary prayer."

So how well do you think the majority of our current crop of CEOs do in keeping their brains fully activated today?

Can you sustain peak performance?

Just like being a top athlete, being a CEO requires that you are as close to your best as much of the time as possible. You have to be able to peak for the big points in a match, but also win a grand slam over a season. States Paul Thompson, "You have to be running at – say – 90 percent so that you can go to 120 percent when the big thing hits." So aside from mastering your emotions and clearing your mind, you need to figure out how to increase your energy levels when necessary – and how to relax and recharge when you have the opportunity. Building capacity requires that you push beyond your normal limits but then factor in time for recovery; many people fail to include this recovery time and so find it difficult to build greater capacity.

As we've seen, emotions have a huge impact on performance. Two of the key hormones that drive results are cortisol, the body's main stress hormone, and DHEA, the performance hormone. Cortisol tends to lead to negative emotional states, while DHEA can make you feel

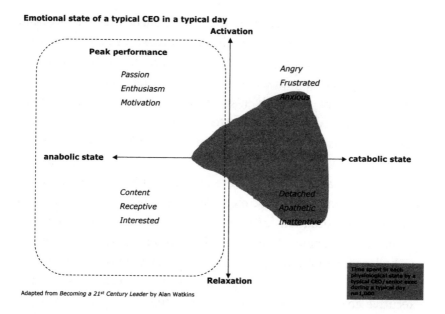

Emotional state of a typical CEO in a typical day

Reproduced with permission from Alan Watkins, *Becoming a 21st Century Leader*, forthcoming.

better. Alan Watkins has spent 15 years researching the impact on CEOs of these hormones and their associated emotions. The diagram above shows that inadequate understanding of their emotional states causes most CEOs to underperform because they spend most of their days in an active catabolic state.

The optimal states for decision making are anabolic. Active anabolic states, such as passion, are critical to performance. In fact, passion is the no. 1 predictor for all types of performance, including health.[4] This is the state the CEO would access before motivating a audience, such as at a new product launch. There are, however, times when a relaxed anabolic state will serve the CEO best, when he or she needs to be receptive, calm, and open to others, for example when making lay-offs.

In contrast, many CEOs spend most of their time in catabolic states. The active catabolic state is that designed by nature for flight – it's what makes a CEO fluff the analyst's question, when the brain shuts down its higher functions to focus on the simple decision to run away from the modern equivalent of a tiger in the trees. A relaxed catabolic state is not much more use – it's designed for playing dead – and exhibits itself today as apathy, detachment, or inattentiveness.

It's all very well recognizing the state you're in, but the real key is to be able to change your state. This is well understood by elite performance coaches, especially in sprinting or contact sports, who have developed methods that allow athletes to move themselves from, for example, a relaxed catabolic state to an active anabolic one.

There is a body of compelling evidence that emotional mastery, mental clarity, and conscious state control can boost executive performance dramatically. At the moment a majority of coaching remains behavioral and situational. However, it is clear that it is only a matter of time before some of the breakthoughs in human performance touched on fleetingly above will be adopted by CEOs who are looking to be at their best and get a edge. This drive will also transform the executive coaching industry as we see it today. Tony Robbins comments: "When people get a taste of personal development, they understand what it feels like to have a sense of mission; a good personal coach can help leaders reinvigorate that insatiable hunger for success in them."

The expectations of personal performance from global CEOs have massively increased. Top CEOs need coaches or coaching teams who can help them always be at their best. The challenge for coaches, then, is not to be narrow specialists but to understand all levels of human performance and to be able to tailor each CEO's coaching intervention to his or specific needs – whatever they may be.

THE ACID TEST

Do you need to take action? We'd suggest a quick self-diagnosis:

- ❏ Are you realizing your career ambitions and enjoying work?
- ❏ Are you aware of how your emotions affect your decision making?
- ❏ Are you tuned into others' emotions?
- ❏ Do you always think clearly?

❏ Are you always able to put yourself into the best state to perform in any situation?
❏ Is your current lifestyle good for your health and wellbeing?
❏ Are you comfortable with the trade-offs you've made between career, family, friends, and yourself?
❏ Are you truly happy and content with life today and your honest expectations for the future?

CONCLUSION

Being a CEO is one of the toughest jobs in the world. It requires exceptional levels of determination and resilience, as well as the ability to cope with stress and not let the role totally dominate your life. It's therefore not a healthy ambition for many successful businesspeople.

The best CEOs are passionate, enjoy the job, and recognize that they are privileged to lead. They are not only strong, with deep-rooted self-belief, but also build robust personal and business support networks, supplemented by coaches and mentors as required. The coaching industry is now beginning to step up and provide the expertise on human performance that is required to complement traditional business coaching.

With a great fellowship and the support to ensure that you're performing at your best, this really is the best job in the world!

EPILOGUE:
WHY NOT YOU?

As a kid, did you dream about how you would change the world? Some of the best global CEOs believe that this will be the decade when you really can. The world has opened up to global markets on a scale not seen for several hundred years and, at the same time, the internet is connecting us all together. In parallel, there is increased awareness of how corporates need to play a bigger and more responsible role in society.

We do have a small number of fantastic leaders who are leading a new generation of great businesses, which have developed more fluid and innovative cell-like organizations and are bonded together not by one person but by a close fellowship. Many of these businesses have featured in this book and form the start of a new breed of champions which are loved by shareholders, have fanatically loyal customers, are magnets for the top 1 percent of global talent, and are sustainable. In addition, the success of these companies will mean that they will go further and start innovatively to address the broader social imbalances in society.

However, as we speak these twenty-first-century global leaders are vastly outnumbered – the majority of corporates, especially in the Western world, are managed in a twentieth-century way. These companies contain legions of trapped people with unfulfilled ambitions and untapped talents. Millions of people only work to live.

Alongside these developments, Generation Y and behind them the so-called dream generation are growing up with fresh aspirations for themselves and the world and striving for a better life than their parents had. These generations will have the mindset and skills to be a vital part of reinvigorating corporates – or they could turn their back on the business world entirely if companies don't change fast.

So whether you're reading this book in the hurly-burly of Hanoi, listening to a podcast in the mountains in Montenegro, or accessing us in Second Life from a coffee bar in downtown Detroit, we hope that this book has stirred you to ask yourself: "Why can't I be a CEO?" If you're an existing CEO, we'd like to think we may have encouraged you to set a new standard of leadership for yourself.

Being a CEO carries a serious health warning, but it's not mission impossible. Imagine working with your fellowship to energize everyone in your company to change your markets and customers' lives around the world. What sort of legacy would that leave for you, your family, your company, and the world? Imagine what your leaving party would be like!

Connect with us at www.theSecretsofCEOs.com and let us know how you get on.

NOTES

Chapter 2

1   *Globality: Competing with Everyone from Everywhere for Everything*, Harold L. Sirkin, James W. Hemerling, & Arindam K. Bhattacharya, Business Plus, 2008.
2   *From "Made In China" to "Sold in China": The Rise of the Chinese Urban Consumer*, McKinsey Global Institute, November 2006; *The "Bird of Gold": The Rise of India's Consumer Market*, McKinsey Global Institute, May 2007.
3   China mobile data from *China Mobile, Direct Line to the Consumer*, CIMB, 4 Feb 2008.
4   Purchasing price parity (PPP) adjusted GDP, WPP Annual Report 2006, p. 87.
5   *The N-11: More than an Acronym*, Goldman Sachs, March 2007.
6   www.hll.com/brands/creating_markets.asp.
7   www.livemint.com/2007/09/12011326/Hindustan-Unilever-draws-up-fr.html; www.unilever.com/Images/ir_Laundry-in-Asia_tcm13-114448.pdf   (Unilever report, November 2007).
8   www.hll.com/brands/creating_markets.asp.
9   *Unilever: Hindustan Lever*, FNV Research Report, 2006.
10   "Winning the Indian Consumer", *McKinsey Quarterly*, September 2005.
11   http://worldbenefit.case.edu/innovation/bankInnovationView.cfm?idArchive=362.
12   www.tata.com/0_about_us/group_profile.htm; www.ft.com/cms/s/0/297c62c2-ea3a-11dc-b3c9-0000779fd2ac.html; www.spiegel.de/international/business/0,1518,476262,00.html; www.businessworld.in/index2.php?option=com_content&do_pdf=1&id=672; www.ft.com/cms/s/2/e8191bda-b0d9-11db-8a62-0000779e2340.html; *Financial Times* 28 March 2008 reported $2.3B acquisition price for Jaguar LandRover.
13   *Globality, op. cit.*

Chapter 3

1   http://unfccc.int/kyoto_protocol/background/status_of_ratification/items/2613.php.
2   www.hmtreasury.gov.uk/independent_reviews/stern_review_economics_climate_change/stern_review_report.cfm.
3   "M&S charge for bags goes national as calls to end plastic spread." *Express and Echo*, 29 February 2008.
4   "Shop around for low carbon," Telegraph, www.telegraph.co.uk/money/main.jhtml?xml=/money/exclusions/supplements/carbonaction/nosplit/shop.xml.
5   www.tescocorporate.com/page.aspx?pointerid=5CDD348F6D5A4833944276F91970D98C; www.tesco.com/climatechange/speech.asp.

6 "Plane truths," Catherine Boyle, *CorpComms* magazine, Issue 22, October 2007.

7 www.easyjet.com/common/img/environment_myths_and_reality.pdf.

8 'Stansted shows that flying really does matter', *Air Transport News*, 11 September 2007.

9 http://news.bbc.co.uk/onthisday/hi/dates/stories/march/24/newsid_4231000/4231971.stm.

10 "British business commits to 'do what it takes' to tackle climate change – major new report," CBI Press Release, 26 November 2007.

11 Carbon Disclosure Project Report, 2007.

12 "Growth through sustainability," Darrell Rigby, Bain & Company, 24 January 2008.

13 *CorpComms* magazine, July 2007, www.thecrossbordergroup.com/cc_archive /pages/1516/June+2007.stm?article_id=11897.

14 www.btplc.com/Societyandenvironment/SocialandEnvironmentReport/ pdf/2007/BT_CSR.pdf.

15 Donna Young, BT Group Head of Environment and Climate Change, conversation with authors, 26 March 2008.

16 "Spreading SRI: Goldman Sachs adds its own twist in social and environmental assessment," William Baue, 5 October 2005.

17 Carbon Disclosure Project Report 2007; Global FT500, on behalf of 315 investors with assets of $41 trillion.

18 "Strategy and society: The link between competitive advantage and corporate social responsibility," Michael E. Porter and Mark R. Kramer, *Harvard Business Review*, December 2006.

19 *Tomorrow's Global Company, Challenges and Choices*, Tomorrow's Company inquiry, 2007, page 4.

20 "Growth through sustainability," op. cit.

21 "Seeing is Believing" supplement, *The Daily Telegraph*, 15 December 2005.

22 www.cadburyschweppes.com/EN/EnvironmentSociety/CadCocoaPartnership/.

23 World Economic Forum at Davos, 2008.

Chapter 4

1 Heidrick & Struggles Breakfast with the Board, 3 December 2007, attended by over 60 CEOs and chairmen.

2 *Ibid.*

3 "The greatest defunct Web sites and dotcom disasters," *CNET*, 5 June 2008.

4 www.facebook.com/press/info.php?statistics (stats downloaded 10 December 2007).

5 "The impact of Web 2.0 and emerging social network models," Chad Hurley, co-Founder and CEO, YouTube, World Economic Forum, Davos, 2007.

6 *Ibid.*

7 *What Is Web 2.0?*, short version documentary by Michael Arrington, TechCrunch Blogger, added to YouTube 10 August 2007.

8 Presentation, Web 2.0 Summit, San Francisco, Mary Meecher, David Joseph, and Richard Ji, Morgan Stanley Global Technology Team.

9   www.forbes.com/free_forbes/2007/0507/138.html.

10 Site names are provided for illustration only. We are not responsible for the content of these sites and do not endorse any of their activities.

11 "The impact of Web 2.0 and emerging social network models," *op. cit.*

12 http://blogs.zdnet.com/BTL/?p=5112, "Cisco CEO John Chambers proclaims the future is Web 2.0 May 2007," account of Network + Interop keynote presentation, accessed December 2007.

13 Speech at Cisco's 2007 Networkers conference in Anaheim, California, July 2007, reported http://networks.silicon.com/webwatch/0,39024667,39167942,00.htm, accessed December 2007.

14 Includes cellphone access; *OECD Science, Technology and Industry, Scoreboard 2007*, 2a, Households with broadband access, 2000–06.

15 'Hooked on the virtual world: A reality in South Korea', Choe Sang-Hun, *International Herald Tribune*, June 12, 2006.

16 www.businessweek.com/magazine/content/05_39/b3952405.htm, retrieved February 2007.

17 'Korea: Cyworld fever cools', Kim Tae-gyu, *Korea Times*, March 7, 2007.

18 Press Release, 22 January 2008, Blizzard Entertainment.

Chapter 5

1   'The signs of a recession are all here', Roger Bootle, *Daily Telegraph*, 7 July 2008.

2   Deloitte, *Global Asset Management Industry Outlook: Issues on the Horizon 2007*; Dealogic data; 'Hedge funds outpace buyout firms in fundraising stakes', *Private Equity News*, 30 April 2007; *The New Power Brokers*, McKinsey Global Institute, October 2007; 'Wealth fund code of conduct proposed', *Financial Times*, 22 February 2008; Notes: asset classes not 100% mutually exclusive; PE funds committed for future use much higher than assets under management.

3   *Lessons from Private Equity Any Company Can Use*, Results Brief 02/06/08, Orit Gadiesh and Hugh MacArthur, Bain & Company.

Chapter 6

1   Forbes CEO Mindset Survey 2007. Sample of 600 CEOs across company size, industry, and country in survey by Millward Brown, Greenfield Consulting, and Forbes.

2   *Mapping Global Talent: Essays and Insights*, Heidrick & Struggles, September 2007, compiled in cooperation with the Economist Intelligence Unit.

3   *Aligning Talent for Global Advantage, How Top Companies Develop the Right Talent in the Right Places*, Boston Consulting Group, September 2007.

4   "The work force of today," Tillie Lima, 5 January 2008.

5   "Managing demographic risk," Rainer Strack, Jens Baier, and Anders Fahlander, *Harvard Business Review*, February 2008.

6   "New global economic challenges: Charting the course for policy responses,"

Angel Gurría, OECD Secretary-General, Lecture at the London School of Economics and Political Science, London, 1 March 2007.

7   Narayana Murthy, Heidrick & Struggles interview, November 2007.

8   Deutsche Bank research, India vs Europe, 2006.

9   "Welcome to Wipro US Analysts/Investors Meet," 30 January 2007, NYSE, New York, page 23.

10 *Mapping Global Talent, op. cit.*

11 http://en.wikipedia.org/wiki/Zuckerberg, accessed 19 March 2008.

12 "Welcome to Wipro," *op. cit.*

13 www.intuit.com/careers/culture.jhtml, accessed 19 March 2008.

14 "From 'professional business partner' to 'strategic talent leader': What's next for human resource management," John W. Boudreau and Pete M. Ramstad, Centre for Advanced Human Resource Studies, Working Paper 02-10.

15 "Making talent a strategic priority," *McKinsey Quarterly*, January 2008.

16 2005 National Management Salary Survey, a survey of approx. 21,000 UK managers by the Chartered Management Institute in 2005.

17 "Wenger – Youth success based on opportunity," 31 Jan 2007, Arsenal.com; "Wenger's way," Alex Fynn, *The Observer*, 12 September 2004.

Chapter 7

1   "Tesco gets more convenient," news.bbc.co.uk, 30 October, 2002.

2   "Tesco acquires Dobbies Garden," *Financial Deals Tracker*, 22 November 2007.

3   "Tesco moves in on the housing market," *The Daily Telegraph*, Nick Britten, 2 July 2007.

4   "Sir Terry Leahy," Andrew Cave, *The Daily Telegraph*, 21 November 2005.

5   *Ibid.*

6   http://news.bbc.co.uk/2/hi/business/4436113.stm.

7   *Ibid.*

8   http://search.ft.com/ftArticle?queryText=Alison+Maitland+Sir+terry+leahy&y=4&aje=true&x=6&id=030730000812&ct=0.

Chapter 8

1   Market data as at May 2008.

2   "The Monday Interview: Mick Davis, Chief executive, Xstrata, Big hitter prepares Xstrata for joining the market's elite," *The Times*, Nigel Cope, 11 March 2002.

Chapter 9

1   www.wpp.com/WPP/About/whoweare/History.htm; "The interview: Sir Martin Sorrell, Chief Executive of WPP," Damian Reece, *The Independent*, 26 March 2005.

2   WPP Annual Report 2007.
3   www.wpp.com/WPP/About/whoweare/History.htm.
4   "Martin Sorrell: Persistence and determination," *Benjamin's Boardroom*, CNN, 16 December 2005.
5   *Ibid.*
6   *Ibid.*
7   "£30m payout for ex-wife eases misery of divorce," *The Times*, 24 October 2005,
8   "The Sunday interview: Charles Dunstone (the TalkTalk man)," Simon Fluendy, *Mail on Sunday*, 5 November 2006.
9   *Ibid.*

Chapter 10

1   www.bp.com/onefeedsection.do?categoryId=773&contentId=2002459; Heidrick & Struggles analysis.
2   *Sydney Morning Herald*, 2 May 2007.
3   Ibid.
4   Management Today Annual Awards.
5   "Sun King of the oil industry," Tobias Buck and David Buchan, *Financial Times*, 12 January 2007 and as updated in conversation with Lord Browne.
6   *Ibid.*
7   *Ibid.*
8   *Ibid.*
9   "BP executive slams strategy," Caroline Muspratt, *The Daily Telegraph*, 19 December 2006.
10 www.chemsafety.gov/index.cfm?folder=current_investigations&page=info &INV_ID=52.
11 www.boardex.com.
12 www.riverstonellc.com.
13 "Browne: Global agency is needed," Clive Cookson, *Financial Times*, 14 September 2007,
14 "Why Barclays banks on this Oxford ascetic," Andrew Davidson, *Sunday Times*, 6 August 2006.

Chapter 11

1   "BT boss has communicated a new vision of his company – but his customers have yet to be impressed," Jane Martinson, *The Guardian*, 22 September 2006.
2   "BT's fourth quarter and full year financial results," BT Press Release, 17 May 2007.
3   "BT boss has communicated a new vision," *op. cit.*
4   *Ibid.*; "Dutch directness boosts BT," Andrew Davidson, *Sunday Times*, 11 February 2007.

5   "Dutch directness boosts BT," *op. cit.*
6   *Ibid.*
7   BT, Annual Report & Form 20-F, 2007.

Chapter 12

1   Google Founders' Letter and Owners Manual, 2004.
2   Tony Robbins, "Unleash the Power Within," London 2008; interview May 2008.
3   *Beyond Authority: Leadership in a Changing World*, Julia Middleton, Palgrave Macmillan, 2007.
4   *Tomorrow's Global Company, op. cit.*
5   Google Founders' Letter, 2005.
6   *The Master Strategist: Power, Purpose, and Principle*, Ketan Patel, Random House, 2005.
7   Tom Peters, London, Autumn 2007.

Chapter 13

1   *Route to The Top: A Transatlantic Comparison of Top Business Leaders*, Dr Elisabeth Marx, Heidrick & Struggles.
2   *Ibid.*
3   Quoted in "The World's Most Admired Companies," *Fortune*, 24 March 2008, page 43.

Chapter 14

1   Heidrick & Struggles survey, 2007.
2   Alan Watkins, Cardio-Coherence, based on >1,000 monitoring sessions with senior executives.
3   *The Feeling of What Happens: Body and Emotion in the Making of Consciousness*, Antonio Damasio, Harvest Books, 2000.
4   Alan Watkins.

INDEX